THE IMPERIAL WAR MUSEUM BOOK OF

THE WAR AT SEA

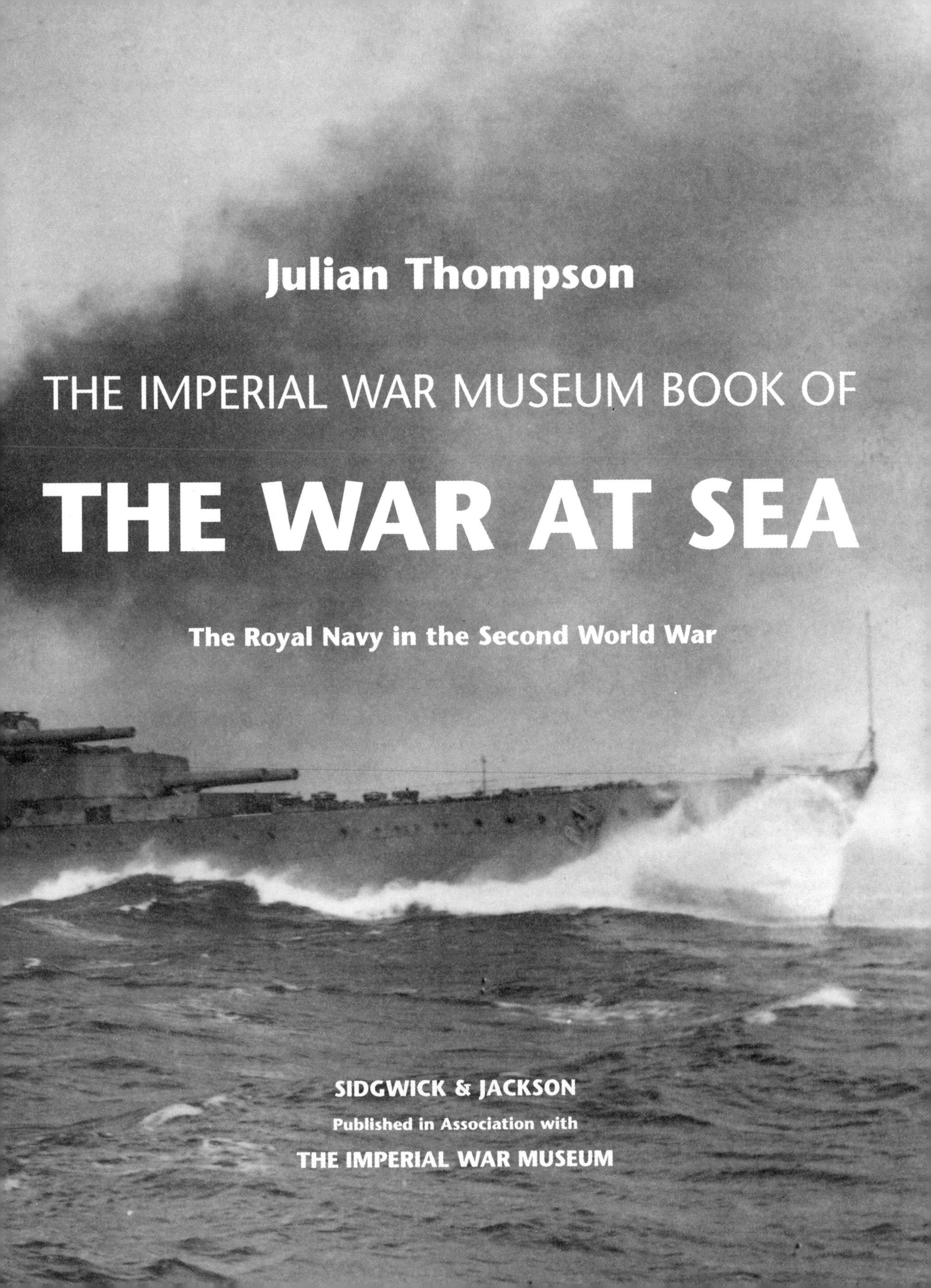

Julian Thompson

THE IMPERIAL WAR MUSEUM BOOK OF

THE WAR AT SEA

The Royal Navy in the Second World War

SIDGWICK & JACKSON

Published in Association with

THE IMPERIAL WAR MUSEUM

First published 1996 by Sidgwick & Jackson

This edition published 1997 by Sidgwick & Jackson
an imprint of Macmillan General Books
25 Eccleston Place, London SW1W 9NF
and Basingstoke

Associated companies throughout the world

ISBN 0 283 06308 4

1 3 5 7 9 8 6 4 2

A CIP catalogue record for this book is available from
the British Library.

Designed by Macmillan General Books Design Department

Photographic reproduction by Aylesbury Studios, Bromley, Kent

Printed and bound in Great Britain by
BPC Consumer Books Ltd, a member of The British Printing Company Ltd

Previous page:
HMS *Hood* undergoing full power trials off the Isle of Arran 1920. She was the longest ship built for the Royal Navy.
(Papers of Admiral Sir John Crace 69/18/4a, negative number DOC 510)

CONTENTS

ACKNOWLEDGEMENTS

This book would not have been possible to write without the letters, accounts and taped interviews of the people I have quoted. My first acknowledgement must be to them. Their names are listed in the Index of Contributors, as are the names of copyright holders. I am equally indebted to the photographers and artists whose pictures I have used to illustrate the book.

Next my thanks must go to the senior members of the staff of the Imperial War Museum, whose support was invaluable. Christopher Dowling, Keeper of the Department of Museum Services, encouraged me throughout. Roderick Suddaby, Keeper of the Department of Documents, was unstinting in his advice and help. I would also like to thank Margaret Brooks (Keeper of the Sound Archives), Jane Carmichael (Keeper of the Department of Photographs), Angela Weight (Keeper of the Department of Art), and Gwynn Bayliss (Keeper of the Department of Printed Books). I am particularly indebted to Paul Kemp of the Department of Photographs for his endless patience and assistance in selecting the photographs. Without his seemingly encyclopaedic fund of knowledge of all matters naval, and unerring eye for detail, I would have been poorly placed to find my way among the vast collection in the Department. He also spent much time and effort commenting on my text, and saved me from committing a number of serious errors. Peter Simkins likewise gave much time to reading and commenting on the typescript. He too steered me away from a number of 'rocks and shoals'.

Michael Moody of the Department of Art was, as ever, a tactful pilot in the matter of selecting the paintings to go in the book. He also headed me away from at least one potentially questionable choice. I must also mention the help given by Peter Hart of the Department of Sound Records.

As before, I found working in the Department of Documents both stimulating and agreeable. For this I must thank Simon Robbins, Nigel Steel, Steven Walton, Penny Goymer, Dave Shaw and Wendy Lutterloch.

As was the case with my previous book published in association with the Imperial War Museum, my friend Linda Kitson gave up time she could ill spare from her very busy life to help me choose the paintings.

I must also thank the Ministry of Defence for allowing me to reproduce the diagram on page 220.

William Armstrong of Sidgwick & Jackson has been a help and support throughout. I am grateful to Claire Evans and latterly Carey Smith my editors. The imaginative design is entirely the work of Wilf Dickie.

Without Jane Thompson the book would never have got as far as having its keel laid, let alone been launched. Her research and editing work were invaluable. Her support was, as always, a vital part of the work.

PROLOGUE

. . . that we might be a safeguard to our Sovereign Lord King George and his dominions, and a protection for such as pass on the seas upon their lawful occasions, that the inhabitants of our islands may in peace and quietness serve Thee our God . . .

from the Naval Prayer

By drawing on the collections of the Imperial War Museum, this book aims to give the reader an idea of what it was like to serve in the most perilous years in the Royal Navy's long history. As far as possible I have let the participants tell the story, providing linking text to set the scene where necessary, or to explain the overall picture. Perforce, the scene setting in a book of this type can only be a précis of what were at times very complex issues. The Imperial War Museum collections are voluminous, and space allows for only a fraction of the available material to be included. Similarly, I can give the reader only a glimpse of the vast tapestry of maritime operations conducted by the Royal Navy in the Second World War. I do not include any accounts by members of the Merchant Navy, whose role in the war at sea was equally important as that of the Royal Navy. The story of the Merchant Navy deserves a book devoted entirely to its activities. For this reason this book is subtitled 'The Royal Navy in the Second World War'.

I do not cover the United States and Canadian Navies, or other Allied participation, other than in passing. Without the United States Navy, the war at sea would not have been won. The same can be said about the Canadian contribution to the Battle of the Atlantic.

Readers, especially those who served at sea during the Second World War, may feel that I have omitted important events, and given scant, or no, mention to particular branches of the Royal Navy. For example, I have given far less space to submarine operations than it might be felt their contribution deserves. For this reason, I have included a special section on submarines. It is lack of space, not deficiencies in the collections in the Imperial War Museum, that must be held to blame for any lack of coverage, and I take full responsibility for my choice of material. The opinions expressed are entirely my own.

By the end of the War in Europe, the Royal Navy had 120 major warships (battleships, carriers and cruisers), 846 destroyers, frigates, sloops and corvettes, 131 submarines and 729 minesweepers, as well as over 1,000 landing craft and minor vessels. The Fleet Air Arm consisted of 69 squadrons of over 2,000 aircraft. Nearly 800,000 men and women were in the Naval Service, including Royal Marines. The seamanship, skill and fighting spirit of the Royal Navy had never been higher. Its performance in the Pacific, despite the imperfections of its logistic system compared with that of the United States Navy, was responsible for the special relationship it enjoyed with the Americans in the Korean War (1950–53), and in the subsequent years of the cold war. The Royal Navy was thus well placed to play a vital role in the formulation of NATO maritime procedures, and was regarded as second to none in its anti-submarine and minesweeping skills, even by its bigger brother the United States Navy. Proof of the Royal Navy's place in the pecking order among America's allies was the crucial role it played at the sharp end of maritime operations in the northern end of the Persian Gulf, in the war against Saddam Hussein. The General Secretary of the Western European Union once boasted that six members of this organization took part in this war. He failed to add that when the shooting looked likely, with one exception, their ships were hastily withdrawn to safer waters. The exception was the Royal Navy. This is not to cast aspersions on the ships' companies of the other five navies, but rather is a commentary on their governments who had, it seems, forgotten that the ultimate purpose of a navy, or any armed service for that matter, when all other means of persuasion have failed, is to fight. The Royal Navy had shown in the Falklands War that it had not forgotten its primary function.

Its record in the Second World War, as the material in the Imperial War Museum bears witness, was a triumph of spirit over adversity. A great deal of that adversity could have been avoided, but for the woeful state of preparedness of all three armed services in 1939; the direct result of the policies of successive governments in the interwar years. It is to the ships' companies and Fleet Air Arm Squadrons of the Royal Navy in the Second World War, who overcame despite the odds, and their successors, that I dedicate this book.

Quotations The text contains many direct quotations from written documentary material and interview tapes. These are reproduced verbatim where possible, but obvious errors have been corrected and minor confusions clarified. It has not been thought necessary to indicate where quotations have been abridged.

Photographs and Paintings All the illustrations in this book have come from the Imperial War Museum, and have been listed with their reference after the appropriate caption.

1

The Royal Navy at the Outbreak of the Second World War: 1939

Previous page: **Boys with Bull Terrier 'Bill', HMS** *Hood.* **This picture was taken early in the War, when sailors still wore their ship's name on their cap ribbon, or cap 'tally'. Soon cap tallies just bore the letters HMS. (A175)**

Went into cells on Thursday 31st August and the War started on Sunday 3rd September, and I promptly put in to see the Officer of the Day with a request that I be returned to duty straight away before the War ended, and I was back on board before dinner, though the Coxswain would not give me my tot as I was still under punishment, so as normal had more bubbly than my ration with all the Sippers.

Able Seaman Fred Coombes

Thus did one member of His Majesty's Navy see the beginning of the Second World War. Fred Coombes was serving seven days' cells for smuggling seven cigarettes out of Portland dockyard. His identical twin Frank, also an Able Seaman, came to the cell window each evening to pass in cigarettes and bars of chocolate. Both served throughout the war, mainly in coastal forces, both were awarded the DSM, and both retired as Petty Officers.

On 1 September 1939 Lieutenant Jack van de Kasteele joined the battleship *Malaya* in the Mediterranean Fleet as assistant gunnery officer. His diary for Sunday 3 September 1939:

After Divisions, Captain addressed ship's company to congratulate them on regatta victory. Mentioned as an afterthought that we should probably find ourselves at war by 13.00!

Our ultimatum to Germany delivered this a.m. War was declared by us at 11.15 (GMT) and by France at 17.00.

Bill Batters, a Petty Officer serving in the elderly cruiser *Danae*, on the South Atlantic station:

September 4th. Well, we saw the official statement re[ference] commencement of hostilities. I'm glad our country made the move and am quite sure Hitler didn't bargain on the Lion waking up. Hope fervently that it doesn't last too long.

On 8 September Paymaster Lieutenant Commander Jackie Jackson wrote to reassure his wife from the battle-cruiser HMS *Hood*:

People have been trying to kill my family for years, but they haven't had a chance, and we've always passed out in our beds when we were old and decrepit. I bet you a much better fur than last time that I'll be back with you before our third anniversary – and I'll try and throw in the wreath on the zircon ring as well if I'm wrong. Make no mistake we've got them on the run already, and they have started moaning about the blockade.

I am looking forward to a quiet and successful conclusion to this skirmish, in a very much shorter time than the majority of people believe.

Rum issue, HMS *Rodney*, sister ship to HMS *Nelson*. (A103)

Writing on 20 September, three days after the aircraft carrier HMS *Courageous* had been sunk by the U-boat U-29:

I shouldn't be too worried in relation to me when you think of the *Courageous. Hood* is a very different kind of ship, and also is constructed quite differently, and so the chances of our being sunk, even if we are hit, can be considered negligible.

Luckily for him, Jackson left the *Hood* in November 1940 on draft to HMS *Glenearn*. But his optimism, reflected in his letters to his 'Darling Booby', was widespread in the Royal Navy. War was expected. 'It came as no surprise,' remembered Lieutenant-Commander Dickie Courage, Fleet Signal Officer in the East Indies. The War which started on 3 September was to last for almost six years. From the very beginning to the very end, the Royal Navy was in the thick of the fight; the first three and a half years were the most perilous in its long history. There was no 'phoney war' from September 1939 to May 1940, as there was for the British Army, nor years when the majority of a greatly expanded Army was out of action, training for the battles to come. Royal Air Force Bomber Command took the battle to the German homeland from early in the war. But it was 1943 before the Army or Bomber Command began the toughest fighting and taking their heaviest casualties. By then, as Correlli Barnett writes:

The Royal Navy at the Outbreak of the Second World War: 1939

1. Corr, Barnett, *Engage the Enemy More Closely, the Royal Navy in the Second World War*, Hodder & Stoughton, 1991, p. xvii.
2. 'The Service' was how many officers referred to the Royal Navy at the time.

. . . the Royal Navy had already fought its most desperate battles and suffered the majority of its wartime losses in ships heavier than a corvette, including all five of those capital ships and all five of those fleet carriers that were sunk.[1]

The Service[2] which went to war in September 1939 was composed almost entirely of regular officers and ratings. Some Royal Naval Volunteer Reserve (RNVR) and Royal Naval Reserve (RNR) had been called up, and were at sea. There were three categories of reserves in the Naval Service. The RNVR consisted, as their title implies, of volunteers from all walks of civilian life, who joined the Naval equivalent of the Territorial Army, sometimes years before the War. Many were commissioned and some eventually commanded ships. The RNR was composed of Merchant Navy officers, who had volunteered to serve in warships in the event of hostilities. The majority were experienced seamen and fine navigators. Many commanded ships. The Navy also called up its reservists. These were ex-regular ratings who, on completing their service, could be recalled in time of war. But when war broke out the huge influx of citizen sailors was yet to come. In the early days, the RN's joke about reserve officers – 'the RNVR are gentlemen trying to be sailors, and the RNR are sailors trying to be gentlemen' – might set a few teeth on edge. But the regulars set the standard of professionalism, discipline, devotion to duty, offensive spirit and wry humour. The RNR and RNVR, officers and ratings alike, took to the life in the Service like ducks to water, and their performance was indistinguishable. The regulars were in no doubt; Bill Batters:

The RNVRs were now doing any and every type of duty in the ship and doing it well. Only they of all the reservists had lacked the advantage of considerable earlier sea experience, but they had had sea time in abundance since joining this ship. We began to wonder how we ever got on without them.

Nelson wrote: 'No captain can do wrong if he places his ship alongside that of an enemy.' The captains and ships' companies of the Royal Navy a century and a half later were to live up to this precept. This spirit, deeply ingrained in a Service with a record of victory at sea going back nearly three centuries, endured throughout the Second World War; gave it its character, and was evident in the uncompromising way in which it fought. The fighting spirit endures to this day, but the Navy of the twenties and thirties, which provided the leadership at the top and the backbone of the Fleet from 1939 to 1945, was very different from the Service of the 1990s.

The training started when many were teenagers. Most officers joined at the age of thirteen, and spent four years at the Royal Naval College at Dartmouth. A lesser number joined Dartmouth at the age of seventeen or eighteen straight from their public schools, and only spent one term there. The regime at Dartmouth was similar to a public school of that time, fairly spartan with cold baths, sport, and beatings for even trivial misdemeanours. Naval discipline made for a tougher environment than most schools. Seamanship, boatwork,

Midshipman Desmond
Cassidi RN (now Admiral
Sir Desmond Cassidi)
in charge of one of
HMS *Cumberland*'s boats
in 1943. (A16669)

navigation and some marine engineering were included in the otherwise typical academic curriculum. Since Dartmouth was a fee-paying school, cadets were exclusively from the middle or upper classes. Promotion from rating to commissioned officer, as opposed to warrant rank, was extremely rare. By the age of seventeen to eighteen, the future officers of the peacetime Navy were at sea in the fleet as midshipmen. For eighteen months they were neither commissioned officers nor ratings. In their late teens they were given considerable responsibility including charge of one of their ship's piquet boats or launches. A young midshipman would often be in command of a tender full of over a hundred inebriated and rowdy libertymen, all older than him, and some old enough to be his father, faced with a journey of several miles to his ship at anchor, at night, in a squall. Eighteen months of boatwork in all weathers was an invaluable apprenticeship for future captains of warships. Despite being given responsibility far beyond that borne by their civilian contemporaries, punishment for infringements of naval discipline or custom by junior midshipmen was often a beating with a dirk scabbard, administered by their seniors, or the sub-lieutenant in charge of the gunroom where they messed. Much of this changed with the outbreak of war. The need for junior officers to fill the expanding number of billets at sea resulted in a large number of ratings being commissioned under the Upper Yardman scheme and, in the early years, direct from the professions in civilian life. Men from either category, often in their mid-twenties or older, would not have taken kindly to some of the schoolboy antics of the pre-war gunroom, although the gunrooms and wardrooms of the fleet could be lively enough, even in the midst of war.

Life below decks was correspondingly tough. Eric Smith joined HMS *Ganges*, a boy training establishment in 1936:

The Gunnery Instructor always carried a length of rubber hose around with him which he used frequently and with relish on any poor unfortunate boy who he considered was not paying sufficient attention, or who was a bit slow obeying an order or answering a question. The rubber hose, or 'Stonarcky', as it was called, was used more frequently in the afternoon training period after he had had his tot of rum.

The Seamanship PO was a different type of person, and had no time for gunners' mates. Any boy not paying attention was rewarded with a slap of his horny hand on the nape of the neck, which while it stung for a while, was not done viciously, and by and large he was popular with us boys.

Life at sea for boys from one of the training establishments was hardly less demanding. The Coombes twins joined HMS *Hood* in 1935:

After being led through some deserted Mess Decks and enclosed compartments, we found all our bags and hammocks heaped at the bottom of a steel ladder, after being thrown a deck at a time, through three decks to the level which led to our mess deck. That rough handling of our hammocks was to be the first indication that life was rough at sea. The Boys' Mess Deck was a small, open area between two compartments. It contained six long scrubbed tables. Overhead ran various electric cables, forced air trunkings, and a variety of pipes. Below these hung a series of bars and hooks from which our hammocks were slung, head to toe at 24-inch spacing over the mess tables and in the gangway. On the Ship's side was fixed a wire framed Mess Cupboard for crockery and cutlery, and underneath, the

Gunroom in HMS *Malaya*, a 15-inch-gun *Queen Elizabeth* class battleship. (A16674)

Sailors in their mess-deck reading mail, HMS *Rodney*. (A162)

Bread Barge, bread bin to us novices, who from custom were looking for something to eat, and finding as on all boys' mess decks there were never any leftovers. We decided to stay in our Messes until 'Cooks to the Galley' was piped at about 4 o'clock, when two duck-suited youngsters came rushing in; one to put a handful of tea into the pot, the other to scatter a few knives on the tables before dashing off to join the queue at the Servery and be handed a numbered tray containing just the correct number of rations required in the Mess. Of food there was no sign, until the Duty Mess Men came running down the three steel ladders to our mess deck, their backs to the rungs, holding the trays with both hands. It took a lot of practice. We pressed the backs of our ankles against the preceding rung to balance ourselves. It was the only way to carry a dish that might contain liquid such as gravy.

In the Fleet, until after the Second World War, there were two systems of messing. Unlike warships today, there was no central dining room for ratings or Chiefs and Petty Officers. Bill Batters:

Big ships were invariably on General Mess. The Paymaster or his deputy drew up a menu for all the lower deck in the ship's company. Each mess sent a 'cook' to collect the rations

Sailors take a jam tart decorated with the 'Saint' emblem to their mess in HMS *Sardonyx*. (A17055)

from the galley at meal times. If there were ten men in the mess, ten cooked meals were supplied, or rather a portion sufficient for ten men. The 'cook' divided up what was in the trays or dishes into the number of portions required. All messes had the same menu, whether Chiefs, Petty Officers or broadside messes. The ship's cooks drew the rations, prepared them and cooked them in bulk.

Hood was on this system. The other system was called Canteen Messing. Each mess had a monthly messing allowance provided by the Service, which they could spend on provisions in the ship's canteen to augment what was issued by ship's provision store. No money changed hands. Once the allowance was spent, the mess was reduced to using only what the ship's store provided: the basics.

The mess 'cooks' drew a ration of meat from the butcher in the beef screen, at the same time drawing potatoes, and sometimes other vegetables. When the mess saw the meat, they decided how best to use it. One day you would have a 'straight bake', roast beef, roast potatoes. The 'cook' prepared the meat and potatoes, and if able to, Yorkshire pudding. He might buy a tin of peas from the canteen. He would take this lot up to the galley in a tray, or trays, each having a brass tally with the mess number. He wouldn't see it again until they piped 'cooks to the galley'. When he arrived, he was handed his food, in the same trays but now cooked. This system allowed more variety and latitude to the messes, some of whom had very skilful 'cooks', or food preparers. When there was food available we lived quite well. Later on in the war, when Batters [he often refers to himself in the third person] had not had a fresh potato for five months or fresh meat for weeks, he wasn't so cocky. The menu then was bully beef, done umpteen different ways and served with rice. Potatoes took up too much bulk and went bad. Fresh meat had to be kept in cold rooms, and anyway, we weren't getting supplies. When we could we ate well, when we couldn't, we had memories of the past and hopes for the future.

Batters' reference to broadside messing evokes the days of sail, and early steam navy. Sailors ate, slung their hammocks, and lived by the guns: the broadside of the ships that provided the 'wooden walls' of these islands for centuries past. A sailor in Nelson's *Victory* would have found canteen messing almost familiar.

Ratings still slept in hammocks, as did the Coombes twins on their first night in the *Hood*:

The long day finished with us slinging our hammocks, holding the 'nettles' [strings] open at our head-end with a short stick, unfolding our heavy woollen blankets lengthways across our hammock before swinging our bodies in; a comfortable bed, with our boots and clothing made into a pillow. We soon got used to it, as we did to the ever-present hum of fan motors pushing stale air from one compartment to the next, and the subdued roar of machinery. The lights were not dimmed until lights out at 10 o'clock. The first night,

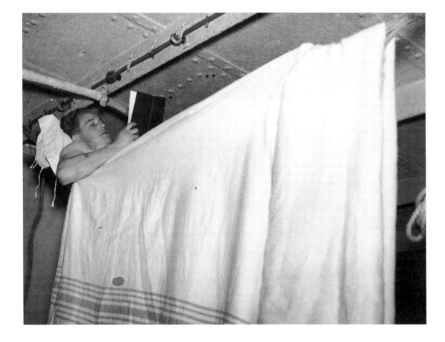

Sailor in his hammock, HMS *Rodney*. (A169)

fitful sleep came to most after a lot of wriggling about, trying to keep our blankets wrapped around us at the same time, and attempting to ignore the bright overhead light. Our long troubled night, broken by odd bumps underneath as passers-by 'headed' our hammocks, as they went about their duties, was ended by the switching on of all lights and raucous shouting of the duty Petty Officer. The time being 5.30 gave us little time to lash up and stow our hammocks, get dressed and find our promised cup of Kye [cocoa] and ship's biscuit. The established mess mates had turned out early to draw the rations, lash up their hammocks, and dispose of the rations in comfort. We were only caught the once, as like all things learned the hard way, only fools get caught twice. The next day we mustered at 6 o'clock, still trying to crunch the hard ship's biscuit before someone robbed us of it. On mustering, the Duty Officer gave the usual order to scrub decks. That morning, in the unusually cold weather for Portsmouth, the sea water turned to icy slush as it was hosed on to the deck.

Even in the 'Mighty *'ood'*, as she was known in the Fleet, steaming at speed into a rough sea was unpleasant for boys at sea for the first time. The Coombes twins were lucky never to suffer from seasickness:

The heavy seas and motion had thinned a lot out by dinner time, with few able to eat their fill for a change. We were among the few able to do justice to the windfall.

Opposite: Scrubbing decks, HMS *Rodney.* (A191)

Humour was rough and ready. The Coombes twins, when *Hood* was in dock at Gibraltar, and ship's facilities could not be used:

The Heads [lavatories] at Gib were long brick buildings on the seaward side of the mole, inside was a long trough with about three inches of water in it, against a back wall. We sat leaning our backs against the wall, while every few minutes an automatic cistern outside the building sent water flowing down the trough. Though not very pleasant places to hang around in, the Heads ashore were much sought after by some as a place to skive in, or perhaps read the newspaper. At busy times in the mornings queues formed. Some anxious person had the idea of crumpling a newspaper, wait for the flush to run, light the paper and drop it in outside the Heads. Everybody soon learned to stand up at the first yell and wait for the flaming newspaper to float by. This harmless form of amusement went on for weeks, and caused many a laugh, but someone always goes too far. He poured petrol in and when it had spread to the other end, threw in a match. There was a huge flash, but this identified the culprit as he was the only one singed round the face, all others being scorched at the other end. It was to be the last time the amusement took that form, although some wit put up a notice that a Delicatessen Meal would be served in the Sick Bay, of Roast Cheek, Grilled Swinging Steak and Curried Dusters. It was a foolhardy trick, but if the Navy wanted crews with plenty of fire in their bellies, who played hard, they had to expect small explosions as devilment fired up.

The Royal Navy was to have need of men with fire in their bellies thanks to the decisions, or often plain lethargy, of successive British governments in the nineteen-twenties and thirties. These decisions had an impact in four areas:

capital-ship design and construction, the size and composition of the fleet, air power at sea, and strategy.

At the Washington Naval Conference of 1922, the British government agreed to American proposals for a ratio of capital ships in the Royal Navy, the United States Navy and the Japanese Navy of 5:5:3. The British thought the Washington Agreement would give them the means to escape the horns of a dilemma. The Anglo-Japanese Treaty was due for renewal in 1922, but to have done so would have offended the United States. The British government's pusillanimity actually had the effect of making a potential enemy of an ally who had exercised sea control of the Pacific for the Royal Navy in the First World War, and did nothing to mollify the Anglophobes in the United States Navy and Congress, although it must be said that Japan was hardly well disposed to Britain in the First World War, only carrying out tasks that suited her. British politicians also saw the Washington Agreement as a way out of a financially crippling ship-construction race with the Americans. The Agreement also imposed a limit of 35,000 tons on the size of battleships built in the future. Finally the British politicians acquiesced with an American proposal for a ten-year moratorium on the building of new capital ships. This, despite Admiral Sir David Beatty's warning that as British ships were older than America's, after ten years, the Royal Navy would be well behind the United States Navy in fighting ability. His warnings of the likely effect on the British shipbuilding industry were also ignored.

When the Royal Air Force was formed in 1918, out of the Army's Royal Flying Corps and The Royal Naval Air Service, despite considerable protest by the Navy, control of maritime air was removed from the service who understood its needs, and how it should be operated. For nineteen years this responsibility would remain in the hands of a service wedded to two strategic theories: the indivisibility of air power, and that all future wars could be won by strategic bombing. The first held that all air assets should be retained centrally by the Air Force, and lobbed out as they thought fit, irrespective of the strategic and tactical situation affecting the other two services. Their requirements were irrelevant anyway, because the Air Force would win the war on its own by implementing its second sacred theory, strategic bombing. The most faithful follower of this creed, Air Marshal Sir Arthur 'Bomber' Harris, would be the cause of much trouble to the Royal Navy at one of its most critical periods in the Second World War.

Although in 1937 the politicians were eventually persuaded to cede to the Royal Navy's oft-repeated requests to regain responsibility for the Fleet Air Arm, much damage had been done in the intervening nineteen years. It was only a partial return to the state of naval aviation in 1918, because the Navy did not win its case to take over Coastal Command. So command of air power in the maritime battle remained divided, with near-disastrous consequences.

Because many of the brightest naval aviators transferred to the Royal Air Force in 1918, the Navy was deprived of men who could influence strategic and tactical thinking on the use of air power at sea, and left the field to the advocates of the battleship. The latter remained almost unchallenged in senior posts in the Royal Navy right up to the Second World War and, in some instances, well into it. They held, among other things, that a battleship with good anti-aircraft guns could survive air attack. That is not to say that the Navy failed to understand that shipborne aircraft had a part to play in maritime warfare. Indeed this is given substance by the ordering of six new fleet carriers of the *Illustrious* and *Implacable* class for the 1936–39 building programmes. However, a question mark hangs over the roles laid down for naval aircraft which are indicative of a very limited tactical approach in the Royal Navy compared with the Japanese and United States Navies, who had retained full control of their air arms. The duties foreseen for naval aircraft were:

1. Reconnaissance for the fleet;
2. Attacks to slow down escaping enemy, to enable the surface ships to come into action;
3. To assist in anti-submarine warfare, against air attacks, and to defend the carriers themselves;
4. Spotting for surface actions and shore bombardment.[3]

3. Roskill, *The War at Sea, 1939–1945*, Vol. 1, HMSO, London, 1954, p. 32.

This list of tasks omits the destruction of major units of the enemy fleet, possibly because the proponents of the win-with-the-battleship school did not think it was possible. How wrong they were to be.

In 1939, the Royal Navy had only one modern aircraft carrier, out of a total of seven: HMS *Ark Royal*, completed in 1938. *Furious*, *Courageous* and *Glorious* were converted from First World War cruisers in 1925, 1928 and 1930. HMS *Eagle* was converted in 1920 from a battleship laid down for the Chilean Navy before the First World War, and never delivered. The first purpose-built aircraft carrier in the world, HMS *Hermes*, was completed in 1923. HMS *Argus*, converted from an Italian liner in 1916, when Britain led the world in naval aviation, was non-operational. The decision to build six new fleet carriers was vital, but late; the first did not take part in operations until 1940. The remark made by Admiral Sir John Fisher to Admiral Lord Charles Beresford in 1902, 'You cannot build a ship in a hurry with a supplementary estimate', held true for the last years of peace, before the outbreak of war in 1939.

The ageing aircraft with which the Fleet Air Arm was equipped were another damaging consequence of Royal Air Force responsibility for the Fleet Air Arm, which included ordering the aircraft. The Fleet Air Arm was the least favoured part of the Royal Air Force, and from 1928 to the end of 1932 only eighteen aircraft were added to the Fleet Air Arm. This, and because the Royal Navy was dominated by the gunnery branch, meant that in 1939 the Fleet Air Arm had 232 aircraft, of which only eighteen were the modern, but inadequate, Skua. The British aircraft industry contributed to this sorry tale well into the Second World War by late delivery and bad design, so that by the time 'new' types such as the Fulmar, Skua and Albacore entered service they were already obsolete, and were hopeless performers compared with their American and Japanese counterparts. Paradoxically, one of the most successful Fleet Air Arm aircraft

Blackburn Skua Mark II fighter and dive-bomber; obsolete before it came into service. Despite this, Skuas notched up two firsts: the first aircraft to sink a major German warship in the Second World War (*Königsberg* at Bergen), and the first ever to sink a warship by dive bombing. (HU2326)

was the rugged Swordfish biplane, with fixed undercarriage and open cockpit, affectionately nicknamed the 'Stringbag'.

The total effective strength of the Royal and Dominion Navies on the outbreak of war in 1939 was:

Battleships and battlecruisers	12
Aircraft carriers	6
Seaplane carriers	2
Fleet cruisers	35
Trade route/convoy cruisers	23
Fleet destroyers	100
Escort destroyers/sloops	101
Submarines	38

British maritime strategy in 1939 was based on the supposition that the French Fleet would look after the western end of the Mediterranean, while the British looked after the eastern end. If a strong British Fleet was needed in the Far East, to deter or counter Japanese aggression, it was planned that the French would take over complete responsibility for the Mediterranean. The sea control task facing the Royal Navy in the First World War had been daunting enough,

Swordfish Mark I, dropping a torpedo. (MH167)

with 61 battleships, 120 cruisers and 443 destroyers. Now, despite Admiralty insistence that 70 cruisers was the minimum to protect convoys against surface raiders, the government had allowed the total, including Dominion ships, to fall to 58. The British Merchant Navy consisted of 3,000 deep sea cargo ships and tankers, and 1,000 coasters, totalling 21 million tons. On any day, there were an average of 2,500 ships at sea to protect.

On 18 June 1935 the British government, alarmed by the threat of a resurgent German Navy since Hitler's accession to power, concluded a Naval Agreement with Germany. Fortunately, the war began rather earlier than Hitler intended, so that with the exception of submarines, the German Navy was actually at 35 per cent of its agreed strength. Given the trouble the German Navy would cause, this was a blessing indeed. The aircraft carrier *Graf Zeppelin*, due for completion in 1940, was never finished. If the war had started in 1944, as Hitler had planned, the German Navy would have consisted of 13 battleships, 33 cruisers, 4 aircraft carriers, 250 U-boats and flotillas of large destroyers. But *Bismarck* and *Tirpitz* outclassed the newest British battleships then being built, the *King George V* class; because, whereas the British complied with the regulations of the Washington Treaty, the Germans did not. The day war began, thirty-nine U-boats, out of a total of fifty-six, were at sea, ready to strike. The German Navy, although much smaller, was all modern; the British had some ships dating back to before 1914. Luckily for Britain, the German U-boat building programme got off to a slow start. Hitler's constant meddling with military and naval construction projects in favour of his pet schemes, and inter-service rivalry, further hindered the German Navy's expansion. Finally, the Luftwaffe, under Reichsmarschall Hermann Goering, was even less disposed to co-operate with the German Navy than the most 'Trenchardian' Royal Air Force air marshals with the Royal Navy. Had the Germans succeeded in building aircraft carriers, the opinion of the British Official Naval Historian of the 1939–45 War is that the survival of Britain would have been problematical.

Frustrating all attempts by the Chiefs of Staff to maintain modern, well-equipped armed forces was the 'ten-year rule'. In 1919, the armed services were told to plan their budgets on the assumption that the country would not be involved in a major war for ten years. The rule was renewed each year. For example, in 1934, with Hitler already in power for a year, and only ten years before the Normandy landings, the Royal Navy had to trim its expenditure, and hence what ships could be ordered, on the assumption that there would be no war for ten years. The rule was finally abandoned in February 1936. Three and a half years before the start of the Second World War, the Royal Navy could at last begin a major shipbuilding programme. There was a great deal of catching up to do.

When Britain declared war on Germany, there were two further potential enemies in the offing. Japan was by now thoroughly hostile to Britain. To keep the Americans sweet, the Anglo-Japanese treaty had not been renewed. The American response was to set their faces against entering into any alliance to counterbalance Japanese naval strength in the Pacific. Italy, an ally in the First World War, was now firmly in the other camp, not least because of Britain's ineffective huffing and puffing over the Italian invasion of Abyssinia (Ethiopia). The loudest huffers and puffers, to the point of pressing for war on Italy, were those who earlier had bent their efforts to emasculate the British armed forces – a feature of political life that persists to this day. Britain had the same maritime commitments in 1939 as in 1914, a global empire and trade routes, but far fewer warships. Now, the Pacific, with British Colonies and the two Dominions of Australia and New Zealand, would not be protected by a friendly Japanese Navy; it would be wide open to Japanese attack. The Mediterranean from 1914 to 1918 was, except for U-boats, virtually an Allied lake. Now Italy, ruled by Mussolini, a fascist dictator with a sizeable modern navy and a large if ageing air force, was poised to challenge British and French passage through that lake. Naval and air forces could sortie from the Italian 'boot', its toe pointing towards North Africa, Sicily and the Italian colony of Libya. Lieutenant Alec Dennis serving in the destroyer HMS *Griffin* based in Alexandria before the outbreak of hostilities remembered:

At that time the Italians, though undoubtedly hostile, were something of an unknown quantity. Although they hadn't much of a fighting record, their larger ships and their aircraft were much more modern than ours.

Furthermore, the Italian colonies of Abyssinia, Eritrea and Italian Somali-land were potential bases from which to attack British shipping in the Indian Ocean, rounding the Horn of Africa, and crossing the Red Sea to and from the Suez Canal.

The Royal Navy harboured two tactical misconceptions at the outbreak of the Second World War. First that the invention of Asdic, or sonar, would ensure that the U-boat would not be able to present the same menace as in 1917. Unfortunately, sonar could not detect a submarine on the surface, and U-boats in the Second World War, as in the First, favoured an approach and attacks on the surface, particularly by night. Second, the Naval Staff considered that anti-aircraft fire from ships would be sufficient to protect them, and convoys, from air attack. The officers serving in the fleet were not so confident. Lieutenant Dennis:

Our anti-aircraft capability was pathetic. When we had the occasional shoot at a radio-controlled 'Queen Bee' aircraft, the target used to fly straight and level through the massed fire of the fleet, emerging unscathed for another run.

In a less than complimentary remark about the standard of anti-aircraft gunnery taught at Whale Island, the Royal Navy's gunnery school, Lieutenant Van de Kasteele's diary on the day war began with Germany:

I get the whole of HA [high angle] armament as my pigeon, and learn more about HA in three days than in 12 months at WI.

Not only were many warships equipped with too few, outdated close-in anti-aircraft weapons, but the fire control system for the larger guns was incapable of giving the correct data to enable the gunners to engage fast-moving aircraft.

But in the end morale is the most telling factor in battle, and the Royal Navy had long recovered from the low state of morale in some ships of the Grand Fleet at the end of the First World War. Ridley Waymouth, a Captain in the Second World War, a midshipman in the First, recalled:

By the autumn of 1918 when the war was drawing to a close, morale in the fleet, or at any rate morale in *Glorious*, was pretty low. The ship was fine, but there was too much drink-ing and too low a standard among the officers. This I realized for the first time when the Forth was swept by a gale of hurricane force and ships began to drag their anchors. Some-time in the night the *Campania* dragged her anchor and dragged down on to the *Royal Oak*, and both dragged down on to us. As the ships slowly approached, the watches were turned out to turn in the boats and prepare the ship for collision stations. It was then that many of the men, when ordered out to man and turn in the cutters, just stayed under cover, and in the darkness, rain, wind and noise, the officers failed to get control and nothing was done.

Because the Germans only came out to fight on two occasions in the four years of the First World War, the Grand Fleet had spent a great deal of that war swinging round buoys at Scapa and Rosyth, or in necessary but boring and fruitless sweeps in the mists of the North Sea. In the cold accounting of Grand Strategy, the Grand Fleet ensured that Britain retained command of the sea, at least on the surface. Without this, she would have lost the war. But to the nation, whose pride was chiefly vested in the Royal Navy, the lack of a latter-day Trafalgar was a disappointment. In the eyes of some less well-informed members of the public, the huge sums spent on the fleet might have been better spent elsewhere. The enforced idleness of the Grand Fleet compared with the terrible sacrifice suffered by the army in France, was all too plain. Some of this feeling, almost of shame, however misplaced, cannot have been lost on the men in that fleet.

Lack of action was not to be a problem for the Royal Navy from 1939 to 1945.

2

From the Outbreak of War to the
Fall of France: 1939–1940

The convoy system was reintroduced immediately on the outbreak of war, but the liner *Athenia* was already outbound from Liverpool. Ten hours after war was declared, the Battle of the Atlantic began when U-30 torpedoed her 250 miles north-west of Ireland on 3 September 1939. Of the 112 lost, 28 were Americans. Mr Jack Coullie and his wife Bella from Chicago were reading in one of the passenger lounges when the torpedo struck:

and we were left in complete darkness. Everybody rushed for the doors, but I held on to Bella until the rush was over, and we made our way on to the deck. It was not quite dark. What a terrible scene. People lying all over the deck, women screaming, children crying, and the crew keeping people from rushing the lifeboats.

After returning to their cabin to fetch their lifejackets, lighting his way with the only four matches he had, he rejoined his wife. After searching in vain for a lifeboat

we went down to the next deck, and a boat came alongside. I yelled to them to take us off. A fire hose was over the side and a man in the lifeboat got hold of the end and told us to slide down. I asked Bella if she could make it. She said she could. I helped her over the rail. She was just at the lifeboat when a wave washed the boat away, the hose was jerked from the man's hands, and Bella fell between the lifeboat and the ship. I jumped far out to clear the lifeboat. In a minute I was at Bella's side and got her to hold on to the rope round the lifeboat. I tried and tried to boost her into the boat, but oil was pouring from a burst fuel tank and everything was slippery. I got one leg over the side of the boat. A man held me as I got hold of Bella's foot. Another man got hold of Bella's lifebelt strap, and we got her into the boat. We were both soaked through with oil, dirty black stuff. There were only five men in the boat, the rest women and children. We got the boat moving and tried to keep it head-on to the waves. We shipped a lot of water and got soaked. Bella and some of the women were sick, and sometime later I was sick. We had swallowed so much oil, the taste was awful.

Jack and Bella Coullie were picked up by the Swedish ship *Southern Cross,* and later transferred to the American freighter *City of Flint*, in which they travelled to Halifax, Nova Scotia.

City of Flint was short of food and water, so we did not fare so well, until we stopped another freighter going the other way, and got some medical supplies and food. We got clothes from the crew. I fixed up Bella with a pair of overall pants [trousers] and two sweaters. Later I got a pair of men's pyjamas and a dress, and we got rid of Bella's oily clothes. I had on my dark suit, and I was just as oily, until I got two shirts, a pair of pants [trousers], and an overall jacket. We were like that until we reached Halifax nine days later; never had our clothes off and no bath.

Hugh Swindley, an ex-sailor from Philadelphia, who had been shipwrecked twice before, was travelling as a passenger, and wrote to friends:

We slid down the falls when our lifeboat was loaded and in the water; three stewards, a cadet, a seaman and myself. I had to use all my strength in getting free the oars, passengers were sitting on them. The capacity of the boat was 40. I was told on board the rescue vessel that our lifeboat held 100 people. After getting away from *Athenia*, our boat was making water badly. There seemed doubt whether the plug was in, it could not be located, and there was no bailing pan. I took off my boots (hand sewn, English made), and began bailing. I had to be rough to keep the packed passengers from standing in my way. I had a fellow passenger from Philadelphia helping me to bail with the boots. He was so patient, steady and willing, I asked him if he was a 'sky pilot' [padre]. He replied, 'No, only a lieutenant in the army.' He was seasick, but he was game. We made the *Southern Cross* of Stockholm at about 5.30 am [seven hours after being hit], and our lifeboat sank about fifteen minutes later.

By October 1939, with the end of the 'phoney war' in Western Europe still seven months away, the Royal Navy was hitting back at sea. Lieutenant Alastair Ewing, First Lieutenant of the destroyer HMS *Imogen*, in company with HMS *Ilex* screening the merchant ship *Stonepool*, on Friday 13 October:

At 6.30 pm [*sic*], *Ilex* suddenly altered course to port, increased speed, and made to us by light, 'submarine this way'. It seemed an odd way of putting it at the time, but *Stonepool*'s masthead lookout being higher than any of ours, had sighted something that looked like a submarine. We followed at once. Almost immediately *Ilex* hoisted the 'submarine in sight' flag, and opened fire.

The submarine (U-42) dived, and after a brisk attack with depth charges by both destroyers:

the U-boat suddenly came to the surface with a tremendous surge at about 20 degrees to the horizontal about 1,000 yards away. It was a most exciting moment. The U-boat righted herself at once and seemed to be in perfect trim. Both ships opened fire with our 4.7-inch guns. The result, *Imogen* one hit and *Ilex* two, one of which knocked the U-boat gun over the side. *Ilex*, who was bows on, went full ahead to ram. Just before she got there, she stopped engines and went full astern to reduce the impact and so the damage which she would sustain. As she passed over [the U-boat], the torpedo gunner's mate fired the starboard depth charge thrower. Almost as soon as *Ilex*'s stern had drawn clear, the conning tower opened and an officer appeared waving a piece of white paper and some sailors with their hands up.

Seventeen crew out of a total of 43 were picked up. Ewing reported that:

Among other information which we got from them was that they could not understand how we had detected them when they were stopped on the surface.

It was lucky that the masthead lookout of *Stonepool* had been so alert. Very few ships in the Royal Navy were equipped with radar at this period of the war, and submarines on the surface were very difficult to spot, particularly at night. Many Allied ships were to be lost to U-boats attacking or approaching on the surface before radar became universally fitted.

By this early stage in the war, U-boats had sunk one major British warship. The aircraft carrier *Courageous* was torpedoed on 17 September by U-29 in the Bristol Channel, thanks to German intercept of Royal Navy radio messages, which they were able to decode until 1943. The day after *Ilex* and *Imogen*'s success, U-47 commanded by Lieutenant-Commander Günther Prien attacked HMS *Royal Oak*, in the Scapa Flow naval base. Prien fired three torpedoes of which one struck *Royal Oak* in the bows. After investigation, the Captain of *Royal Oak* thought that the explosion was merely a minor internal one. Eighteen minutes later Prien struck again; all three torpedoes hit. Able Seaman Don Harris:

A heavy explosion awakened me. I asked a seaman running past what was the matter. 'Explosion up forward,' he replied.

'Oh well,' I thought, 'the watch on deck will soon fix that', and drifted back to sleep. It never occurred to me that the explosion was the first torpedo striking home. But there

Kapitän-Leutnant Günther Prien, who sank *Royal Oak*, shakes hands with Admiral Alfred Saalwachter, Flag Officer Group West.
(HU2226)

was no mistaking those that followed, when three more tore into our ship. All lights went out, and in a matter of minutes she listed to starboard. I hauled myself out of my hammock and into my shoes. A further sudden list made me realize that the situation was getting desperate. The piano [borrowed by Harris's mess for a concert] grazed me as it slid past and crashed into the combing fitted to hold six-inch shells. Had I been standing a foot closer, it would have crushed me against the bulkhead.

Being at night defence stations, most routes to the upper deck had been battened down and there were only two paths of escape for the majority of the ship's company. Slowly – and how interminably slowly it seemed – I made my way to the ladder at the bottom of which stood the first of many heroes I was to know that night. Torch in hand, he calmly guided sailors to the upper deck, gently urging them on in a cool, reassuring voice. I will never forget his 'steady boys, keep moving boys, keep calm'.

Harris was rescued, but 833 of the ship's company were lost. U-47 escaped. It was a daring and devastating blow at the Royal Navy's principal Home Waters base. Peacetime parsimony had resulted in failure to maintain or replace the defences built in the First World War.

By the end of 1939, the Allies had lost 114 ships to U-boats, of which only 11 were in convoys. But this was only a foretaste of the grim struggle ahead. By the end of the year, another menace was engaging the Admiralty's attention.

Just before the outbreak of war, two of Germany's pocket battleships, *Admiral Graf Spee* and *Deutschland*, had sailed for their operational stations. Their aim was to disrupt the sea-lanes on which Britain depended for her existence. Armed with six 11-inch and eight 5.9-inch guns, they outgunned the heaviest cruisers, and were faster than all but three of the Royal Navy's capital ships in commission. To seek and destroy these two ships before they wreaked

HMS *Royal Oak* in Plymouth Sound pre-1939. Identification stripes on B Turret show that she is under orders for the Mediterranean Fleet while the Spanish Civil War was in progress. These markings were to avoid being attacked by mistake by either side in this war, including German and Italian 'volunteer' air squadrons fighting on Franco's side, and Soviet pilots fighting on the Loyalist (Communist) side. (A5730) havoc on seaborne trade in the North and South Atlantic, the Royal and French Navies had no alternative but to form eight hunting groups, totalling five aircraft carriers, four battleships and fifteen cruisers. This was of course exactly the purpose for which the pocket battleships had been built: to force the British and French into dispersing their strength searching the vastness of the ocean. Only a handful of Allied ships were equipped with radar and their land-based and carrier-borne aircraft were limited in range. It is not a cliché to say that it was like searching for a needle in a haystack.

In November the German Navy added to the strain on the already hard-pressed British Home Fleet, when the battle-cruisers *Scharnhorst* and *Gneisenau* sortied from Wilhelmshaven with the intention of attacking North Atlantic shipping. With nine 11-inch guns, they were outgunned by British battleships and battle-cruisers, but were more than a match for the armed merchant cruiser *Rawalpindi*, which they encountered between the Faroes and Iceland, and battered into a blazing hulk in ten minutes; but not before she had radioed their position to the Home Fleet, while she fought back. The Captain and 270 of the crew of *Rawalpindi* paid with their lives for pre-war political decisions whose outcome was liners armed with 6-inch guns for lack of cruisers.

The Germans, aware from radio intercept that their position had been divulged, turned for home; the first of many tactical retreats by units of the German surface fleet, whose superbly equipped ships were not equalled by a willingness to 'mix it' with the enemy on the part of their captains and crews. Although brave and sturdy seamen, the attacking spirit so prevalent in the incomparable German Army was lacking in their surface fleet, possibly because, unlike the U-boat crews in the First World War, they had no tradition of success.

In mid November, *Deutschland*, having sunk two merchant ships, returned to Germany. *Admiral Graf Spee*, commanded by Captain Langsdorff, remained at sea, and by 7 December had sunk the last of nine merchant ships. It was the sinking of SS *Doric Star* on 2 December that led to his undoing. *Doric Star* managed to transmit a distress signal, giving her position in mid South Atlantic. Sweeps ordered by the Commander-in-Chief South Atlantic, acting on *Doric Star*'s signal, achieved nothing. But Commodore Henry Harwood, commanding hunting group G, with a combination of common sense and percipience, sketched out on a signal pad a possible destination for *Graf Spee* off the River Plate. Harwood acted in the great tradition of the Royal Navy, whose commanders were expected to use their initiative.

SS *Doric Star* had reported being attacked by a Pocket Battleship in position 19 degrees 15 minutes south, 05 degrees 05 minutes east during the afternoon of Dec. 2nd, and a similar report had been sent by an unknown vessel 170 minutes SW of that position at 05.00 GMT Dec 3rd.

From this data, I estimated that, at a cruising speed of 15 knots, the Raider could reach the RIO focal area a.m. Dec 12, the PLATE focal area p.m. Dec 12th or a.m. 13th, and the FALKLANDS area Dec 14th.

I decided that the PLATE, with its very vulnerable grain and meat trade, was the vital area to be defended, and I therefore arranged to concentrate sufficient force in advance of the time at which it was anticipated the Raider might start operations in that area.

One can imagine a similar situation today. The ether would be thick with signals from Whitehall. Ministers would be demanding detailed briefings on the manoeuvres of each ship, while officials hovered gloomily counselling caution for fear of defeat or, even worse, causing offence.

Harwood's squadron, consisting of HMS *Exeter* (six 8-inch guns) and two light cruisers (each eight 6-inch guns), *Ajax*, wearing Harwood's broad pendant, and *Achilles*, manned by New Zealanders, encountered *Graf Spee* at 06.14 on 13 December. Langsdorff had turned to investigate the smoke of Harwood's ships, and when he realized he was running into British cruisers, increased speed to close to firing range to bring his 11-inch guns to bear, in the hope of crushing them before they could retaliate.

Ordinary Seaman Eric Smith's action station in HMS *Ajax* was B Turret; he was in his cruising station, the 4-inch gun director above the bridge:

Soon I could see the outlines of a large warship. At first I had a feeling of numbness, that this was the real thing, then as I heard action stations sounded, I scrambled down the side of the director, shot down two ladders leading from the bridge, knocking into Commodore Harwood clad in his pyjamas leaving his sea cabin. Shouting 'Sorry Sir', I rushed to B Turret just as *Exeter* opened fire.

Harwood's squadron steamed at full speed to obey his instructions signalled to them the day before: 'Attack at once by day or night.' *Achilles* and *Ajax* raced to take up position on the far side of *Graf Spee*, in accordance with Harwood's battle plan to engage her from two sides.

Graf Spee opened fire first, hitting *Exeter* with her third salvo. Unlike the British, *Graf Spee* had gunnery radar to assist in correcting the fall of shot. *Exeter* struck back, but her 8-inch shells did little damage. For some twenty-five minutes Langsdorff concentrated his main armament on *Exeter* in an attempt to crush Harwood's strongest ship. *Ajax* and *Achilles* were treated to heavy fire from *Graf Spee*'s 5.9-inch secondary armament as they crossed to take up station on the far side. Fire from the two light cruisers' 6-inch guns was having little effect at this stage. By now *Exeter* had fires below deck, all communications destroyed, only one turret in action, the bridge had been badly damaged, and her Captain was conning her from the after steering position.

Eric Smith in *Ajax*'s B Turret:

I did have the opportunity occasionally to glance out of the sighting ports. Poor *Exeter*, she bore the brunt of the enemy's fire, and I had the occasional glimpse of her blazing furiously and listing, but still firing one of her after guns from time to time.

Exeter was still steaming at full speed, when water flooded in through a shell hole in her side, and cut power to her remaining turret. Her Captain had no alternative but to turn away and try to save his ship. Instead of closing and finishing off *Exeter*, Langsdorff was distracted by the fire of the two light cruisers who had closed to harry him with some very effective shooting. Harwood later wrote to his friend Admiral Crace describing German tactics:

He wriggles like an eel behind very cleverly laid smoke screens. Uses full wheel and lists over. Don't think you've got him beat as we did, he comes upright again when he steadies. His fire is very accurate.

The Royal Marine band's action station was, as in all cruisers and capital ships, the transmitting station (TS) in the bowels of the ship. Here they manned the 'table' (an early form of computer manually operated rather than electronically). The gunnery officer in the director high above the bridge passed range and bearing electrically to pointers on dials on the 'table' in the TS, where bandsmen by winding handles fed in the necessary data to produce range and bearing for the guns. This had to be computed so that the shells would land on the spot where the target would be after the interval between guns firing and

HMS *Ajax* seen from HMNZS *Achilles* heading for the River Plate chasing the *Graf Spee*. (HU205)

Captain Edward Parry RN,
Captain of HMNZS *Achilles*,
on the bridge with a leg
wound after the action with
Graf Spee. **Taken during the
pursuit to the River Plate.**
(From papers of Admiral Sir
Edward Parry 71/19/12
negative number DOC509)

the shells arriving, during which time both firer and target would have steamed
hundreds of yards, and the earth would have spun, however infinitesimally.
The range and bearing was 'transmitted' to each turret electrically. Each layer,
the man who cocked the guns up to achieve the range, and trainer, the man
who swivelled the turret to the correct bearing, wound a wheel to keep his
pointer on a dial over a pointer controlled by the TS; in doing so the guns and
turret moved accordingly. At the command 'broadsides' from the TS, which
indicated that the 'table' was 'set', the guns were all fired together electrically
by the gunnery officer in the director when his sight was dead on the target.
Correcting the fall of shot was done visually from the director in the Royal
Navy at this time. Only later did gunnery radars become commonplace.

Bandsman J. Nicholls, in HMS *Ajax*:

We in the band were closed up at action stations in the 4-inch and 6-inch transmitting
stations. Although we could see nothing of the action, our Captain Royal Marines in
4-inch director gave us a running commentary on the action through the phones with
such remarks as, 'another one on the way'. Between his remarks, shells could be heard
bursting and falling all around the ship. We also received reports from the 6-inch TS of
casualties and damage. 'A' Turret was reported to have fired 300 rounds, and the guns
were so hot that they did not go back into place after recoiling. They had to be pushed
back by hand.

Eric Smith:

We received a direct hit on X Turret, the one manned by the Royal Marines, killing some
of the crew and putting the turret out of action. Y Turret had also suffered damage. The
Graf Spee was firing everything at us, 11-inch and 5.9-inch guns, and torpedoes, which our

Rear-Admiral
Sir Henry Harwood,
soon after his promotion
from Commodore,
photographed on board
HMNZS *Achilles*. He is
standing in front of
Achilles's battle honour
board which has been
suitably updated.
(From papers of Admiral
Sir Edward Parry 71/19/12
negative number DOC508)

Seafox [floatplane] reported so we were able to turn away, so they missed us completely. At about 08.00 it was reported that we had only 20 per cent ammunition left, X turret was still out of action, and the hoist in B turret had jammed.

By 07.38, Harwood, with *Ajax* apparently short of ammunition and with only three guns in action, decided to break off day action, and close in again after dark:

It subsequently transpired that the report of shortage of ammunition in *Ajax* referred only to A turret, which had been firing continuously for 81 minutes, but this was not realised at the time.

Langsdorff, instead of following and finishing them off, continued to run to the west. Harwood turned and harried him as he ran for shelter into Montevideo in neutral Uruguay.

We could not believe it when we saw him heading for the Plate. It was a surprise when he anchored in Montevideo, we certainly expected him to bolt at any moment. That waiting was the worst of all. On the Sunday we heard of a transfer of crew to *Tacoma*. We hoped and still thought he would bolt with a death or glory rush. When he sailed, I sent an aircraft up to watch and oh such a long time elapsed before we got any reports and then, suddenly, *Graf Spee* has blown herself up. We passed this through the loudspeakers, and the cheering!

Everybody poured up on deck and on the tops of the turrets. I saw *Achilles* was the

same, so I told her to take station ahead, and as we passed we cheered and cheered. The New Zealanders sang their Maori songs. Then we formed up and trailed our coats past the wreck, a wonderful sight. She burnt beautifully.

Three days later Langsdorff, worn out by the strain of command, committed suicide.

Langsdorff's decision not to turn on the two light cruisers when *Exeter* had to haul off is still the subject of debate, as is scuttling his ship without a further fight. *Graf Spee* was not mortally damaged, and Langsdorff does seem to have lacked fighting spirit. He also seems to have believed reports that the fleet carrier *Ark Royal* and the battle-cruiser *Renown* were in the offing. In fact this was a British deception plan, because they were some days' steaming away.

On 17 February 1940, in Jossingfjord in neutral Norway, there was a dramatic footnote to the destruction of *Graf Spee*. Here lay the *Altmark*, one of *Graf Spee*'s supply ships, loaded with prisoners taken from merchant ships sunk by Langsdorff.

The diary entry of Herbert Saville, taken from MV *Newton Beech*:

Thurs Feb 15th 133rd Day
Stopped by Norwegian patrol. We made all the noise we could in the hope of attracting attention. Allowed to proceed on our way.

She was about to sail for Germany:

Before Vian's rescue of merchant navy crews imprisoned in *Altmark* she was shadowed by the destroyer HMS *Intrepid*. This shows her entering Jossingfjord in Norway. Both *Intrepid* and *Altmark* infringed neutral waters, as did *Cossack*. (HU45257)

Frid Feb 16th 134th day
Rescued by Destroyer *Cossack* about 11.30 p.m.

Captain Vian, in the first of his numerous distinguished actions in the Second World War, laid HMS *Cossack* alongside *Altmark*, and the boarding party swarmed across shouting, 'The Navy's here.' It was to be the last good news from Norway for some time. The rescue tipped Hitler into deciding to invade Norway, having hitherto resisted Grand Admiral Raeder's pleas to seize Norwegian ports and airfields to deny them to the British.

Ever since the Soviet Union's attack on neutral Finland in November 1939, the British government, under Chamberlain, had been dithering over going to Finland's assistance. How the British would have coped with a new powerful enemy, the Soviet Union, in addition to the Germans, was never put to the test, because the British were still havering when the Finns finally conceded defeat in mid March 1940. British support for Finland was not entirely altruistic. The Germans imported large quantities of ore from the Gällivare iron fields in Sweden. When ice closed the northern Baltic to shipping, this vital commodity was transported by rail to the Norwegian port of Narvik, for shipment to Germany. Much of the route lay down the 'leads', between mainland Norway and the numerous offshore islands. The British hoped to use the excuse of assistance to Finland to choke off the supply of ore to Germany. The Baltic was closed to the British, but they planned on demanding right of passage by land through Norway and northern Sweden, backed by force if necessary. How, given the lack-lustre performance of the British in Norway in the spring, a winter campaign would have fared, in the face of Norwegian and Swedish resistance, probably with German assistance, is another intriguing but unanswered question. Churchill, still First Lord of the Admiralty, had also been pressing for some time for mines to be laid in the leads to deny them to ships taking ore to Germany, as well as wholeheartedly supporting the proposed military expedition to Norway, with landings by British and French troops at Narvik, Trondheim, Stavanger and Bergen. However, with the collapse of Finland, these operations were cancelled.

Hitler invaded Denmark and Norway on the morning of 9 April. Denmark, totally unprepared, and unaware of Germany's intentions, surrendered by lunchtime. The Norwegians fought back with spirit, although simultaneous German landings at Oslo, Kristiansand, Stavanger, Bergen, Trondheim and Narvik taxed their limited and unprepared military resources to breaking point. British and French troops, originally earmarked as aggressors in Norway, now arrived as allies. Forces that landed in Namsos and Alesund, each side of Trondheim, were rapidly pushed back and evacuated through Andalsnes and Namsos. At Narvik the Germans suffered a set-back, when in two actions British destroyers sank German destroyers and ships with large numbers of troops on board. The German commander, General Deitl, was left holding Narvik with about 4,000 men, half of them sailors, against 24,000 Allied troops, including the best Norwegian formation, 6th Division. Despite overwhelming superiority,

the Allies took so long to capture Narvik that the German invasion of the Low Countries and subsequent collapse of France necessitated their withdrawal.

The first blow against German forces in Norwegian waters was struck by five ships of Captain Warburton-Lee's 2nd Destroyer Flotilla, which was detached to proceed up the Westfjord and enter the Ofotfjord leading to Narvik on 10 April. In a brilliant action, against superior forces, Warburton-Lee sank six supply ships, two big German destroyers, and damaged five for the loss of two of his small destroyers. Warburton-Lee was killed in the *Hardy*, and was posthumously awarded the Victoria Cross.

A stronger sortie up Ofotfjord was made on 13 April, this time with the battleship HMS *Warspite* in support. The diary of Arthur Turner, a rating in HMS *Hero*:

12:4:40 When darkness fell, *Warspite*, with the destroyers *Icarus, Hero, Foxhound, Kimberley, Forester, Bedouin, Punjabi, Eskimo* and *Cossack* were detached.

13:4:40 *Hero* became 'guide', and with *Icarus, Foxhound* and *Forester* swept the channel for mines. All hands closed up at action stations at 05.15. Weather very cold, slight mist and snowing at intervals. The entrance to the Fjord was very narrow with snow covered mountains on either side.

10.50 Battle ensigns hoisted.

12.25 Enemy in sight. One destroyer coming towards us out of the mist.

12.30 *Forester* and *Foxhound* opened fire and enemy destroyer withdrew. A minute later the mist lifted and more enemy destroyers were sighted and engaged. Land batteries opened up and *Warspite* engaged with 15-inch. Narvik in sight.

13.35 One German destroyer suddenly burst into flames and sank. Another with smoke

Destroyers heading for the Second Battle of Narvik. Taken by hand-held camera from *Warspite*'s Swordfish, hence the poor quality of the picture. (A33)

HMS *Eskimo*, with her bows blown off after being torpedoed by *Georg Thiele* in the Second Battle of Narvik. (N233)

coming from her engine room was aground. Her after gun kept firing so *Warspite* blew her out of existence.

14.22 The enemy retired up Rombaksfjord under cover of a smoke screen. The next destroyer we were engaging received several direct hits. She stopped, and the crew abandoned ship.

14.23 *Eskimo*, *Forester* and *Hero* followed the enemy into Rombaksfjord. The entrance was barely 50 yards wide, so we could enter only one at a time. *Eskimo* entered first and reported two destroyers which she engaged. *Forester* followed and opened fire as soon as she was clear of the hillside. We could only get our bows into the fjord, as it was only 3,000 yards long and 300 wide. Only one enemy was in sight, the other having retired round the corner.

14.52 The enemy destroyer fired six torpedoes, then beached herself and the crew abandoned ship. *Forester* was able to dodge, but *Eskimo* was unable to swing for lack of room. A sheet of flame shot up from *Eskimo*, and her bows disappeared. B gun's crew, with the bows shot away from beneath them, continued to fire. They deserved the cheer we gave them.

15.10 Aircraft from *Warspite* reported three more German destroyers round the corner. *Hero* took the lead to investigate. One destroyer was sighted which we immediately engaged. No reply from the enemy, so we went round the bend, *Icarus* and *Kimberley* astern. After a few rounds, the crews abandoned ship. Shortly afterwards two of the three destroyers turned over and sank. The third remained afloat with fire raging.

16.15 *Hero* sent a boarding party to the remaining destroyer, the *Hans Ludeman*. One of the boarding party entered the wireless office, and saw the two operators sitting by their desks with their heads blown off. One wounded man brought back to *Hero* died later and was buried at sea.

17.20 Fired a torpedo into *Hans Ludeman*, and retired out of Narvik.

Seven large German destroyers were sunk.

The evacuation of troops and the movement of ships out into the open sea were conducted under the lash of German land-based air power. The gallantly flown, outnumbered, obsolete, carrier-borne aircraft, and the handful of Royal Air Force Hurricanes, shot down a number of enemy aircraft, but could only make a dent in the swarms put up by the Luftwaffe. Lieutenant John Mosse in the destroyer HMS *Havelock*:

Above the general din, we heard the scream of a dive bomber as it roared out of the sky and dropped two bombs just astern of *Southampton*. Arriving in formations of fifteen or twenty planes at a time, they bombed us incessantly for two hours. Everyone increased to full speed and manoeuvred independently within the narrow limits of the fjord which was only three miles wide. The valley reeked with the bitter stench of cordite fumes from the guns. Time and again the ships were hidden from one another by vast columns of water. For a few moments a curtain of water completely bridged the entrance to Rombaksfjord. The conversation on our bridge went:

'One's coming in on the starboard side sir.'

'He's diving, sir.'

'Hard astarboard. Three hundred revolutions.'

'Bombs dropped sir.'

'Three coming from astern, out of the sun sir.'

'Port thirty.'

'*Southampton*'s getting a bit close sir.'

'Hard aport.'

'One bearing green nine o – he's diving, sir.'

'I'll kill the next —— who says that. Starboard thirty.'

'Down everybody.'

'*Cairo*'s hit.'

She had caught two bombs, one just before the bridge, one just abaft. She stopped short for a time, smoke and flames pouring out of her, then, to our relief, she got under-way, and smothered the flame.

Ordinary Seaman Herbert Messer RNVR, in HMS *Curlew*, an anti-aircraft cruiser:

I was taking a shell out of the magazine, when the stick of four bombs hit us on the starboard side, below the waterline and abreast of where I was standing, blowing the ship's

Damage to the bridge of the anti-aircraft cruiser *Cairo*.
(N329)

bottom out. The shells bounced out of the magazine clocking me in the face and balls; the blast from the explosion propelled me over the port guardrail into the sea.

Messer was hauled back in, and a few minutes later volunteered to search the after end of the ship for anyone who might be alive. The hatch cover was closed over his head:

There was no other noise other than my splashing through the dark, cold, oily water. The water was not level, and I discovered later that the ship had run, out of control, on to a reef in the middle of the fjord. In the wardroom flat, there was a great hole where the deck should have been. Skirting round the ragged edge, I saw the body of the Paymaster Commander lying below. Beyond the body was a tangle of metal in which there were several other bodies. I shouted several times, but could hear nothing that might be a human voice. I made a half-hearted attempt to climb down, but it seemed pretty obvious nobody was alive, and I was becoming very worried about my own safety.

Eventually he made his way back to the hatch, gave the agreed signal,

quite flattered at the looks of relief on the faces of the gun's crew who had stayed by the hatch.

Able Seaman Charles Hutchinson, in another anti-aircraft cruiser, HMS *Carlisle*, supporting the withdrawal from Namsos:

I saw five planes make a swoop for the French destroyer *Bison*, and a bomb burst on the fo'c's'le. Soon she was a cloud of smoke, but we still stuck tight to the troop ship. It seemed strange not racing to her, but that's the Navy, we had our job to do. Three destroyers went to stand by her. *Afridi* was the last to leave her, when a fresh batch of planes came. I saw a huge explosion on *Afridi*, she heeled over, her bows dipped low into the water. We steamed slowly on, guarding the troopships. It wasn't long before *Afridi* went down. What a tragedy after picking up the survivors of the French destroyer.

Almost the final act of the Norwegian campaign was the unnecessary loss of the aircraft carrier *Glorious*. On 8 June she was detached from the main body of the ships leaving Norwegian waters and sent ahead, with two escorting destroyers, to return to Scapa Flow. That morning she had recovered ten RAF Hurricanes and ten Gladiators evacuated from Bardufoss airfield in north Norway. The Captain, an authoritarian submariner with no previous carrier experience, scorned advice from the Fleet Air Arm. There is a suspicion that he was obsessed with returning to Scapa to press court-martial charges against his Commander (Air), whom he had disembarked earlier after a violent row over the employment of his aircraft earlier in the campaign. He had no aircraft on patrol, although he had six Swordfish, and ten Sea Gladiators of the Fleet Air Arm in addition to the RAF aircraft. No aircraft were on deck alert, or even ranged on deck. The ship was at cruising stations (the fourth degree of readiness), there was no lookout in the crow's-nest, although she was not fitted with radar. The ship's company were taking a 'make and mend', the Royal Navy's term for a half holiday. In perfect weather, *Glorious* was sighted by the *Scharnhorst* and *Gneisenau* some twenty minutes before she spotted them.

Air Mechanic Vernon Day:

Action stations went. I went to the hangar. Armourers were busy changing the bomb racks on the Swordfish to torpedo racks. A shell came through the hangar and set the Hurricanes on fire.

Glorious's reactions were so slow that although thirty-eight minutes elapsed between sighting the two German battle-cruisers and their first shells hitting her, only two aircraft had been brought on to the flight deck. None were launched. She was sunk within an hour and a half, taking to the bottom 1,474 of her own ship's company, and every one of the Hurricane pilots, so soon to be desperately needed in the Battle of Britain. There were thirty-seven survivors from *Glorious*, and one rating from each of the destroyers. Vernon Day jumped into the sea:

I saw a Carley raft and swam to it. There were about twenty-four people on it. In the end there were only four left. The next morning we got dried out a bit, and put on jerseys from the dead. We were picked up by a Norwegian fishing boat after two and a half days and taken to the Faroes.

The captains of the escorting destroyers both attacked *Scharnhorst*, without hesitation. HMS *Ardent* was sunk first, followed by *Acasta*, one of whose torpedoes knocked out two of *Scharnhorst*'s three engine rooms. Perhaps this damage saved the vulnerable troop convoys from a similar fate, for the German admiral took *Scharnhorst* back to Trondheim, before returning with *Gneisenau* and *Hipper*. Able Seaman Rodger Hooke of HMS *Ardent* found himself in a raft with five others:

Opposite: **The carrier HMS *Glorious* in heavy weather off Norway.** (BRO541)

After one day, one man died from cold. During the day, another man passed away. With no food and water things were not too good for us. Another man passed away leaving three of us. During the early hours of the following morning we saw quite a lot of smoke on the horizon. The ships turned out to be troopships withdrawing our troops from Norway. With only two paddles we tried to get towards them. Although we could see them plainly, none spotted us. Later, a flying boat flew over a trawler a matter of two or so miles from us. It came nearer and nearer, before turning and heading back towards the convoy. We shouted and waved to the trawler, but they failed to see us. Another ship passed, and did not stop. Another comrade passed away. Now there were only two of us left.

Eventually the two were picked up by a German seaplane and taken to Trondheim.

We were given very good treatment, and, after nine days moved on to Oslo. My last surviving comrade passed away after a fortnight in Oslo, leaving myself the last survivor of HMS *Ardent*.

The Royal Navy lost an aircraft carrier, two cruisers, seven destroyers, one sloop and a submarine in the Norwegian campaign. The Germans lost three cruisers, ten destroyers and six U-boats; three battle-cruisers, two cruisers and some smaller vessels were damaged, several of them badly. Much of the damage to German heavy units was the result of attacks by the Fleet Air Arm, at considerable loss in aircraft and crews. The damage would probably have been permanent had more modern aircraft been available, and the right bombs used.

The earliest German setback in the Norwegian campaign was the loss of the cruiser *Karlsrühe*, sunk by the British T-class submarine *Truant* on 9 April en route to attack Kristiansand. The report by Lieutenant-Commander Christopher Hutchinson, commanding officer of *Truant*:

18.33 Cruiser *Köln* class screened by 3 *Maas* class destroyers, range 4,500 yards.

18.56 Fired dispersed salvo of 10 torpedoes at six second intervals.

18.58/45 Heard loud explosion.

18.59/45 Heard second loud explosion.

19.02 Two depth charges exploded close. Went to 150 feet. The hunt by two enemy destroyers now began and between this time and 23.30 thirty-one depth charges were fired, nearly all of them unpleasantly close.

Enemy appeared to be uncomfortably efficient at hunting, and most persistent. I hoped, forlornly, that they would retire after dark on more important business. After the first attack, which was unpleasantly close, the submarine was taken to 320 feet in a depth of 260 fathoms [1,560 feet]. Water was too deep for bottoming. The submarine was making water too fast to attempt to hold a stopped trim. The rudder had to be used blind as the Sperry was stopped [noisy gyro compass], and both magnetic compasses were going round in circles as the magnetism of the boat was shaken up.

Truant was taking water aft, and had lost full use of her hydroplanes, which control the angle of dive or ascent. Because of the weight of water aft, she assumed an angle of 15 degrees up. The water could not be pumped out for fear of the pump being heard and oily water being seen on the surface.

23.25 By now the battery was low, air foul, and a pressure of four and a half inches made breathing laboured after nineteen hours dived. The submarine was very slowly and quietly brought to the surface, and nothing more was heard of the enemy.

23.50 With an overcast sky and no compass at all, it was difficult to decide how best to clear away from the vicinity, especially when so near to the now enemy coast.

Hutchinson signalled his intention to return to base because of damage, but changed his mind when he reassessed the state of his boat, having made such repairs as were possible. His signal to Vice-Admiral Submarines ended with:

Six torpedoes remaining. Morale high. Shall I return to patrol?

To which his Admiral replied:

All in good time. I want to see you first. Again well done.

The superlative armament of the T-class, with ten forward facing tubes able to fire a salvo of ten Mark VIII torpedoes, was not matched by any other submarine in the world.

Troops were still being withdrawn from Norway when a far greater disaster loomed. On 10 May Hitler invaded the low countries; by 25 May, a German corridor had been driven through to the Channel coast and Calais isolated. Lord Gort's British Expeditionary Force (BEF), the Belgian Army and two French armies were cut off from the main body of the French Army south of the corridor. With the imminent collapse of the Belgian Army, the BEF began to withdraw to the only Channel port not in German hands: Dunkirk. On 26 May, Vice-Admiral Ramsay, Flag Officer Dover, was ordered to organize the evacuation of the BEF. Operation Dynamo was launched. Churchill, by now Prime Minister following the Norway débâcle, thought that at best some 45,000 Allied soldiers would be evacuated before the Germans fell upon the exposed beaches. The Prime Minister feared that it would be his 'hard lot to announce the greatest military disaster in our long history'. Although Von Kleist's Panzer Group was closer to Dunkirk than most of the BEF, Hitler had intervened on 24 May to stop the final 'sickle stroke' which would have spelt the end for the British and all their allies north of the corridor. We now know it was the earlier British counter-attack at Arras which had alarmed Hitler, and he wanted to bring up infantry to hold the flanks of the corridor, which until now mostly consisted of armoured formations. Hitler also saw the French as the main enemy, and had no intention of allowing them to stage a last-minute recovery as had happened on the Marne in 1914. By the time he had lifted the 'stop' order to his army, the British and a large part of the French 1st Army had reached a line behind the Aa and Colme Canals, and were well placed to hold the panzers at bay while withdrawing from the beaches.

The Royal Navy was already involved in the battles in progress at Boulogne and Calais, whose garrisons had been reinforced with troops hastily scraped together in Britain. There was to be no evacuation from Calais. The troops had been ordered to hold out to the last, to buy time for the BEF to get away from Dunkirk.

The shipping put at Ramsay's disposal for the evacuation of Dunkirk was of a magnitude inconceivable today after half a century of erosion of British maritime power. Despite the demands of the Narvik battle still in progress, the Atlantic convoys, the Mediterranean and the Far East, Ramsay had 38 destroyers, the AA cruiser *Calcutta*, 38 minesweepers, 61 minesweeping craft, 18 anti-submarine trawlers, 6 corvettes, 1 sloop and 79 other small craft, including MTBs, gunboats, and Dover flare-burning drifters. The Merchant Navy provided 36 passenger ferries, 7 hospital ships converted from passenger ferries, and 262 tugs, trawlers, barges and dredgers. In addition there were the 'little ships', civilian-owned yachts and motor cruisers. The French, Belgians and Dutch also provided craft, including 19 French destroyers, 65 French civilian craft; and 43 Dutch skoots with RN crews. In all, some 848 vessels of all descriptions served on Operation Dynamo under Vice-Admiral Ramsay.

Boulogne had been evacuated before Dynamo was under way. Lieutenant Graham Lumsden was the navigator of the destroyer *Keith*, which with HMS *Vimy* was ordered into Boulogne. Both were alongside the quay:

Trawler evacuating troops from Dunkirk. (HU2108)

We had begun to embark the mass of people into the two ships, until they were blocking all gangways and ladders.

At this critical moment, the town and harbour were attacked by a wave of enemy aircraft.

Thirty Stukas in a single line wheeled to a point about 2,000 feet above us, and poured down in a single stream to attack the crowded quay and our two destroyers. The only opposition was some scattered rifle and Lewis gun fire, mostly from soldiers ashore, and the single-barrelled two-pounder pom-poms in each destroyer.

The Captain ordered the crews of the 4.7-inch guns to take cover because they were useless against aircraft. He also ordered the bridge people below. The bridge was just above quay level and exposed to splinters from bombs bursting there. I stood back to allow him down the ladder to the wheelhouse, as courtesy and seniority demanded, but he signed to me to precede him; no Captain likes to leave his bridge when under attack. I took one or two steps down when he fell on top of me, shot in the chest by a German sniper. The doctor arrived and pronounced him dead. Our First Lieutenant, now in command, was shot in the leg. He ordered everybody in the bridge structure to lie down, because German small arms fire and splinters from mortar bombs fired from weapons sited in houses over-looking our berth were piercing the sides of the wheelhouse, and hitting frightened men and women struggling to get down the steep ladder to the mess decks below.

It seemed a miracle that the ship had not been hit directly by bombs, but lying there she and *Vimy* alongside were open to further air attack and our bridges and upper decks were already swept by small arms fire from positions we could not identify in an area we had understood to be occupied by British troops.

Don Harris, having survived the sinking of *Royal Oak* in Scapa, was on *Vimy*'s bridge.

I noticed our Captain, Lieutenant-Commander Donald, train his binoculars on a hotel diagonally opposite but quite close to our ship. I heard another burst of fire from the snipers in the hotel, and saw our Captain struck down. He was choking on his own blood, so I moved him on to his side. I received his final order: 'Get the First Lieutenant on to the bridge urgently.' As I rose to my feet, more shots from the hotel swept the bridge. The sub-lieutenant fell in front of me, with four bullet holes in line across his chest.

Vimy's First Lieutenant took her out to sea, followed by *Keith*, also under command of her First Lieutenant. Lumsden took HMS *Keith* out of Boulogne harbour stern first, conning the ship from the chart house, looking out of a small porthole.

No communication was possible with men on the upper deck to slip our wires, so after ringing on main engines, I shouted orders to the Signal Officer and Chief Yeoman who were manning the engine telegraphs, to make the ship surge ahead and part the wires. This achieved, it was not too difficult to swing the stern off the quay, and start the ship moving astern. I rushed up to the bridge more than once to increase my view astern, but soon clattered down again, when bullets whistled past as I showed my head. Keeping as close as I dared to the stone pier on the northern side of the channel, I was mightily grateful to round the corner successfully. Knowing the rudder would be more effective at higher speed, I increased shaft revolutions to give 14 knots. Outside the harbour we manned the bridge and sorted out our load of disorderly refugees. Captain Simson and some dozen others were quietly buried at sea as we scanned the skies for enemy aircraft. It was decided to return to Dover to land our evacuees and wounded.

The meticulous organization by Ramsay and his staff for the evacuation of Dunkirk, which followed that of Boulogne, included the issue of charts to the skippers of a mass of craft, many of whom had never crossed the channel in their lives, and whose knowledge of navigation was sparse. Lieutenant George Grandage RNR worked in the Naval Control Office at Ramsgate.

A London taxi drew up outside our office and three large boxes of charts were brought in. As I had not ordered them, I telephoned the Hydrographic Office at the Admiralty, to be told, 'you will need them'; 1,500 charts in all, 500 in each set, covering the route from Ramsgate to Dunkirk.

Grandage was told by the Senior Operations Officer at Dover over the tele-phone that the Ramsgate Naval Control Office was responsible for despatching all the small craft from Tilbury, London, and ports on the Essex coast across to Dunkirk.

I reported to my senior officer who was living in a nearby hotel. The only place we could discuss the situation was the gents lavatory. The next morning I soon had the route made out, and the typist got busy producing four hundred copies; one copy and a set of three charts for each craft. Three light buoys had been laid on the route from north-east of the Goodwin Sands to Dunkirk. But they were not marked on the charts. The types of craft for which we were responsible included Dutch coasters and tugs, some of which were towing lifeboats. Most of these had some navigational equipment. In addition there were many river steamers, motor pleasure cruisers, fishing boats, etc. Few had any navigational gear. I decided to lay off the courses and positions required ourselves on the charts before issuing them. Two of us did this all day and well into the night on about 1,000 charts.

To begin with the evacuation was slow. Some 400,500 troops were with-drawing to the perimeter. It was estimated that the operation could be sustained for only two days, and that about 45,000 men might be lifted out. On the first day only 7,669 were evacuated. Fortunately, Captain W. G. Tennant RN, appointed the Senior Naval Officer ashore, arrived with a beach party of 12 officers and 150 ratings (some 200 more were sent across later).

Until the beach parties arrived, and for a little while afterwards, the Official Narrative of Events for Operation Dynamo records:

As regards the bearing and behaviour of the troops, both British and French, prior to and during the embarkation, it must be recorded that the earlier parties were embarked off the beaches in a condition of complete disorganization. There appeared to be no military officers in charge of the troops, and it was soon realized that it was vitally necessary to despatch naval officers in their unmistakable uniform with armed beach parties to take charge of the soldiers on shore immediately prior to embarkation.

Extracts from reports by naval officers working on the beaches and in inshore boats:

On approaching the beach she [the boat] was promptly boarded by a crowd of French soldiers, who so overloaded the boat that she grounded. In the meantime the Coxswain of ALC 17 procured the assistance of some British troops, who with fixed bayonets drove off the French when these again attempted to rush the boat as the tide rose.

On another beach:

Some difficulty experienced through persistent attempts of large masses of French troops to intercept boats and demanding passage. Assisted by British troops succeeded in holding off French by means of rifle fire 50 yards along beach.

At the start of the evacuation, and before Tennant's arrival, Dunkirk harbour

had been the main embarkation point until as Rear Admiral Frederic Wake-Walker recorded:

On 25 May a heavy bombing attack was made on Dunkirk when the harbour was full of ships. *Grenade* was sunk and *King Orry* and several others alongside the pier were hit. As a result, a junior member of the naval party ashore, whose judgment had been affected by the events of the day, dashed off in a car to La Panne where he saw Lord Gort and telephoned to the Admiralty that further embarkation from Dunkirk itself was impossible. In consequence Dover was sending all ships over to the beaches and none into Dunkirk.

Seeing that the embarkation from the beaches was desperately slow, Tennant ordered a destroyer to come alongside the East Pier. From that moment on, thousands of men, British and French, were embarked in ships skilfully laid alongside the East Pier and West Quay by their captains and crews. The next day Ramsay ordered the bulk of the embarkation to be moved from the beaches to the harbour, using larger ships, mostly destroyers and some civilian transports.

Rear-Admiral Frederic Wake-Walker who was working in the Admiralty arrived in the Dunkirk area on 30 May:

On my return to the Admiralty from lunch on Wednesday 29th May, I was told that I was wanted by Rear-Admiral Phillips [Vice Chief of Naval Staff]. He asked me if I would like to go to Dunkirk to try and get some organisation into the embarkation there. I said I would be delighted. Some discussion followed as to my appointment, it was not intended that I should supersede Captain Tennant who was already Senior Naval Officer Dunkirk. It was decided I should be Rear-Admiral Dover, and be in charge offshore at Dunkirk.

HMS *Vivacious*, a V-class destroyer, alongside the pier at Dunkirk with a sunk ship just outboard of her. (HU1149)

Lieutenant S. A. Nettle RNVR was a beachmaster:

Coming in from seaward we could see the enormous pall of smoke rising up to the west of the harbour from the oil storage tanks set on fire by bombing. An intense aerial bombardment was in progress when we arrived. This was the first time I had experienced that devastatingly frightening 'screaming bomb'. It seemed to screech into your brain, and you felt it was coming straight for you.

When not embarking troops from the Mole, we spent the time like troglodytes in the cellars of the building in company with local residents listening to the drone of planes and crump of bombs, while the duty officers in the rooms above sent and received signals, and liaised with the Military Control Staff.

Lieutenant Jack Neale RNVR, in the minesweeper HMS *Speedwell*, picking men off the beach:

At 09.00 we were ordered by W/T [radio] into Dunkirk Harbour, so off we set at full speed to pick up troops from the jetty. The destroyer *Ivanhoe* came past us at 30 knots. Two hundred yards ahead of us a bomb scored a direct hit on her amidships, and she came to a stop, belching clouds of steam. *Speedwell* went alongside her starboard side to take off her troops. A large diesel yacht went to the other side. I said to the Sub [sub-lieutenant], 'Look, they got the paint locker.' He replied, 'That's not paint, you fool.'

I felt foolish at mistaking blood in the scuppers, from some 40 sailors and soldiers dead on the deck, for red lead paint, but was otherwise unmoved by the sight. We had become so inured to death and destruction in the last five hours.

We took off about 150 soldiers. Just as we were about to push off, one or two of *Ivanhoe*'s ratings started climbing over too. *Ivanhoe*'s Captain looked down and said, 'Where do you think you are going?'

'I thought she might sink, Sir.'

'Oh no she's not, you come back here.'

From the tone of his voice, you would have thought he had just bumped the quay and scratched his paint.

The yacht on the other side pushed off, but was sunk as she left for home.

We abandoned the destroyer, and entered Dunkirk, securing to the East Jetty alongside our senior officer in *Halcyon*. A little *Duck* class corvette berthed outside us. We took off several wounded and more soldiers until we had about 800 to 1,000 troops on board. We were now very fidgety to get going. But we were under orders of the beachmaster and had to await his pleasure. Number One [First Lieutenant] found a bunch of women, whether nurses or what I don't know. The Old Man [Captain] was adamant he was only going to take soldiers, so Number One smuggled them on board and locked them in the Captain's pantry.

At last we got permission to proceed. Getting away was not easy. Our mooring wires were all fouled up with other ships' wires, so we slipped and left them hanging. I doubt if the Old Man knew this. He was all in by now, and our 'pilot' [navigating officer] took the ship astern out of the harbour, threading his way through wrecks and other ships. There were wrecks all over the place, and crewless boats drifting around.

Opposite: **Troops on board the destroyer** *Vanquisher.*
(HU1152)

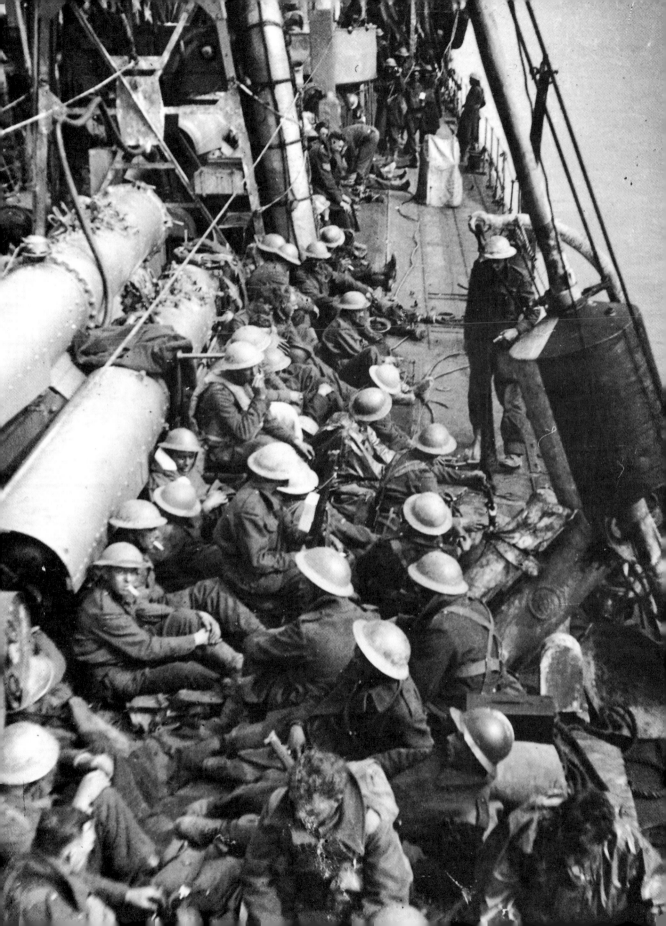

As soon as we got clear, there were droves of Gerry planes about, and *Speedwell* had a lively time dodging bombing attacks. The method in sweepers was to put the helm hard over as soon as the bomber was committed to his run. Normally a fleet sweeper will hardly heel at all when in a tight turn, but with over 800 extra men *Speedwell* heeled alarmingly when dodging bombs. However, the soldiers were an asset. Fifteen of them were Bren gunners, and eager to contribute to the AA fire. Two of these Brens never went ashore, and were most useful in the coming months.

About this time the destroyer *Keith* was sunk near us. We would see bombers bent on mischief, and tense up. On realising that it was not us but a ship nearby that was to be attacked, we relaxed and watched with interest.

We berthed alongside in Dover at about 15.00 on 1 June. We knew we would have to go back for more troops and didn't think we could possibly survive another day like that, so we officers all sat down to make our wills together in the wardroom, amidst a certain amount of hilarity. Our navigator was a solicitor in civilian life, and advised us to let him look them over for errors. He was later killed in the *Algerine*.

HMS *Speedwell* made two more trips to Dunkirk.

Some troops were still being embarked from the beach at La Panne and Bray, respectively ten and five miles away from Dunkirk. Lieutenant Lumsden in HMS *Keith*, now under command of Captain Berthon, back in Dover after one trip to Dunkirk mole:

We were ordered to return to Dunkirk and embark the Admiral in command of ships afloat [i.e. all Allied shipping in the Dunkirk area], Rear-Admiral Wake-Walker. On 31 May we cruised up and down the beach from Dunkirk to La Panne in the shallow and narrow stretch of water between beach and shoals offshore, avoiding known mined areas and trying to marshal the various boats working there. Long lines of soldiers, dark against the white sand, stretched for miles from the area of La Panne to the harbour, and in queues down to places on the tide-line where rough, almost unusable, piers of abandoned vehicles had been built, or where some boat was trying to embark men direct off the beach. Movement of these masses of men seemed very slow. A good number of small ships, destroyers, minesweepers and paddle ferries, were lying off the beaches close as they could in view of the very shallow water. Loaded boats, mostly clumsy ships' lifeboats towed over from London with one or two young naval ratings in charge, were pulling, oh so slowly, from the beach to the ships, where soldiers clambered aboard as best they could up nets or ladders. This operation was dreadfully inefficient. As each heavy boat moved into the beach under the efforts of one or two men at the oars, and finally grounded a little way out from the water's edge, it was rapidly filled with soldiers clambering over the side. The boat sank a few inches and stuck on the sand. A young sailor, or perhaps an army officer or NCO would instruct the last men to get out again to lighten the boat, but such an order in the dreadful circumstances, and when every man's thought was of reaching home, was very hard to accept. When boats did float off, it was very difficult for soldiers, tired and untrained at sea, to find space to man the oars and row to the waiting ships. Once there, many of the boats were abandoned to float aimlessly and uselessly offshore.

With variations this is the picture of the Dunkirk beaches, and accounts for the fact that the great majority of men who were successfully evacuated were properly marshalled from the beaches onto the pier in the harbour, and thence into fast ships with disciplined and trained crews. This is not to belittle the bravery and determination of the volunteer crews of yachts and other small craft who sailed straight into the maelstrom of war and did their uttermost to help their country in its hour of need; they lifted some 10,000 men.

During 31 May, still in glorious calm weather, a few cars drove down on to the beach and signalled by lamp that the General Staff needed a lift to England. We sent in a whaler and motor boat to fetch them, and circled offshore. More than 100 enemy aircraft appeared and attacked everything in sight, including our boats; but they escaped damage. Lord Gort was transferred to a minesweeper [*Hebe*], while most of his staff stayed in our Captain's cabin.

Our ancient 3-inch High Angle Gun, so newly fitted, was without any effective fire control system and was firing virtually over open sights. By the evening of 31 May, we had expended all our ammunition.

Early next day, 1 June, which again dawned calm and clear, a very large enemy aircraft formation appeared. A number of Stukas dived on us. The first three aircraft missed, but close explosions jammed our steering gear, and we were in hand steering from the tiller compartment when a further and heavier attack came in. A bomb from the second aircraft exploded and holed our starboard side between the engine room and boiler room, causing heavy casualties there and a total loss of power. The ship listed heavily and slowly came to a stop. We anchored her near a wreck. The Admiral and his staff boarded a fast launch to continue their work. *Keith* was subjected to a further Stuka attack; a bomb started a fire aft and a number of men were wounded by machine-gun fire.

The ship continued to list and settle, so the Captain decided to abandon ship, but asked me to stay with him, in case a tow could be arranged back to Dover. The crew were taken by a Dutch coaster to Ramsgate. As *Keith* sank deeper, the Captain summoned an Admiralty tug alongside and she embarked our wounded and everyone else alive. As the tug pulled away, another onslaught by bombers blew *Keith* apart, and she sunk instantly, for we never saw her when the bomb splashes subsided.

At last all the enemy aircraft seemed to have gone, except for one twin-engined bomber returning from Dunkirk. In case he had any bombs left, we made one more circle to starboard. As we did so, the world stood on end. The tug split in half. As the forepart sank in less than 30 seconds, all those under the forecastle were trapped; those of us lucky enough to be on the bridge scrambled out into the sea. I struck out for the beach, about three-quarters of a mile away. Swimming in full uniform and inflated lifebelt was slow and laborious. Thinking of something that would reinforce my will to swim on, I found myself picturing my wife's small but beautiful backside. I aimed at a squat red brick fort in the dunes at Bray. About 100 yards from the beach, I scrambled on to the deck of a wrecked yacht. Finding that I was still wearing my heavy binoculars, I hurled them into the sea.

Eventually, Lumsden landed and was taken to the fort by some French sailors. After a rest and a cognac, he set off for Dunkirk, dressed in a French sailor's uniform, complete with flat hat and pom-pom, to replace his soaked uniform. Here, after further adventures, he found Rear-Admiral Wake-Walker in his launch alongside the Dunkirk pier, who offered him a lift back to Dover.

Wake-Walker:

By this time it was beginning to get light, and as the morning was very clear, I decided to get the ships away at 03.00 instead of 03.30 as originally planned. Men were still coming down the pier, but it was no use running the risk of having ships sunk alongside and blocking the pier and harbour. To seaward lay the ships visible as dark blurs only, waiting off the harbour entrance for their turn to come in. Looking shoreward, the whole town and harbour were shut in by a pall of smoke overhead, lit up by the glare of fires in several places inland. Against the piers, harbour and town were sharply silhouetted. On the piers and quays an endless line of helmeted men. The funnels and masts of ships showed clear as they lay alongside, their hulls dark and invisible. There was not a great amount of noise; sirens hooted occasionally when ships moved, shells bursting with sharp cracks, distant crashes of bombs, machine-gun fire faintly heard, and nearby at times when someone fired at a plane overhead, engines throbbing as a destroyer moved past, occasional orders and hailing of boats.

On his return to Dover:

I slept heavily and woke suddenly as two fellows came into my room – it was Captain Berthon of the *Keith* and his First Lieutenant. They were black with fuel oil, but they had come to let me know they were safe. I dropped off to sleep again with a feeling of thankfulness.

Graham Lumsden:

I reported to Naval Headquarters in the Castle, and went straight to the Cipher Room to see if Daphne was on watch. I poked my head round the door, asked after her, and then saw her. She replied 'Yes, here I am', but didn't recognise me, for, apart from the disguise of my French uniform, my face was black with oil.

It was not only some French who were ill disciplined. Lieutenant Nettle RNVR was sent to the beaches for the last days of the evacuation. Having watched two ship's lifeboats drifting in on the tide capsized by soldiers over-loading them,

a third boat appeared, the troops again started wading out, so I went alongside them shouting to them to wait until it came into shallower water. They took no notice of a young RNVR Lieutenant. I drew my revolver and fired it into the water about three yards in front of the leading man. They all stopped. I waded across to them, waving my revolver indicating that they should return to the shore. Here I pay tribute to the British soldier and the natural discipline of the Services. They accepted the orders and moved slowly back. I detailed two men to go out and tow the boat in to shallow water so the others could embark. I asked for two men to row it back, and said I would ensure that they stayed in and went back to the rescue ship. But no one did, and we had to rely on boats drifting in on the tide. As for the troops, there was no depression or panic, just a quiet resignation to fate, and uplift of spirits when a boat floated in.

One afternoon all the beachmasters were called together and told that the commander of the perimeter could not hold out later than the next evening. Three out of the six of us were told to be off the beaches by dawn, and I was to be one of those to leave. We dispersed to our sectors. We had been told that no Naval Officer was to be taken prisoner, but this had never entered my mind. I had been ordered to leave, so I continued embarking soldiers until about 3 o'clock the next morning, and got into one of the boats myself. We climbed aboard a ship already crammed to overflowing which made course for Ramsgate.

Wake-Walker at Dover:

After a bath and breakfast and a few moments in the sun outside, I felt fit for anything and made my way to the dungeon office to discuss the next night's operation. There were still 5,000 of the BEF to come and an unknown number of French, thought to be from thirty to forty thousand. A scheme was produced which provided a carrying capacity of 37,000 men in addition to those got off in small craft.

There were a large number of wounded in Dunkirk, and orders were that fit men were to be got away in preference. Embarking wounded would have taken up too much time. But it was decided to try and get some wounded away in daylight in Hospital ships, hoping the Germans would respect them. One was bombed and sunk and the other so badly damaged she had to return [before loading at Dunkirk]. The wounded, other than those who could walk to the pier, had to be left behind.

Tennant and the last of his party left on an MTB as soon as the last British troops had gone.

Wake-Walker remained to supervise the embarkation of the French. A total of 54,000 were embarked over the last two nights, in addition to the French troops already evacuated earlier. More might have been taken off, but for a lack of organization by the French Navy:

After the [Royal] Naval ratings had left, there was difficulty in getting ships berthed as the French did nothing to replace our men, although the port was the headquarters of a French Naval Command and there was always a considerable number of French marines in evidence.

By the time Operation Dynamo ended on the afternoon of 4 June, 338,226 soldiers, including 123,095 French, had been evacuated, instead of the 45,000 that had been predicted originally. But the Royal and Merchant Navies had suffered grievously. Six destroyers had been sunk, fourteen damaged by bombs, and twelve by collision out of a total of thirty-eight. Twenty-four other RN ships or craft were sunk. Nine ferries were sunk, and eleven damaged out of a total of forty-six.

There were other evacuations, as the last remnants of the BEF were brought out of other parts of France in the wake of the final collapse of the French Army, and the Franco-German armistice which took France out of the war.

At St Nazaire, Lieutenant Mosse was on board the destroyer *Highlander*, with the Naval Officer in charge of evacuation:

The air raid was still in progress, and we made our way to the bridge just in time to see [the liner] *Lancastria* hit by two bombs. She had just embarked five thousand troops. We watched her roll over and sink. For a while, the side of her hull remained above water with hundreds of men sitting on it, singing lustily before they floated off. Soon there were thousands to be rescued. Yet two thousand in *Lancastria* perished. Some undoubtedly were bomb casualties, but many more must have been trapped below in a strange ship, unable to find their way out in the darkness. It was the worst individual sea disaster of the War, and, not surprisingly, the least publicised.

Now the Germans were in control of all the French airfields, from which they were infinitely better placed to bomb Britain than they had been from Germany, only a month before. In addition, they had the whole Atlantic coast-line from North Cape in northern Norway to the Spanish border on the Biscay coast of France from which to launch their assault on Britain's Atlantic life-line, and on shipping in the English Channel and North Sea. U-boats had nearly brought Britain to its knees in 1917, when Germany controlled a mere strip of coast from Ostend to Schleswig-Holstein, excluding Holland. Grim days lay ahead.

3
1940: After the Fall of France

Previous page: **HMS *Ark Royal* under air attack off Sardinia, 27 November 1940.** (A2325)

On this tenth day of June 1940, the hand that held the dagger has struck into the back of its neighbour.

President Roosevelt

On 10 June 1940, Italy declared war on France while her back was turned desperately attempting to stem the German tide. With the fall of France and entry of Italy into the War, Britain, fighting alone, found her maritime strategic plans in ruins. Not only did she face an enemy only twenty-one miles away across the English Channel, but she had acquired a new foe with powerful forces in the Mediterranean and territories in north-east Africa. No longer would she have the assistance of the French Fleet in the western part of the Mediterranean. Indeed, the French Fleet was now a potential enemy, or would be if it fell into German or Italian hands. Although Article 8 of the Franco-German Armistice stated that the French Fleet, except that part left free for safeguarding French colonial interests, 'shall be collected in ports to be specified and there demobilized and disarmed under German or Italian control', they would pass into that control fully armed. The German Government had declared that they would not use them for their own purposes. But Hitler and Mussolini were not to be trusted. They would use any pretext, or none at all, if it suited their purpose.

When the French signed the Armistice, the First Sea Lord, Admiral of the Fleet Sir Dudley Pound, sent a personal signal to Admiral Darlan, the C.-in-C. of the French Navy. Lieutenant Patrick Whinney RNVR was an Assistant Naval Attaché on the staff of the British Ambassador in France, with special responsibility as the British liaison officer to Darlan.

A long signal came in addressed to Darlan personally and I had to decode it personally. It was from Admiral Pound. The contents were a straightforward invitation to Darlan to send every ship he could to the West Indies where they would receive full, open-armed support from the British. When I had finished [decoding] it, I drove out to the barracks. I spotted Darlan's robust figure walking towards me across the barrack square. I walked to meet him, ready with my salute. I held out the envelope containing the signal, 'Here, Admiral, is a personal signal for you from Admiral Pound.

There was no return salute. No 'good morning'. Instead, he looked me up and down as if he had never seen me before, grabbed the envelope from my hand, his only acknowledgement to snap out 'Bien', before turning on his heel and walking away.

'If there is any reply, Admiral,' I began, but he never looked back.

The French Navy was deployed widely. At Portsmouth and Plymouth there were two battleships, four light cruisers, some submarines, including *Surcouf*,

the largest in the world, eight destroyers and a number of smaller craft. These were impounded. At Alexandria, under the guns of Admiral Sir Andrew Cunningham's Mediterranean Fleet, lay one French battleship, four cruisers and some smaller ships of Admiral Godfroy's Force X. At Oran, in the military port of Mers-el-Kebir, were the battleships *Dunkerque* and *Strasbourg*, two of the finest ships in the French Fleet. With them were two older battleships, some light cruisers, destroyers and submarines. At Algiers were seven cruisers. An aircraft-carrier and two light cruisers were at Martinique, in the West Indies. The new battleship, *Jean Bart*, but without her guns, lay at Casablanca, where she could not complete fitting out, so was temporarily out of action. *Richelieu*, nearer completion and almost ready for action, was at Dakar. As well as numerous minor ships in several French ports, there were some warships at Toulon, which were beyond the Royal Navy's reach.

The force at Oran posed the greatest threat. In a little known incident, the Flag Officer North Atlantic, Admiral Sir Dudley North, was sent in the destroyer HMS *Douglas* to the French Admiral Gensoul, commanding at Oran, to put the British Government proposals to him. Sub-Lieutenant Geoffrey Brooke RN in *Douglas* wrote an account of the visit to Oran; the following are extracts:

June 23–24 1940
Admiral North came on board at 20.00 accompanied by SO1 Commander Birley, FLOG (French Liaison Gibraltar – The Comte de Brissac), and a cypher officer. His task, Admiral North's, was surely one of the strangest ever performed by a fighting man on active service, to ascertain the attitude of the French Admiral and his command at Oran in the light of the French submission to Hitler's all conquering hordes.

Two very rare, if not unique, photographs of the French Fleet in Oran before the attack by Force H on 3 July 1940. The large ships by the mole are, left to right: the seaplane carrier *Commandant Teste*, the battleships *Bretagne*, *Strasbourg*, *Provence* and *Dunkerque*. Six destroyers are moored further inshore. From the photograph album belonging to the then Commander R. A. Currie RN, gunnery officer of the Battlecruiser Squadron. The photographs were probably taken by HMS *Hood*'s spotter aircraft and given to her gunnery officer, who subsequently sent them to Currie. It is possible that all other copies of these photographs went down with *Hood* when she was sunk by *Bismarck*. Later *Hood*'s gunnery officer wrote in a letter to Commander Currie: 'As you have heard we were in that melancholy business at Oran. What a way of firing our main armament for the first time for business purposes!' (From the collection of Rear- Admiral R. A. Currie, Department of Documents 66/291/1–2)

On arrival off Oran:

Since the terms of France's capitulation were unknown to us, our position at Oran might have been anything between a welcome ally bringing plans for future collaboration to an undefeated colony and an enemy warship approaching a newly captured base.

After being admitted to Oran with due ceremony Admiral North left to call on Admiral Gensoul in *Dunkerque*. The French ships in Oran at that time, according to Geoffrey Brooke, were

2 capital ships, 1 carrier, 2 cruisers, 9 destroyers or escorts, 6 submarines and many smaller craft.

Frenchmen stood or leant and watched us with a listless air. The two *Dunkerque* class battleships were now plain in the adjoining anchorage of Mers-el-Kebir. I could not forget some of *Dunkerque*'s officers whom I had met at Rosyth during a French courtesy visit before the War. They had been so confident and proud of their ship. I could not but imagine them now, in the beautifully panelled wardroom with paintings by well-known artists, waiting for a future that could bring little beyond despair. Unless of course they joined with us, but somehow it didn't seem likely. It is easy, as explained to us by FLOG, for an outsider to say, 'disobey the Government', but the practical difficulties are immense. Questions of nationality, especially relatives at home, and many other points would be unsupportable to all but the most courageous and united crews.

Admiral North returned after an hour, and a further conference was held in the Captain's cabin.

The French would not accede to the British proposals, and if attacked would fight their way out to a home port. HMS *Douglas* left for Gibraltar.

On 3 July 1940, Vice Admiral Sir James Somerville, commanding Force H based at Gibraltar, was off Oran with his Force. He had been ordered to offer Admiral Gensoul at Oran the following options, which were the same, but for the addition of point number five, as those offered by Admiral North on 24 June:

1. Sail with us and continue to fight for Victory against the Germans and the Italians.

2. Sail with reduced crews under our control to a British port. The reduced crews will be repatriated at the earliest moment.

3. Alternatively, if you feel bound to stipulate that your ships should not be used against the Germans or Italians unless these break the Armistice, then sail them with us with reduced crews to some French port in the West Indies, where they can be demilitarised to our satisfaction, or perhaps be entrusted to the United States, the crews being repatriated.

4. If you refuse these fair offers, I must, with profound regret, require you to sink your ships within six hours.

5. Finally, failing that above, I have the orders of his Majesty's Government to use

whatever force may be necessary to prevent your ships from falling into German or Italian hands.

Captain Francis de Winton RN, commanding 17th Destroyer Flotilla in HMS *Keppel*, part of Force H:

The news that we might be expected to fire on our late allies was repugnant to all of us. Admiral Somerville made a final protest to the Admiralty and submitted his own amended proposals based on the reports of our liaison officers who had been with the French. He was promptly rapped on the knuckles and told to get on with it.

In the forenoon [of 2 July] another meeting of Flag and Commanding Officers was held in *Hood* [Somerville's flagship] to discuss final arrangements for 'Catapult' [codeword for the operation]. The Force sailed at about 17.00, the heavy ships screened by two destroyer flotillas. On 3rd July at 03.00, *Foxhound* was sent ahead to arrive off Mers-el-Kebir at 07.00. She had on board Captain Cedric Holland (Captain of *Ark Royal*), to act as emissary, he having been recently Naval Attaché and having many friends among French officers.

After a long delay and exchange of signals, Captain Holland was finally allowed to board *Dunkerque* to see Admiral Gensoul.

Although de Winton was unaware of this, Gensoul was playing for time. Admiralty decrypts of French signals during the negotiations made plain that all French ships had been ordered to meet fire with fire. These decrypts also revealed that Gensoul had been guilty of duplicity, telling his superiors that the British offer was merely 'join us or scuttle'.

The Admiral kept all ships informed of the progress of the negotiations, and also of the numerous signals from the Admiralty. Deadlock on board *Dunkerque*, despite negotiations until 17.30 [the final deadline signalled to Gensoul by Somerville]. Captain Holland left in *Foxhound*'s motorboat, being picked up at sea.

The Admiral ordered fire to be opened at 17.54, with aircraft spotting, range being about 15,000 yards. The battleships' fire was extremely accurate, and hits could be clearly seen. The French ships and the forts replied to our fire, and though they made no hits, at least two salvos straddled our ships. I had a complete view of the action for some minutes till about 18.01. Just before this there was a tremendous explosion and a large plume of smoke (this was *Bretagne* blowing up). Our fire ceased at about 18.04. There was a heavy pall of smoke over the harbour and fire from the French gradually died away.

One ship, the *Strasbourg*, was reported leaving with an escort of destroyers. Too late, Somerville, who at first discounted the report, followed in *Hood*. But *Strasbourg* was too fast, and reached Toulon under the cover of darkness.

Richelieu at Dakar was put out of action temporarily by one hit from a torpedo bomber which distorted a propeller shaft.

At Alexandria Admiral Cunningham by his courtesy and patience managed to persuade Godfroy to render his ships non-operational, without a fight. There were some tense moments. Lieutenant Jack van de Kasteele, the assistant gunnery officer of the *Malaya*, who was friendly with a French officer in *Duquesne*:

Wednesday 3rd July

Sent for by Captain. C.-in-C. has been instructed this a.m. to place certain alternatives before French Fleet, and good watch to be kept in case they start to slip or scuttle.

At 20.45, by which it was dark, C.-in-C. made a signal 'Carry out Operation PF' (initials for Prevention of Flight, or as Fergy suggested, 'Persecution of the French'). A and B turrets closed up, and about 21.15 were ordered, 'With HE and a full charge, load'. *Tourville* was our particular responsibility. Turrets trained on her – range 700 yards! RM platoon, together with ER [engine room] party prepared to prevent scuttling, stood by. No apparent movement in French ships, while we watched and raised steam for 18 knots, furled awnings and prepared for sea.

Mad to dissipate our energies by fighting our erstwhile allies – and they should see how it is letting us down to hand over their fleet.

Honoré [French officer] was on board at 11.30, very disappointed I had to cancel lunch appointment in *Duquesne*. Assured me the occasion was an *anniversaire* – mine – and cake and 27 candles awaiting me.

Admiral Sir Andrew Cunningham, C.-in-C. Mediterranean Fleet, on HMS *Warspite*. He was one of the great fighting sailors of the Royal Navy in the Second World War. (E488E)

Thus concluded a series of operations that caused much anguish in the Royal Navy; and a corresponding bitterness in the French Navy, which lingers to this day.

Cunningham ended a signal to his Fleet:

This is a difficult situation for us all, but it must be cleared up so that we can get on with the war against the Italians, and get to sea to exploit our successes of last week.

The successes referred to by Cunningham included the bombardment of Bardia, and the sinking of three Italian submarines and an Italian destroyer. This was just a beginning.

Four days later Cunningham took his fleet to sea to cover the passage of two convoys from Malta to Alexandria. He knew that the Italians, who called this stretch of the Mediterranean '*Mare Nostrum*', 'our sea', would react. His force consisted of three battleships, HMS *Warspite* (Flag), *Malaya* and *Royal Sovereign*, the carrier *Eagle*, five cruisers and seventeen destroyers. The next day, 8 July, reports from the submarine *Phoenix* and flying boats from Malta indicated that an Italian battle squadron with cruisers and destroyers was escorting an Italian convoy from Tripolitania. Cunningham altered course to get in between them and their base at Taranto. All that day, Italian land-based aircraft bombed the British ships, a foretaste of what became commonplace in the Mediterranean for the next three years. HMS *Gloucester* was hit by a bomb, killing everyone on her bridge.

The next day, air reconnaissance reported two Italian battleships, twelve cruisers and a host of destroyers off Cape Spartivento, Calabria. Cunningham, with three battleships, five cruisers, including the damaged *Gloucester*, and *Eagle*, steered to close the enemy.

Lieutenant van de Kasteele in *Malaya*:

By 15.00 course altered to SW, and Captain said; 'I can feel it in my bones', and Action Stations was sounded off. We hoisted battle ensign at the main. Enemy fleet reported as only thirty miles off. At 15.07 was sighted by *Neptune*.

At 15.20 a cloud of brown smoke from *Warspite* as she opened fire. At 15.31, we could see the smoke of the enemy battle fleet on the port bow. *Malaya* was ordered to join. At 15.59 first enemy salvos fell. Both ranging and line were excellent. *Warspite* straddled twice. At 16.00 sighted four enemy cruisers on starboard bow and two right ahead. Three minutes later we opened fire, being this time astern of *Warspite*, who was engaging right hand battleship of two.

About 17.11, after nearly two hours, Italians had had enough and turned away – though if they stayed to fight it out they could have tanned us well, for they had all the advantages of range, speed, light and wind. They could have made rings round us from 25,000 to 30,000 yards, for we never got within range, and *Royal Sovereign* never even opened fire with main armament. *Warspite* and *Malaya* turned to chase, but it was no good, the Italians running for Messina were soon out of sight.

Warspite's shooting had been excellent, hitting the Italian flagship at thirteen miles [22,800 yards]. This had been enough for Admiral Riccardi.

The Italian Air Force now took a hand. Cunningham was only twenty-five miles off Calabria, so very vulnerable indeed. He had taken enormous risks approaching so close, but had the advantage of being able to read the Italian Naval codes, thanks to the capture of an Italian codebook and Enigma coding machine taken from an Italian submarine. From signals intelligence he learned that the Italians had hoped to trap him. He had walked into it with his eyes open, and gained the upper hand. His battleships, all First World War vintage, were outranged and could be outrun by the Italian modern warships, except for their flagship the 1911 vintage *Giulio Cesare*. Fortunately on this, as on so many future occasions, the Italians used their superior speed to run away.

The advantage of being able to read Italian signal traffic lasted only a few weeks. The Italians changed their codes, and the Mediterranean Fleet was reduced to low grade signals intelligence on the Italians thereafter.

But most important, Cunningham had established the Royal Navy's moral ascendancy over the Italian Fleet, by going straight for them, despite their technical superiority. The next engagement was ten days later. Commander T. J. N. Hilken, the Executive Officer of HMAS *Sydney*:

19 July

At 07.30 on Friday morning we were about 40 miles north of Cape Spada. *Hyperion* was reporting two enemy cruisers about ten miles to the west of her. It became clear that 2nd Destroyer Flotilla was being chased towards us by the enemy, who had no idea we were in the vicinity. The Italian cruisers were faster than our destroyers by about 3 knots. But a stern chase is a long one, and we ought to arrive on the scene before our ships were overtaken. The situation was interesting: one cruiser and five destroyers, all capable of about 32 knots, against two cruisers capable of about 35 knots. Having the legs of us, it was reasonable to suppose that if the enemy accepted or was surprised into battle, he would fight it out at long range and refuse to allow the destroyers to get into action, so the Captain decided to go straight into action as soon as he had made contact with 2nd Destroyer Flotilla.

I piped the dress of the day 'battle dress', warned the ship's company we would be going to action stations in about twenty minutes and had a hurried breakfast before going to my action station in the lower steering position. [The Executive Officer, as second-in-command, manned this position below decks, from which the ship could be steered, although not conned (directed). Here he waited to take over should the Captain be killed, and, until that moment arrived, was in charge of damage control.]

At 08.20 we altered course to close 2nd Destroyer Flotilla, and six minutes later sighted the enemy. We had seen their smoke some minutes earlier, but the first they had seen of us was the flash of our guns, when we opened fire at 20,000 yards [eleven miles]. This was also the first our destroyers had seen of us, and they were very relieved to see our shells falling near the enemy. At 08.35, we appeared to be hitting the leading ship, the *Banda Nera*.

Able Seaman Arthur Turner was in the destroyer *Hero*, one of five who until now had been fleeing from the two cruisers:

The enemy altered course and retired at high speed.

08.40 Rear cruiser came within range again and we opened fire in concentration and positioned ourselves for attack with torpedoes.

Hilken in *Sydney*:

The enemy turned away making all the smoke they could. *Sydney* formed on the starboard wing of the destroyers who were in line abreast. I would have given a great deal to have been on the bridge. It must have been a grand sight, the five destroyers throwing up great bow and stern waves, and *Sydney* with shells bursting all round her, and her guns belching flame. I sat listening to the roar of our salvos and the dull thud as shells burst close in the water.

Because of the enemy's zigzagging, the range had closed to less than 18,000 yards [ten miles]. At 09.15 we altered course and a few minutes later one of our shells cut the *Colleoni*'s steam pipe, although we did not know this at the time. She was heavily on fire forward. Even before she stopped a great part of her ship's company jumped over the side.

Turner:

Although she was stopped and had ceased fire, the cruiser's ensign was still kept flying therefore we carried out the attack with torpedoes. Bows shot completely away.

Hyperion, *Ilex* and *Havoc* stopped to pick up survivors, while *Sydney*, *Hasty* and *Hero* continued to chase the other cruiser.

Sydney continued the chase until 10.37:

He [the *Banda Nera*] drew out of range, and gradually disappeared into the haze. Five minutes before the Captain broke off the pursuit, we sighted and opened fire on an Italian reconnaissance plane – a most unwelcome sight, as it meant that before long the bombers would be over.

We were in a dangerous position, with practically no ammunition (four rounds per gun in A Turret, and one per gun in B). It seemed likely that enemy forces were at sea to the southward, because *Banda Nera* had held on to the south, when her obvious course was to the west. *Havoc* signalled, 'survivors report cruisers were expecting to meet large supporting forces in this area this morning'. We could expect a bad time from the bombers whose bases were in Tobruk and the Dodecanese, between us and Alexandria. However there was nothing to do but make for Alex at our best speed. We had been cheered by a signal from 2nd Destroyer Flotilla Leader saying that *Bartolomeo Colleoni* had sunk at 09.59. We reduced to 25 knots to allow the other three destroyers to catch up, but they delayed for a long time picking up 545 survivors, including the Captain who was wounded.

The Italian Air Force put in an appearance in the early afternoon. Arthur Turner in *Hero*:

14.53 *Havoc* with over 200 prisoners on board bombed and had one boiler put out of action.

Sydney had been informed by signal of *Havoc*'s damage:

She was about 60 miles astern of us, still close to Crete, able to make 24 knots. The Captain ordered *Hero* and *Hasty* to go on to Alexandria, and altered course to join *Havoc*. This, I think, was the hardest decision he had to make all day. We were nearly through the danger zone north of Tobruk, the fleet was at sea coming to our assistance, and we should have been in touch at about 20.00. Now we had to turn back into bombing range, away from our own fleet, and towards the 'large supporting force'. We had practically no ammunition left. I must admit my heart sank at the prospect, but there was no alternative. *Havoc* was alone (*Hyperion* and *Ilex* were far ahead), and having no AA armament would be a sitter when the attacks were renewed. We turned back at 15.04, and a few minutes later a stick of bombs fell each side of the ship, so close that spray and splinters came inboard. Other attacks followed, but we dodged them successfully.

At 16.30 we made contact with *Havoc*, who was making about 20 knots, throwing up a huge column of spray from the rent in her side. At 18.30 2nd Flotilla Leader joined in *Hyperion* with *Ilex* in company. A few minutes later, we had another severe air attack, without result although the bombs fell very close. This was the end of our ordeal, as the sun set shortly afterwards. We still felt far from safe, not knowing that the 'large supporting forces' were actually in harbour.

Hero and *Hasty*, sent on ahead, had also been bombed twice, but without damage.

Hilken:

20 July

We met the *Liverpool* at dawn and followed her back to harbour. As she approached the boom, she ordered us to pass ahead and gave us three cheers. We entered Alexandria harbour at 10.30 and found each ship's company massed on the forecastle to cheer us as we passed. We never dreamed of such a reception. Our feelings: a blend of disappointment that one enemy ship had escaped, and thankfulness that we had done the same.

Midshipman Johnny Carter RNR, aged nineteen, writing to his parents in England to tell them of his ship HMS *Ilex*'s part in the Cape Spartivento battle and the sinking of the *Bartolomeo Colleoni,* added:

I hope I never grow up more than I am now. This is the ideal age, and I've always longed for it. I get my stripe [promotion to sub-lieutenant] in six months.

In the Western Mediterranean, Admiral Sir James Somerville's Force H had also been busy. Somerville was a fighting admiral with a cool analytical brain and good strategic sense, as well as being famous for his salty language. Based at Gibraltar, he was not only responsible for the Western Mediterranean, for escorting convoys as far as Malta, and for guarding the Straits to bar enemy shipping, but also had to be prepared to sortie out into the Atlantic to support operations hundreds of miles from Gibraltar. Midshipman Charles Friend RN, a Fleet Air Arm observer in 810 Naval Air Squadron flying in Swordfish from HMS *Ark Royal*:

The Italian cruiser *Bartolomeo Colleoni* hit and sunk by HMAS *Sydney*, 19 July 1940. (A219)

Sir James was an amiable man, if slightly eccentric, and he was an able director of our affairs. In my opinion he was one of the few Admirals who used aircraft really well at that stage of the war. He had taken the trouble to learn to fly, which helped his understanding of the limitations as well as the capabilities of aeroplanes, and he also called our squadron commanding officers together to learn from them. He was appreciative of the successful efforts of both Swordfish and fighter squadrons, and of the ships under his flag, and tolerant and understanding of our occasional failures. He used to come to fly in the back seats of all three types of aircraft just for fun.

After Oran, on the very next day, we left Gibraltar on the first club run [Mediterranean sorties] and made for Sardinia, encouraged by an aptly worded signal from Flag Officer Force H: 'The object of the operation is to test the price and quality of ice-cream'. [One of the nicknames for the Italians at the time was 'ice-cream merchants'.] Two or three days out we were sighted by Italian reconnaissance aircraft and shadowed. The Cant Z506B three-engined seaplanes, which were a feature of our life in the Mediterranean, simply made off at high speed when they saw the Skuas taking off to deal with them. Although the rudiments of a fighter direction system had been set up, the Skuas, operating entirely by sight, had very little chance of catching the shadowers, who continued to keep us under scrutiny in a very determined way.

Their bomber colleagues in Savoia Marchetti SM79s were also brave and determined men. Their aircraft were named Sparviero (Hawk), but like us with the Swordfish, they nicknamed the type 'il Gobbo' (the Hunchback), so perhaps they felt much as we did, frustrated, exasperated, amused and affectionate about our aircraft. Those of us who saw their attacks from the air were very impressed by the Italians' courage and apprehensive for the safety of our ships, especially dear old *Ark* on whose deck we had to land. Seen from on board, these events were very noisy. The bombs fell so close and showered us with water and fragments, but our 4.5-inch guns, multiple pom-poms and machine-guns were going hell for leather, as were the other ships' guns.

Until the surrender of Italy three years later, the battle for sea control of the Mediterranean followed the form set in the first few days after Italy's entry into the war. Each side needed to run convoys through: the British from west to east and back again; the Italians, and later the Germans as well, from north to south. Geography could either be an advantage or disadvantage to one or other of the protagonists at sea, depending on the progress of land operations. The ebb and flow of the British Army along the North African coast of the Western Desert began with O'Connor's offensive in December 1940, and ended with the arrival of the Allied Armies in Tunis, from both west and south, in June 1943. As the British advanced, the Axis lost airfields in North Africa; as the Axis advanced, so they regained them. So the ability of each side to attack the other's convoys from air bases in the North African littoral waxed and waned with the success or otherwise of each offensive. The Mediterranean can be pictured like an hourglass on its side, the western bulge consisting of the area from Gibraltar to Tunis, the eastern from Tunisia's east coast to Syria and Palestine. The neck of the hourglass is the hundred mile gap between Sicily and Cape Bon, Tunisia; the Sicilian Narrows. Right up until June 1943, the Axis powers had airfields on both sides of the Narrows. Sixty miles south of Sicily, and 200 miles east of the Narrows, lay the British island base of Malta. Although Malta had been the Mediterranean Fleet Base for over a century, pre-war parsimony meant that the island was woefully equipped for modern air defence, and so vulnerable that the Mediterranean Fleet was moved to Alexandria. One of the most onerous duties for Somerville's Force H and Cunningham's Mediterranean Fleet was the resupply of Malta with every commodity needed for defence, maintenance of the ships that used the harbour (mainly convoy escorts and submarines), and for the garrison and civilian population: food, ammunition and fuel, the last especially for fighter aircraft.

Cunningham, one of the great fighting admirals in the long history of the Royal Navy, was a legend in his lifetime. 'Cuts', as he was known to the lower deck, had spent most of his life in destroyers, and handled a battle fleet like a destroyer flotilla. He loathed staff work. He never had a staff job until, as a Vice-Admiral, he was appointed Deputy Chief of the Naval Staff to the First Sea Lord, Sir Roger Backhouse; a notorious nit-picker, who never delegated anything. Backhouse fell sick, to be relieved by Admiral of the Fleet Sir Dudley Pound, himself obsessed by detail. He was replaced as C.-in-C. Mediterranean Fleet by Cunningham in June 1939. So when the Mediterranean Fleet faced its sternest test since Nelson's day, it was commanded by an admiral who delegated everything to his staff, and concentrated his considerable energy taking the fight to the enemy, regardless of the odds.

Cunningham and Somerville had a high regard for each other, which was just as well because the complicated and hazardous operations they embarked upon called for mutual trust. One such was Operation Hats, whose aim to

Vice-Admiral Sir James Somerville, commander Force H, and later C.-in-C. Eastern Fleet, in his day cabin with his Siamese cat Figaro who always accompanied him to sea. (A6258)

reinforce Cunningham involved ships transiting the whole length of the Mediterranean. Somerville with Force H was to steam to a point between Sardinia and Sicily, and there detach the reinforcements, called Force F, to the east. On his return trip to Gibraltar Somerville would bomb the airfield at Cagliari in Sardinia. Cunningham was to meet Force F, and at the same time take the opportunity to send in supplies and reinforcements to Malta. Lieutenant-Commander George Blundell, the First Lieutenant of the 8-inch gun cruiser HMS *Kent,* in his diary:

Friday 30th August

We are leading *Liverpool,* and *Gloucester* with three destroyers in attendance. Way over to port was the battlefleet comprising *Warspite, Malaya, Eagle, Sydney* and *Orion,* with all available destroyers. The fleet is on a very interesting operation steaming Malta-wards to welcome and escort reinforcements in the shape of *Valiant, Illustrious* plus two AA ships, *Calcutta* and *Coventry.* They'll be a welcome addition to our air offence [defence?]. At the moment the Ities are predominant in the air and are completely cramping our style. *Illustrious* and *Valiant* have the latest equipment. This reinforcement is being escorted from Gib by our Western Med forces under Sir James Somerville with *Renown, Resolution, Ark Royal, Sheffield, Enterprise* and about 14 destroyers. We are both making a feint at attacking Italy, to cover the transfer.

The latest equipment referred to by Blundell was radar. This enabled Cunningham, for the first time, to detect the approach of the enemy through fog, haze, at night, and at a greater range than the human eye; certainly out to fifty miles. *Illustrious* was the first of a new class of fleet carrier. With her armoured flight deck she was a heartening sight to a Fleet whose opinion of the Italian air force echoed Blundell's. Now the Mediterranean Fleet with two carriers and their air groups could strike back, as they did on the leg of their voyage to Alexandria in a night strike on two Italian airfields. Some Italian attacks got through; Blundell:

Action stations was sounded off. It was a bit premature, done on RDF [radar] reports of large enemy formations approaching. Apparently about 50 machines approached the fleet, then went away again. I suppose they didn't like the look of all the fighters ahead of us.

Later:

I had the last dog [watch from 18.00 to 20.00]. At 19.05 *Gloucester* opened fire with her port 4-inch. There overhead were seven to eight bombers at 10 to 12 thousand feet. *Eagle* was ahead of us and I think they were attacking her. When they seemed almost overhead they let their bombs go. It was a wonderful sight. One could almost count the number of bombs as they hung in the blue sky, unhurriedly suspended like a row of immense rain drops, gradually getting larger and larger. Everybody lay down on the bridge – there wasn't much room. I lay on my back and watched them coming. The noise was rather like an express train coming from a distance, and as they hit the water there was a terrific crrrump.

While escorting the convoy bound for Alexandria which had passed north of Crete, through the Kaso Strait, east of the island:

They dropped about nine bombs, big ones all around us, and the splashes were huge, much higher than the masts. By evening the convoy was in the Kaso Channel screened by four destroyers and two AA cruisers. We expected the Ities to do something here. But did we or anybody get any opposition or even see a blooming Itie? Not a bit: it is simply astonishing the lack of Itie enterprise. Most of us are disgusted at not having met anything or had a scrap, but the Admiral [commanding the Cruiser Squadron – not Cunningham] and Captain were both tremendously relieved.

Blundell, a senior Lieutenant-Commander, was regularly passed over for promotion to Commander, possibly for his irreverent views on his seniors and ill-concealed dislike of certain flag officers.

Friday 6th September
Pandemonium raged on the bridge yesterday evening when forming up after leaving the convoy. The Admiral read out an enormous signal to Flags [his flag lieutenant] who, after writing down a page and a half of hieroglyphics, pushed his cap back, scratched his head and said, 'Don't you think we could just hoist the Disregard, Sir?' Skips [the Captain] was terrible – making poor jokes one minute and cursing the next – and he is no help.
Sunday 8th September
A Day of Prayer ordered by the King, so we must expect some major disaster. Every day a Day of Prayer has been ordered by that villainous Cosmo Cantuar [Cosmo Lang, Archbishop of Canterbury], we've been visited shortly afterwards by some terrible reverse.

The lower deck's views on Sunday, as overheard by Blundell, an excellent First Lieutenant and in touch with the ship's company and their opinions, was as one would expect pithy and to the point:

And six days shalt thou labour and do all that thou has to do, but the seventh is the Sabbath; on it thou shalt work a fucking sight harder.

Although Blundell laments:

Why is it that I, a naturally lazy, indolent and quiet loving fellow should be pitchforked into infernos of hard work and bother?

He was sharp enough when HMS *Kent* was hit bombarding Sollum. The ship was dead in the water, but thanks to his energy and initiative electric power was restored to the engine room. The Engineer Commander was exhausted, and like many of the officers and ratings had passed out with the heat caused by the extractor fans failing for lack of electric power. HMS *Kent* made it safely to Gibraltar, and eventually to Plymouth just after Christmas 1940.

On 11 November 1940, Cunningham struck the Italian Fleet a devastating blow at Taranto. Commander Manley Power RN on Cunningham's staff wrote to his wife:

My Darling

It has been a week packed with events since I last wrote to you – all spent at sea. We are just on our way home after a very pleasant spell on the briny which has had excellent results. You will have seen in the papers what a crack our air boys hit the Wop Fleet in Taranto.

It all started when we got in from our last trip. Things had been talked out a bit at sea and I had a rough scheme in my head and a few dirty bits of paper in my pocket. The C.-in-C. goes off with COS [Chief of Staff] to confer with the heads of other Services as the Greek War is under way and matters of high policy are involved. C.-in-C. gets back late and we have a meeting about 23.00 in his cabin – various members perched on the club fender and chairs, with glasses to taste, while we get the broad outline of policy; but not the go ahead without final orders tomorrow. We get the go at noon next day. My orders are finally drafted by 2.30 next morning.

The thing was approved in principle from my draft at about 9.30, so we go to press about 18.00 with orders complete so as to reach the first ships who are sailing in the wee sma' hours next morning. Aircraft are told off to carry orders here and there about our scattered parish. Convoys sail for various destinations – ships rendezvous with other ships at sea – air patrols go off to quarter the thousands of square miles of Mediterranean and watch the Wops in their bases.

Then we have days at sea, covering all the movements, wondering whether everything is going to plan or if the weather, bombs or torpedoes are going to upset the business.

Reports come in slowly. Ships we expect to join us turn up over the horizon, sometimes early, sometimes late. The usual, almost monotonous reports from the carrier come in: 'shadower shot down'. We have a bombing attack, very frightened Wops, shining like silver in the sky, drop their bombs miles wide as the AA fire turns them, and then the rats get at them, and there is a plume or two of smoke on the horizon where they crash in flames. So it goes on for several days, until the grand moment comes when all our crawling convoys are reported in, and we are free to fight at last.

C.-in-C., COS, Tom and I in the chart house have a final confabulation – then off go Tom and I to write the signalled orders and work out courses for the night. Off go the orders by flashing searchlight.

Great excitement: 'shadower reported' – relief: 'shadower shot down'. Signals go up from time to time: 'So and so part company, proceed in execution of previous orders. Rejoin me at . . .' Until we are left at midnight with only our solemn row of battleships plodding along in brilliant moonlight, with a ring of watchful destroyers, as a cover and rallying point for the striking forces. We are near the enemy's bases now, and keeping a watchful eye out for enemy ships or torpedo aircraft. No sound except the wash of the bow wave and occasional orders as the guns train to a new bearing to keep the crews alert. All night wondering how things are going.

Then the morning. The carrier turns up. Two aircraft missing. Aircraft report three enemy battleships torpedoed, and some small craft damaged, seen burning. Masthead hoist [of flag signal from C.-in-C.], 'Manoeuvre well executed. Resume station previously ordered'.

Sparse words, but high praise indeed from Cunningham, whose watchword was: 'Duty is the first business of a sea officer'; and crisp as one would expect from a Service trained in short and to the point communication.

Manley Power continues in his letter:

Slowly as the day wears on the other detached units come over the horizon and make their reports. A shadower or two turns up, and gets shot down – one after a thrilling chase right over our heads, and down to the water behind us.

Finally we are collected and head for home, full of good cheer and thinking out more schemes to confound the King's enemies and wondering if we shall find any mail when we get into harbour. It will be a miracle if we all get in without the loss of a single ship or man after hitting the enemy so hard.

I feel like holding my breath until we get there, but am writing to you instead, which makes me hold my breath almost as much with loving and wanting you.

The 8-inch-gun County class cruiser HMS *Kent* off Bardia, just before she was hit by a torpedo. (E558)

Anyhow we've struck a big blow this time which may shorten the war a bit, and bring us together earlier. I expect the Top Wop is raving mad, and we shall probably get a lot of bombing back in harbour – not that we stay there long these days, thank goodness. These long sea trips are absolute bliss after the office in harbour.

The air strike against the Italian Fleet in Taranto was launched from HMS *Illustrious*. Originally *Eagle* was also to have taken part, but was damaged while in action off Calabria; so some of her aircraft were transferred to *Illustrious*. Twenty-one aircraft in two waves were launched from *Illustrious* at 20.40 and 21.00 on 11 November. They achieved complete surprise, sinking three battleships at their moorings. Admiral Cunningham wrote:

The 11th and 12th November 1940 will be remembered for ever as having shown once and for all that in the Fleet Air Arm the Navy has a devastating weapon. In a total flying time of about six and a half hours carrier to carrier, twenty aircraft inflicted more damage upon the Italian Fleet than was inflicted on the German High Seas Fleet in the daylight action at the Battle of Jutland.

Manley Power fails to mention that the idea of a strike against Taranto was first mooted by Rear-Admiral Lyster, who commanded Cunningham's carriers.

Sketch of Taranto harbour after the raid by the Fleet Air Arm, showing the position of sunk and damaged ships. (CM165)

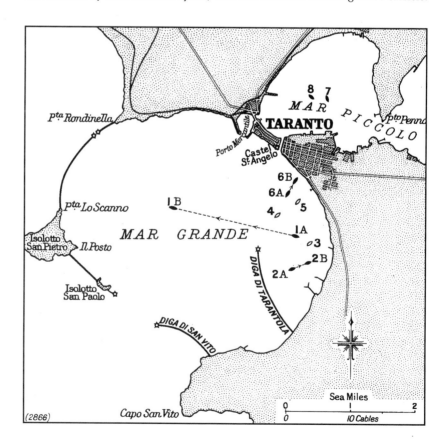

He had first thought of the idea when Captain of *Glorious* in 1938. But it had found little favour with the then C.-in-C., Pound, a battleship admiral. The strike at Taranto vindicated all those who had been saying for years that the aircraft carrier was the prime means of taking the battle to the enemy at sea, or in his harbours; a practical demonstration whose significance the Japanese were not slow to digest. Unfortunately the Royal Navy at this early stage of the war was not too well placed to take advantage of the experience, thanks to too few modern carriers being built pre-war and, until American aircraft were available, obsolete or unsuitable types. It is to the credit of the Fleet Air Arm that they achieved so much in the years ahead, despite such poor equipment. The success of aircraft against battleships had still to be properly understood by the big gun protagonists too, among whom the First Sea Lord, enthusiastically supported by Rear Admiral Tom Phillips, Vice Chief of Naval Staff, was prominent.

Phillips from behind his desk in the Admiralty was prone to criticize the operational admirals, and was a prime mover in ordering the Board of Inquiry into Somerville's actions in failing to pursue the Italian Fleet at the end of November 1940. Before leaving Liverpool for Gibraltar, Commander Jocelyn Salter RN, commanding the destroyer *Foresight* and a divisional leader in the 8th Destroyer Flotilla, was handed a letter for personal delivery to Admiral Somerville.

I came to think the world of him [Somerville]. As a wartime leader he was superb, second only to Andrew Browne Cunningham. I discovered later what it was about. Some months previously, Force H had been escorting a very important convoy from Gibraltar to the Eastern Mediterranean. Force H was to be met midway by the Mediterranean Fleet from Alexandria. To the east of Sardinia a sizeable Italian force, two battleships, seven 8-inch gun cruisers and sixteen destroyers were reported by aircraft reconnaissance coming south, an infinitely more powerful force than Somerville's *Renown, Ark Royal, Sheffield, Despatch* and nine destroyers. Action was joined and Somerville turned towards the enemy and increased to high speed, but after ten minutes the enemy turned to the north-east towards Naples, and retired. Force H followed for about an hour, but were rapidly approaching the Italian coast, and Somerville had to consider whether pursuit would assist his main object, the safe passage of the convoy. He realised that he was unlikely to catch up with the enemy, unless their speed could be reduced, and that a headlong pursuit would endanger the convoy, so he abandoned the chase and ordered his forces to rejoin the convoy, the most hazardous part of whose passage was now approaching.

Somerville came in for considerable criticism from the Admiralty, but instead of waiting for his return to harbour and calling for a written report, Admiral of the Fleet Lord Cork and Orrery was sent to Gibraltar to set up a Board of Inquiry before Somerville had even returned. The Board, once possessed of all the facts, entirely upheld Somerville's action, but both Cunningham and Somerville were more than a little indignant at the impetuous action initiated by the Admiralty.

I delivered the letter to the Flag Lieutenant who met me as I stepped on board *Renown* [Somerville's flagship]. I subsequently received an Immediate Most Secret Signal, for Addressee (i.e. me) Only, telling me that the letter was not, repeat not, to be delivered, and

Two of the cruisers of Force H which took part in the fleet action off Sardinia, 27 November 1940. (A2408)

that it was to be held for the present, and returned to the Admiralty under MOST SECRET cover.

Salter does not mention that a further threat to Somerville had he closed the Italian coast would have been Italian land-based aircraft. The moving spirit behind the Admiralty's questioning of Somerville's action seems to have been the Vice Chief of Naval Staff, Phillips. Barely a year hence, secure in his belief that capital ships could survive in the face of air attack, he would approach within striking distance of land-based enemy aircraft, without any air cover. He and many others would pay for his error.

Winston Churchill, whose understandable desire that commanders took aggressive action wherever possible, and sometimes when it was not, had a part to play in the Admiralty criticism of Somerville. Although the Admiralty was back-seat driving, it must also be remembered that as well as being a great department of state, it was also an operational headquarters, unlike its counterparts, the War Office and Air Ministry. So the temptation to interfere was strong, particularly when headed by an officer of Pound's temperament.

Despite the ructions on high, success against the Italian Navy, combined with British offensives in the Western Desert beginning before Christmas 1940, made the outlook in the Mediterranean considerably brighter than six months earlier, following the fall of France and entry of Italy into the war.

At home the end of 1940 saw the threat of invasion diminished almost to nothing. However, between the end of June and early November half the Royal

Navy's destroyer force was deployed on anti-invasion duty, instead of escorting convoys. The U-boat crews called this the 'happy time' as they wreaked havoc on the trade routes. The destroyers operating in the English Channel came under air attack from the Luftwaffe based just across the narrow strip of water, although the RAF was very much in evidence too, a welcome sight after the evacuation of Norway and France. Lieutenant Alec Dennis in the fleet destroyer HMS *Griffin*:

Our job was partly to cover the brave coastal convoys which were still operating through the Straits [of Dover], and partly to be a first warning, particularly at night, of any seaborne threat. So we settled into a pattern known as the 'prostitute's patrol'; out every night, and when our turn came, out by day as well. The day patrol meant almost certain air attack, and it was hard to distinguish friend from foe. For the first time in our experience some of the aircraft could be, and often were, friendly.

Naturally we were a little bit edgy. Any object to seaward could be the advance guard of the invasion. Being 'watch and watch' [on watch every other four hours], when not at action stations meant one got little sleep, so on return to Dover one tended merely to eat and sleep.

On the evening of 6th July we endured our heaviest air attack yet. Thirty-six Dorniers made straight for us. We were a lone destroyer on patrol. However, we had plenty of time as they approached at a steady height. Johnny [Captain] weaved her around at high speed, and the first three groups missed satisfactorily. But the last one didn't. With the ship swinging at 30 knots, a torrent of bombs came straight down on us. There was a series of mighty explosions all round. The ship jumped, and a drenching shower of dirty black water through which we steamed without a scratch, apart from a few leaks below. Within half an hour we were off to chase some E-boats, without success.

Our next solitary patrol on Sunday 14th July had us covering a convoy off the Downs. We were all heavily attacked by Heinkel 111s, and went to the assistance of a small steamer called the *Balder*, which was hit aft and on fire. We went alongside and put the fire out with hoses. All the while there lay in her well deck, a dead man, stark naked, all his clothes blown off by blast, but otherwise looking uninjured. He had an aggrieved expression as though someone had interrupted his sleep.

On Friday 19th, it was our turn to be in harbour when it was bombed, by ten JU 87s. I was in my cabin about to go to sleep when the alarm bells rang, and almost immediately after, the familiar scream of bombs. When all the water subsided, we found no one was hurt. But several compartments were flooded including the Asdic compartment, which meant a dockyard job for which Dover was not suitable. So off we went to Chatham, just as well because the next attack sank the *Codrington*, our new leader, and the port had to be abandoned by destroyers. Repairs took about ten days, so each watch had five days' leave.

I think we all had the feeling that one must live the life while one could. I had a lot of fun and drank and smoked a lot. Taking Faith to the movies, my hand shook so much, she had to help me light my cigarette.

In hindsight, the German plans for the invasion of Britain are unconvincing. The Germans had no specialized landing-craft, and no experience in

HMS *Griffin* hidden by bomb
bursts in Dover harbour;
taken from Cinque Ports
Yacht Club June 1940.
HMS *Boreas* in foreground.
(Papers of Commander
J. A. J. Dennis RN 95/5/1
negative number DOC523)
[Author's comment: this may
be a composite photograph]

amphibious operations. Their plans included using barges, towed across the Channel by tugs. The chaos that would have ensued once these barges were released to proceed to the beach without an adequate source of propulsion, can be imagined. If one contemplates the Allied effort required to get ashore in Normandy only four years later, albeit against far stronger forces and better prepared defences, with total air supremacy, total command of the sea, a massive bombardment, a vast array of special equipment, waterproofing techniques, the ability to land tanks straight on to the beach, and a host of other skills learnt the hard way after a number of successful landings – and disasters; a German invasion of Britain in comparison never stood a chance. Unless, perhaps, they had totally destroyed Fighter Command. Even then, given their rudimentary landing-barges, and inability to wade and drive armour straight on to the beach, the rate of build-up ashore, the key to success in any amphibious operation, would have been problematical. The German lack of mechanization would have imposed additional delays; they required 4,500 horses to be lifted in the first wave of barges. German amphibious techniques were hardly better than Napoleon's.

Before the year was out, the British were given some practical revision in amphibious operations, and especially the pitfalls that await those whose plans are half-baked. The aptly named Operation Menace was an attempt to bring the Vichy French garrison of Dakar into the war on the British side. It was a pet project of Churchill's, sold to him by General de Gaulle, supported by the ex-British Consul General in Dakar. Intelligence about French morale, defences, shore batteries and the beaches was rudimentary, wrong, or non-existent. Such up-to-date information about defences that was available was not passed to the commanders charged with the operation. The plan called for a landing by the Royal Marines Brigade and about 2,400 Free French soldiers, while Royal Navy and Free French warships tackled the defences including two cruisers and the battleship *Richelieu*, not fully seaworthy after the earlier attack on Dakar, but still able to fire her guns. The opening gambit, on 23 September, by de Gaulle's emissaries who were to attempt to persuade the authorities to change sides without any fighting, failed. The Free French landing was a farce. Fire from *Richelieu* damaged the cruiser *Cumberland* and two destroyers. The next day the British resumed bombarding, and *Ark Royal* launched dive bombers and torpedo aircraft to attack *Richelieu*. Midshipman Charles Friend took part in the abortive attempt to win the garrison over without bloodshed. Free French officers also flew to Dakar, either in French Luciole aircraft or in the back cockpits of British Swordfish.

Some of us flew about over the town, dropping leaflets tastefully printed as a red, white and blue tricolour and bearing a message from de Gaulle which began, *'Français de Dakar! Joignez-vous à nous pour délivrer la France!'* We were unopposed at first, but the affair went sour almost immediately after they (the Free French) had landed, and the Stringbags which had been peacefully guiding them or dropping leaflets were escorted out to sea by fighters.

He took part in the strike on *Richelieu* the following day:

I was in the sixth aircraft of a six Stringbag striking force, armed with semi-armour-piercing (SAP) bombs and briefed to attack the shore batteries. 'Tail end Charlie' again, this time with Hartley and Huxley. As we were waiting on deck, engines running, for the ship to turn into wind to fly us off, the duty boy came down from the Air Intelligence Office with a small blackboard and braved the slipstreams and other hazards to show it to each crew. On it was chalked, 'change target to *Richelieu*'.

We took off, formed into two sub-flights, and as the harbour came into sight, high angle gunfire began to explode around us. As we lined up to dive-bomb the *Richelieu* – I suppose our SAP would have done some damage to the guns which were troubling the fleet – I was facing forward looking over Jock's shoulder. I saw one Stringbag ahead hit by flak and fall out of the line in flames. I was thumped on the back by Huxley, who was heaving up the rear gun as I looked round. He pointed astern to a section of three or four Curtis Hawk fighters, one of which was obviously bent on attacking us. Pointing and shouting were the only means of communicating with the air gunner then. But I was linked to Jock by the Gosport tube voicepipe, and I said, 'There's a fighter on our tail.'

'Christ, tell me when to turn.'

Huxley opened fire just before I saw the first flashes of cannon firing at us through the Hawk's propeller, and I said, 'Now!'

Next thing, Huxley and I were up on the ends of our 'monkey chain' harnesses as Jock stall-turned over to starboard and back. The fighter shot past in a wide turn, unable to follow us round. He or one of the others attacked the Stringbags further ahead, and one more of them was shot down before our eyes. Jock jettisoned our bombs outside the harbour, and we flew back on our own to land on *Ark*. Three of the strike were lost.

General Charles de Gaulle in
a pith helmet on board the
Westernland, travelling to the
abortive Dakar expedition.
(A1474)

In the afternoon, 820 Squadron attacked the cruisers with torpedoes, without loss to ourselves, but without discernible damage to the French.

A final bombardment the next day was equally fruitless, resulting in the battleship HMS *Resolution* being torpedoed by a French submarine, but managing to limp home. The total score in damage to their opponents was, British, nil; French, one battleship damaged and out of action for a year, and nineteen aircraft. On the way out, the cruiser *Fiji* had been torpedoed by a U-boat and was out of action for six months. The Royal Marines Brigade never set foot ashore.

Although in early October Hitler postponed his plans for invading Britain, permanently as it transpired, another threat to Britain's very existence loomed larger. The Battle of the Atlantic grew in intensity, although it had a long way to go before it reached its grim peak. By the end of 1940 shipping losses for the year totalled 3,991,641 tons, 3,599,242 in the Atlantic and Home Waters. U-boats had claimed the lion's share of these losses, sinking 2,186,158 tons of shipping. In the Second World War the average displacement of a merchant ship was 5,000 tons. The winning of this battle would decide who would win the war.

4
The Atlantic: 1941

Previous page: **Depth charges exploding.** (A4570)

1. Churchill, *The Second World War*, Vol. V, Cassell, London 1962, p. 6.

The Battle of the Atlantic was the dominating factor all through the war. Never for one moment could we forget that everything happening elsewhere, on land, at sea, or in the air, depended ultimately on its outcome, and amid all other cares we viewed its changing fortunes day by day with hope or apprehension.

Winston Churchill[1]

In order to survive, and build the ships, aircraft and weapons to equip its fighting services, Britain needed to import thousands of tons of raw materials each month. The oil under the North Sea still remained undiscovered, so every gallon of fuel burned by aircraft, tank and ship came from North and Central America or the Middle East. Non-ferrous metals, machine tools and warlike equipment from the United States and food were brought into British ports by merchant ships at a huge cost in lives and shipping. Britain produced enough to feed only half its population, and had sufficient reserves for a few months. In 1939, of which only during the last four months were we at war, Britain had to import 55 million tons of raw materials by sea.

The greatest threat to merchantmen at sea, whether in convoy or not, was the U-boat. Surface raiders, both warships and converted merchant ships, also accounted for some losses, although the numbers were small compared with U-boat sinkings. The most successful German armed merchant ship, the *Atlantis*, was sunk by HMS *Devonshire* after sinking twenty-two ships. German

A lookout in a destroyer in bad weather in the North Atlantic in February 1941. (A3157)

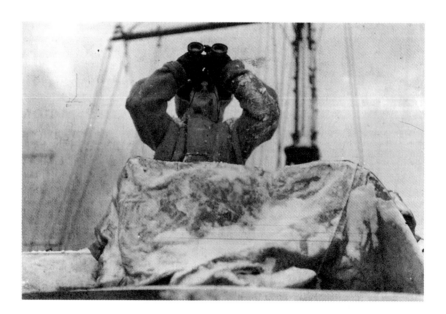

capital ships and cruisers made some forays out into the trade routes, but most of their time was spent lurking in harbour or the Norwegian fjords. Here they posed a constant threat at minimum risk to themselves. Their presence could never be ignored, and great efforts were made to destroy them in their bases. When they left their lairs, the effect on the war in the North Atlantic was often out of all proportion to their numbers. In the English Channel and North Sea, E-boats (fast patrol craft) and aircraft menaced convoys by direct attack and minelaying. U-boats, too, could and did lay mines. But their principal and most deadly weapon was the torpedo; until mid 1942, it was the First World War model, which had to hit the target to activate the firing mechanism. Later the magnetic pistol, activated by the magnetic field of the target, was brought into service. One mine or torpedo could sink the largest ship, whereas it often took several shells or bombs; it was more cost effective to sink a ship by letting water into the bottom than air into the top.

The convoy was the best protection against the U-boat. Ships sailing independently, unless very fast, were at great risk. There were insufficient escorts to spare one for each ship. The U-boat captain merely had to position himself astride a shipping route; if he missed one ship, another would soon be along. Because the submerged speed of a U-boat was seldom greater than that of the slowest convoy, a captain who was badly positioned for attack would find the whole convoy passing him before he got into range to fire his torpedoes. If he did get within range, he risked attack by the convoy escorts.

The Commander-in-Chief U-boats, Admiral Karl Doenitz, introduced the 'wolf pack' tactic, tried out in the Mediterranean in the First World War. He positioned a chain of submarines across likely convoy routes. They remained on the surface, where they had the advantage of speed, and either submerged out of sight of the convoy, to attack by day, or, more usually, attacked by night on the surface. Mass attacks often overwhelmed the efforts of the escorts, especially in the early days, when there were far too few to provide more than a handful to look after convoys of over a hundred ships. For the wolf pack system to work, Doenitz needed to direct his boats into the correct area of sea. To do this he had to discover the routing of convoys, different on each occasion, and vector his boats by radio to their patrol line. Thus began the battle for supremacy in radio intercept, a battle within a battle. The German Naval Intelligence Division, the B-Dienst, intercepted and decrypted British, and later American, radio traffic to obtain convoy routing and re-routing signals. The Government Code and Cipher School at Bletchley Park and Admiralty Intelligence monitored Doenitz's orders to his boats, and re-routed convoys out of their path. The fortunes of this secret battle swayed back and forth as one side or the other gained the upper hand in breaking the codes, which changed daily, and the methods used for enciphering which also changed frequently.

The machine most commonly used by all the German Armed Forces was Enigma. Before a message was transmitted the text was punched in on a keyboard, activating a system of wheels which 'scrambled' the letters. When

Admiral Karl Doenitz. A dedicated Nazi, he was a Captain, Commander U-boats, until promoted Rear-Admiral C.-in-C. U-boats in 1940. On 30 January 1943 he relieved Grand Admiral Raeder as C.-in-C. of the German Navy, retaining command of U-boats. Before committing suicide in April 1945, Hitler appointed Doenitz to succeed him as Führer of the German Reich. (A14899)

transmitted, the text was a meaningless jumble to the enemy listener unless he knew the day's wheel settings – and there were up to four wheels – and what type of Enigma was being employed. The authorized receiver merely typed in the text of the message on his Enigma with the day's settings, which 'unscrambled' it. Later, a further refinement was introduced whereby the message was encoded before it was punched in on the Enigma. There were months when the Germans were reading the Admiralty radio traffic, and the German traffic could not be broken, and equally long periods when the boot was on the other foot. Throughout the War, Doenitz, and indeed all other German commanders of all three services, never knew that their traffic was being read; they believed that the secrets of the Enigma machine were impenetrable.

Convoys from Britain into the Atlantic were generally routed north of Ireland, because Eire's neutrality denied bases to the Royal Navy. Winston Churchill:

Owing to the action of the Dublin Government, so much at variance with the temper and instinct of thousands of Southern Irishmen who hastened to the battle-front to prove their ancient valour, the approaches which the Southern Irish ports could so easily have guarded were closed by hostile aircraft and U-boats. This was indeed a deadly moment in our life, and if it had not been for the loyalty and friendship of Northern Ireland we should have been forced to come to close quarters or perish from the earth. However, with a restraint and poise to which, I say, history will find few parallels, His Majesty's Government never laid a hand upon them, though at times it would have been quite easy and quite natural, and we left the Dublin Government to frolic with the Germans and later the Japanese representatives, to their hearts' content.[2]

2. Prime Minister's Victory Broadcast, 13 May 1945.

The rate at which merchant ships were sunk set against the speed with which they could be replaced was critical. To begin with they were sunk faster than the shipyards could build them.

On the British side operations in the Atlantic were directed from Liverpool. In June 1940 Lieutenant-Commander John Mosse was drafted there from HMS *Havelock*:

The operational headquarters of the C.-in-C. Western Approaches, Vice-Admiral Sir Percy Noble, was now in Derby House, where a strong reinforced concrete operations room had been installed. C.-in-C. and his RAF opposite number [Air Vice-Marshal J. M. Robb, Commanding Number 15 Group Coastal Command] each had an office with a glass wall through which they could overlook the huge Atlantic plot in the operations room. Here Wrens moved symbols depicting convoys, striking forces, U-boats, casualties etc. climbing sliding ladders when necessary. This was the inspiration of the cartoon in which the Chief Wren said, 'Well, Admiral, either the Wrens must wear trousers or the convoys must be routed further south.'

Mosse was later sent to the staff of Captain Stevens RN to train the command teams of escorts in tactics.

Though flattered, I was not pleased to be grounded again, but the job proved to be most interesting.

His job included interviewing incoming captains and trying to assess the tactics of the U-boats.

It had always been the official belief, strongly supported by our own submariners, that U-boats operated independently, and that if more than one attacked the same convoy, this was fortuitous.

We were now becoming increasingly suspicious of this doctrine, and following a study of recent events, we were able to tell the Director Anti-Submarine Warfare in the Admiralty (Captain George Creasy RN), that U-boats were operating in co-ordinated packs at night, attacking from different bearings and making their escape on the surface, thus minimising their detection by Asdic.

Although Mosse did not know it at the time, his shrewd deductions were confirmed by intercepts of German naval signals, known as Ultra, the code-name for Bletchley Park's code-breaking of all enemy Services. For this was a

A Wren up the ladder in front of the 'plot' at Derby House in Liverpool, the Headquarters of C.-in -C. Western Approaches, from where the Battle of the Atlantic was directed. Photographed during the shooting of a film by the Army Film Unit, hence the floodlighting. (A25746)

THE WRENS

The WRNS played a vital part in winning the war at sea.
These photographs show some, but by no means all, of their roles.

Left: June Mortimer, a farmer's daughter from Northern Ireland and member of a WRNS boat crew, on a 60-foot harbour launch.
(A26514)

Right: Members of the WRNS served ashore in every theatre of war. This is Wren D. J. Currie in the Middle East.
(A20263)

Below: Wrens pushing a torpedo out for loading on a submarine at HMS *Dolphin*, Portsmouth.
(A19471)

The Western Approaches Tactical Unit, an early form of simulator for training escort commanders. Wrens became experts at U-boat and anti-submarine tactics.

Above left: Wrens laying out the floor for a tactical exercise. The 'students' sat at desks behind drawn curtains, and from time to time were allowed to see part of the floor through eyepieces in what look like bags suspended on two sets of uprights between each door curtain. (A27823)

Above right: Behind the curtains, the 'students commanding escorts or ships' sat with chart, dividers and parallel ruler, while orders and information were passed in. Their orders to their ships were passed out to the Wrens who moved the convoy and ships accordingly. (A27820)

Right: A Leading Wren radio mechanic being assisted by another Leading Wren loading a radio into a Lysander of the Fleet Air Arm before taking it up for an air test. (AP12709)

period when the British had the upper hand in the war of the decrypters, although it would be grossly unfair to claim that every success can be laid at the door of Bletchley Park. In the end much depended on the skill of captains and ships' companies of attacking escorts:

Merchant ship losses had increased to about forty a month, and Admiral Doenitz was boasting the success of certain 'Ace' U-boat commanders who had each sunk more than 250,000 tons of shipping. But the enemy was not having it all his own way. The greater efficiency and new tactics adopted by the escort forces [and Ultra] began to pay off. Sinkings of U-boats increased, and in March 1941 we had a spectacular success.

Early that month an unknown U-boat was sunk by *Wolverine*. A few days later, two more of our ships, *Vanoc* (Commander Denese), and *Walker* (Commander Donald Macintyre) fought a remarkable action in which two U-boats were sunk. Following a convoy attack, *Vanoc* gained a fleeting radar contact on a surfaced U-boat trying to escape. She rammed and sank U-100 and picked up a few survivors, but her CO perished. He was Joachim Schepke, one of the wanted men. Almost simultaneously, *Walker* gained Asdic contact with another U-boat, which seemed to be virtually underneath *Vanoc*. She carried out a depth charge attack and caused sufficient damage to force U-99 to the surface. The crew jumped overboard, and *Walker* picked them up, including her CO. He was Otto Kretschmer, lionized in Germany as the 'Wolf of the Atlantic'.

To complete this remarkable hat trick, we learned later that *Wolverine*'s victim was U-47 whose CO was none other than Günther Prien, another ace who had not only sunk a quarter of a million tons of shipping, but had carried out the brilliant exploit of penetrating Scapa Flow and sinking the battleship *Royal Oak*.

Despite these encouraging results, the Battle of the Atlantic was not being won by either side. By the end of 1941, the accumulated shipping losses in all theatres in two years and four months of war were ten million tons of Allied shipping, of which over half were sunk by U-boats. New construction had replaced less than half that figure. Doenitz had lost thirty-five U-boats. But only in the first quarter of the year did the number sunk exceed those available for operations. The total number, including those training and on trials, was well in excess of the losses.

The year had also been marked by one of the greatest dramas of the war. On 18 May, the new German battleship *Bismarck* (Captain Lindemann) left the Baltic, in company with the heavy cruiser *Prinz Eugen*, bound for commerce raiding in the Atlantic, under the command of Vice-Admiral Lütjens. Grand Admiral Raeder, C.-in-C. of the German Navy, had hoped that the force would also consist of *Scharnhorst* and *Gneisenau*. But both were in Brest: *Scharnhorst* for an engine overhaul, and *Gneisenau* had been badly damaged, first by a torpedo from a Beaufort of Coastal Command, and subsequently by aircraft of Bomber Command. Lütjens had requested Raeder that the sortie be delayed until *Scharnhorst* was repaired, or even better until *Bismarck*'s sister ship *Tirpitz* was fully worked up. In the light of subsequent events, it was perhaps fortunate that both great battleships did not go out together. Although formidable, *Bismarck* was not the miracle of design portrayed in some accounts. The Japanese *Mutsu*, American *North Carolina* and British *Rodney* were bigger, better armed and protected, and in the case of the first two faster. *Bismarck* was basically a First World War design with Bauhaus styling. Her protection was poorly distributed and non-existent in some areas, all internal communications ran above her armoured deck, and her machinery was unreliable. She was, however, to cause the British Admiralty considerable angst.

As Lütjens' squadron passed between Denmark and Sweden on 20 May, it was sighted by a Swedish cruiser. This information was passed via the Norwegian attaché in Stockholm to the British Embassy and thence to the Admiralty.

Lütjens' orders from Raeder were to destroy enemy shipping but not to engage warships unless he could do so without excessive risk; very much in the tradition of the German surface fleet. Neither Lütjens nor Lindemann was cast in the mould of Cunningham, Somerville, Vian, Warburton-Lee and the host of other fighting leaders in the Royal Navy, whose instinct was to go for the enemy whatever the odds.

Lütjens, instead of heading straight up into Arctic waters to rendezvous with the tanker *Weissenburg*, took his squadron into Bergen to refuel, but neglected to top up *Bismarck*'s tanks. She had sailed with less than a full fuel load, and now had about 80 per cent in her bunkers. By putting into Bergen he not only lost a day, but risked detection by air reconnaissance. From Bergen he set a

Bismarck from *Prinz Eugen*, during RAS trials in the Baltic. (HU374)

Vice-Admiral Günther
Lütjens. He went down
with his flagship, *Bismarck*.
(A14897)

course for the Denmark Strait, the 180-mile-wide gap between northern Iceland and the pack ice. In doing so he ignored the advice of Group North (the German Maritime Headquarters responsible for operations north of the English Channel) to head for the Iceland–Faroes gap. He also cancelled his plans to meet *Weissenburg*. Thus he chose a longer route, and at the same time failed to take on more fuel. He did not survive to justify his actions, but they bear the hallmarks of indecision and lack of confidence perhaps brought on by exhaustion.

On the day Lütjens was refuelling in Bergen, the Home Fleet, alerted by Ultra decrypts of Luftwaffe radio nets, was a hive of activity. The C.-in-C. Home Fleet, Admiral Sir John Tovey, ordered Rear-Admiral Frederic Wake-Walker commanding 1st Cruiser Squadron to maintain his watch on the Denmark Strait. Vice-Admiral Holland sailed in his flagship, *Hood*, with the new battleship *Prince of Wales* and five destroyers to join Wake-Walker. The cruisers *Manchester* and *Birmingham* were ordered to keep watch in the Iceland–Faroes gap. Tovey brought his flagship HMS *King George V* and the 2nd Cruiser Squadron to short notice. Meanwhile the Admiralty placed the battle-cruiser *Repulse* and the new carrier HMS *Victorious* under Tovey's command.

After an air reconnaissance report on 22 May that Bergen was empty Tovey knew that Lütjens had sailed; and that he must be headed for the North Atlantic convoy routes. Ordering the cruiser *Arethusa* to reinforce *Manchester* and *Birmingham*, Tovey in *King George V* with *Repulse*, *Victorious*, four cruisers and six destroyers, headed west towards Greenland. He asked Coastal Command to fly air reconnaissance over the Denmark Strait, the Iceland–Faroes Gap, the Faroes–Shetland Gap, and across to Norway.

Tovey's ships, although outnumbering Lütjens' force, were not as overwhelmingly superior as one might think. The newly commissioned *Victorious* had been on the point of sailing for the Middle East carrying crated Hurricanes, leaving room for only nine Swordfish and six Fulmars. Her aircrews had not had time to work up. The *King George V*, also recently commissioned, had never tried her new design 14-inch gun turrets in action. The battle-cruiser *Repulse* was of 1916 vintage. Although her armour had been increased, and anti-aircraft guns added, she was essentially little better than Beatty's battle-cruisers which had taken such a pasting at Jutland twenty-five years before. The mighty *Hood*, pride of the Royal Navy, had never been modernized since her launching in 1918. The newest of all, the *Prince of Wales* [*King George V* class], sailed with Vickers' technicians who were still working on a number of mechanical defects, including the main armament.

The weather in the North Atlantic could not have been more favourable to surface raiders. Only in the immediate vicinity of the pack ice ringing Greenland was the visibility good; elsewhere thick mist, heavy rain and snow squalls made the hunters' job desperately difficult.

In the evening of 23 May, HMS *Suffolk* of Wake-Walker's 1st Cruiser Squadron was closing the ice near the British minefield in the Denmark Strait, as ordered. Extracts from Wake-Walker's Official Report:

Admiral Sir John Tovey,
C.-in-C. Home Fleet, on
board his flagship, the
battleship *King George V.*
(A14840)

While doing so she made contact at 19.22 with the enemy, reporting one battleship and one cruiser, bearing 020 degrees, seven miles, course 240 degrees. At 19.57, *Suffolk* reported the enemy's speed at twenty-eight knots.

Norfolk [flag] closed with the intention of making contact with *Suffolk* when clear of the minefield, but at 20.30 while steering 030 she sighted the enemy at about six miles on an opposite course. On sighting *Norfolk* turned away and made smoke, under fire from the leading ship. Salvos fell very close and splinters came aboard.

The report by 1st Cruiser Squadron gave *Bismarck*'s and *Prinz Eugen*'s positions to all ships and to the Admiralty. Eleven convoys were in the North Atlantic, including one of five troopships bound for the Middle East, escorted by the *Exeter* and *Cairo* with five destroyers. To protect this convoy, Somerville, who on his own initiative had brought Force H to short notice, was ordered to sail from Gibraltar. Within an hour and ten minutes he was steaming west at 25 knots with his flag in the battle-cruiser *Renown*, the carrier *Ark Royal*, the cruiser *Sheffield* and six destroyers.

Meanwhile *Suffolk* and *Norfolk* shadowed the enemy. Only *Suffolk* had radar. Wake-Walker:

The enemy appeared from *Suffolk*'s reports to be skirting the edge of the ice.

I continued to draw ahead on the enemy and informed *Suffolk* at 23.11 of my intention to endeavour to cover any move the enemy might make to the eastward away from the ice. At midnight *Suffolk* reported the enemy hidden in a snowstorm. At this time visibility from *Norfolk* was one mile.

At 04.45 on 24 May:

A report was received from *Icarus* [one of *Hood*'s escorts] giving the position of herself some distance astern of us. This was the first intimation I had of the Battle Cruiser Force being in the vicinity. *Suffolk* continued to keep in touch at a distance of about fifteen miles. The enemy was making good a course of about 220 degrees at a speed of 28 knots, but frequently made large alterations of course of as much as thirty degrees.

At 05.16 smoke was sighted on the port bow, which later proved to be the battle-cruisers. At 05.41 *Norfolk* sighted the enemy at a distance of sixteen miles, at about the same time as she was reported by *Prince of Wales* and *Hood*.

Vice-Admiral Holland steered at high speed to engage the enemy. Both *Hood* and *Prince of Wales* were taking water 'green' over the bows as they smashed into high seas. Spray blinded their main range-finders. The *Prince of Wales*'s gunnery radar was jammed by her own high-power radio transmitting the enemy movement reports to the Admiralty. Holland manoeuvred his ships to close the range as quickly as possible and present the smallest possible target. He had just ordered a turn to port to unmask *Hood*'s after turrets, when *Bismarck*'s fifth salvo found its mark.

Able Seaman Albert Briggs was Holland's Flag Lieutenant's messenger.

The Admiral decided to command from the Compass Platform, rather than the Admiral's bridge. The Captain was fighting the ship from the compass platform. I was in a position to see everything that was going on. I kept pestering the Flag Lieutenant, and he was very helpful. The Admiral intended *Prince of Wales* and *Hood* to take on *Bismarck*, and the two cruisers *Norfolk* and *Suffolk* to engage *Prinz Eugen*. The six destroyers we had to leave fifty miles behind would carry out torpedo attacks, when they arrived.

We fired about six salvos before she replied. Her gunnery was extremely accurate. Her shells made a noise like an express train going through a tunnel. Everybody on the bridge was very calm. Her fifth salvo hit us, at the base of the main mast. The ship shuddered, and we were thrown off our feet.

What struck me was the unreality of it. It just seemed as if it wasn't happening. It seemed as if you were watching a film. The gunnery officer reported it as if it were a routine.

Just as we were altering course the next salvo hit us. Again the ship shuddered, I didn't hear any explosion. All I saw was a gigantic sheet of flame which shot round the front of the compass platform. The ship started listing to starboard. She'd gone about ten degrees, when she righted herself and started going over to port, and carried on going over. I heard the quartermaster report, 'Steering gone, sir.' The Captain ordered, 'Change to emergency steering.' By that time we realized she wasn't coming back. I went to the starboard door of

The last known photograph of *Hood* before she was sunk, taken from *Prince of Wales* on 23 May 1941. (HU50190)

the compass platform, as I got there, the gunnery officer was going through before me, and the navigating officer stood to one side to let me through. I was about half way down the ladder to the Admiral's bridge, when I was dragged into the water. I had to get clear of the deckhead above, I kicked out, but felt myself being dragged down. I couldn't do any more. I felt quite a feeling of peace. Suddenly I shot to the surface. The ship was vertical, and B Turret was just going under, about fifty yards away. I swam as fast as I could away from her.

There were three survivors. Albert Briggs eventually climbed into a Carley float and found the other two. Midshipman Dundas had been on the compass platform, and Ordinary Seaman Tilburn had been on the boat deck. They were rescued by the destroyer *Electra*. The subsequent Court of Inquiry concluded that a boiler may have burst as *Hood* was sinking and an air bubble brought the three of them up.

Admiral Holland, her Captain, and more than 1,400 of her ship's company went to the bottom. It is now believed that a 15-inch shell penetrated her side below the armoured belt on a submerged trajectory. The shell caused an explosion in a 4-inch magazine, blowing out the bulkhead into the engine room inflicting massive structural failure. Some who were present in other

Ordinary Seaman Bob Tilburn, one of the three survivors from *Hood*. (HU50191)

**HMS *Glorious* in the Arctic
by Eric Ravilious.**
Glorious embarked Hurricanes
shortly before she was sunk
by *Scharnhorst* and *Gneisenau*
off Norway. This painting
may depict this event.
Ravilious was killed during
the War. (LD283)

**At the controls of
a submarine
by Eric Ravilious.**
(LD15213)

Withdrawal from Dunkirk, June 1940 *by Charles Cundall.*

(LD305)

Attack on convoy seen from the air, 1941 *by Richard Eurich.*
The artist has put himself in the position of a German airman attacking a channel convoy as it passes the
Isle of Wight. The Needles can be seen in the top left of the picture. (LD1326)

A destroyer rescuing survivors, 1942 *by Richard Eurich.*

(LD2297)

The Garrett landing *by Anthony Gross.*

Major Ralph Garrett Royal Marines (with map board under arm) on the beach near Sidi Barrani in Egypt. Garrett with Australians and Royal Marines covered the final embarkation of troops from Crete. When the last ships had left, he gave his men the option of surrendering or attempting to escape. He refloated a derelict landing craft, and with 137 volunteers from many regiments reached Egypt after a voyage of nine days, much of it using makeshift sails. (LD2751)

HMS *Repulse*, 15-inch gun turret *by Barnett Freedman*.
Unusually the turret crew are not wearing anti-flash gear, possibly because the artist wanted to see their faces. The battle-cruiser
Repulse was sunk by Japanese aircraft with *Prince of Wales* off Malaya on 10 December 1941. (LD2295)

Hoisting the black pennant: the black pennant is hoisted when going in to attack submarines *by Roland Pitchforth.*
(LD4869)

Submarine Patrol HM Submarine *Upholder* leaving the base for the Mediterranean *by Leslie Cole.*
Actually this was painted in the Mediterranean in Malta. *Upholder* was commanded by Lieutenant-Commander
M. D. Wanklyn, the first submarine VC of the Second World War. She was subsequently lost with all hands in
mid-April 1942 on Wanklyn's last patrol. (LD3232)

ships remember a huge puff of smoke up her funnel before she broke in half, which would support this theory. Some witnesses recall seeing her forward turrets firing vertically skywards as her forepart slid, bows up, into the sea. Some quirk in the electric firing connections might have made this possible. The scene in the two forward turrets, shell-handling rooms and magazines, with hundreds of men flung in heaps against the after bulkheads, with no hope of getting out, beggars description.

Wake-Walker:

Prince of Wales continued the action and a hit was seen on her and at 06.13 she turned away and made smoke.

In fact her bridge was wrecked, and she had a hole aft which let in 400 tons of water. To add to her troubles her after quadruple turret ring jammed, so that it could not be trained. It took the Vickers staff and the turret crew over two hours to bring it back into action.

With Holland's demise, and Tovey still 360 miles to the south-east, Wake-Walker was now the senior officer on the scene:

At 07.06 I ordered *Prince of Wales* to remain in company.

At 07.57 *Suffolk* reported that the enemy had reduced speed and appeared to be damaged and on fire.

About 08.10 a Sunderland flying boat was sighted and I ordered him to report whether *Bismarck* was on fire, and at 08.45 I received his reply, 'No fire seen course 220 degrees, speed 30 knots.' At 08.50 the Sunderland reported 'losing oil', which was taken to refer to an unfortunate personal ailment affecting the aircraft.

In fact *Prince of Wales* had hit *Bismarck* with two 14-inch shells. One holed her near the bow, ruptured a forward fuel tank leaving a long slick astern, allowed in 2,000 tons of water, and damaged the forward oil pumps so the 1,000 tons of fuel in the bow tank could not be pumped to the boilers. The other put one engine room out of action. This combined with the need to counterflood to level her trim reduced *Bismarck*'s speed to 28 knots. At 09.00 Lütjens decided to detach *Prinz Eugen* to attack convoys, and head for St Nazaire in *Bismarck*.

Wake-Walker hung on to *Bismarck*'s coat-tails. The Admiralty meanwhile sent a signal to him asking him for his 'intentions' as regards re-engaging with *Prince of Wales*:

The question whether I should re-engage with *Prince of Wales* had been exercising my mind for some time before the receipt of this signal. The factors to be considered were: the state of efficiency of *Prince of Wales*. I had seen her forced out of action after 10 minutes' engagement at the end of which her salvos were falling short and had a very large spread indeed. She was short of one gun and her bridge was wrecked. She was a brand new ship, with new turrets in which mechanical breakdowns had occurred and were to be expected.

I had been unable to observe any hits on *Bismarck* and her shooting had given striking proof of her efficiency. To put it in a nutshell, I did not, and do not consider that in her then state *Prince of Wales* was a match for *Bismarck*. This was in no way a deciding factor. My object was the destruction of *Bismarck*, and I knew that other forces were on the way to intercept her. I therefore had two broad alternatives, one to ensure that she was intercepted by the Commander-in-Chief, the other to attempt her destruction with my own force.

Wake-Walker, a cool, brave sea officer, decided

to keep touch with the possibility that we might fail to do so, though with *Prince of Wales* in support I had no fear of being driven off.

Afterwards, Pound, probably egged on by Phillips, demanded that Tovey court martial Wake-Walker and Leach, the Captain of *Prince of Wales*, for not engaging *Bismarck*. Tovey refused, saying that he would act as Prisoner's Friend. No more was heard on this subject.

Through the early part of the night 24/25 May Wake-Walker shadowed *Bismarck*. By then a total of four battleships, two battle-cruisers, two aircraft-carriers, twelve cruisers and dozens of destroyers were moving from almost all points of the compass and from hundreds of miles away to attempt to intercept *Bismarck*.

By now Tovey had detached *Victorious* ahead with an escort of four cruisers of 2nd Cruiser Squadron in the hope that a strike by her aircraft would slow *Bismarck* down sufficiently to enable him to catch up with her the next morning. At 22.00, still 120 miles from *Bismarck*, the *Victorious* launched nine Swordfish under Lieutenant-Commander Eugene Esmonde RN, with four Fulmars as a reconnaissance force. Rear-Admiral Curteis commanding 2nd Cruiser Squadron signalled to *Victorious*:

Please convey my sincerest good wishes to all who are flying tonight. They have a wonderful chance to avenge *Hood* and gain a success which will be invaluable to our cause. Good luck.

The weather was showery, with squalls, and a fresh north-westerly wind which sent streamers of spray across the heaving flight deck as *Victorious* ploughed into wind to launch aircraft. With great determination Esmonde's crews pressed home their attack on *Bismarck* under a massive weight of fire from her flak batteries. Amazingly no Swordfish were hit, probably because *Bismarck* was twisting and turning violently to avoid the torpedoes. One hit was observed, but the torpedo had run shallow, despite being set for 31 feet. It detonated on the armoured belt, causing no damage.

At 03.06 on 25 May *Suffolk* lost contact with *Bismarck*. For most of that day Tovey, believing that she was headed back for the Denmark Strait, steered in that direction. He was not helped in his assessments of *Bismarck*'s course by

a series of muddled signals from the Admiralty. Not until the evening did he turn back on to the correct track, by which time he was 150 miles astern of his quarry.

Early on 26 May, Somerville's Force H coming up from the south launched a search of ten Swordfish from *Ark Royal*, in appalling weather. Midshipman Charles Friend:

Swordfish ranged on the after end of *Victorious* before the strike on *Bismarck*, 24 May 1941. (A4090)

The wind was gusting over the deck up to fifty knots, even though the ship had reduced speed to moderate the deck movement. The after end of the flight deck was pitching something like fifty feet up and down. The waves were so high that even sixty feet tall [height from waterline to flight deck] *Ark Royal* sometimes took it 'green' over her bows. *Renown*'s weather decks were continually awash, and *Sheffield* could not be seen at all through the spume and spray. The aircraft, as their throttles were opened, instead of charging forward on a level deck, were at one moment breasting a slippery slope, the next plunging downhill towards the huge seas ahead and below. Some seemed to touch the wave tops as they fell off the bows, others were nose up as they 'unstuck', but thanks to the skill of our pilots they all flew safely away.

They all returned safely, but had seen nothing.

Then, at 10.30 on the 26th, a Catalina of Coastal Command sighted *Bismarck* 690 miles north-west of Brest. The Air Officer Commanding-in-Chief of Coastal Command had decided to push his reconnaissance further south than the Admiralty had thought necessary, in case estimates of *Bismarck*'s track were incorrect. Later that day, thanks to the Catalina's report, Swordfish from *Ark Royal* in Force H also found and shadowed her.

Bismarck, heading for Brest, soon to be under land-based air cover, could use up all her fuel to get there. Tovey, who had now been joined by the battleship *Rodney*, was not only well astern, but his ships were running short of fuel, and had a long voyage home. At that time the Royal Navy did not have an effective system for resupply at sea (RAS) from tankers, and ships almost always refuelled in port. Occasionally oiling was done at sea from a hose towed astern, or, if the sea was calm, by making fast to a tanker alongside. Resupply underway with beam RAS rigs would not be executed by the Royal Navy until the very end of the war in the Pacific.

Tovey, 130 miles behind, and having reduced speed to conserve fuel, would have to slow *Bismarck* down, or lose the race. Somerville was now about forty miles north-east of *Bismarck*. The Admiralty, dreading that Somerville's flagship, the lightly armoured *Renown*, might go the same way as the *Hood*, had signalled:

Renown is not to become heavily engaged with *Bismarck* unless the latter is already heavily engaged with either *King George V* or *Rodney*.

Somerville detached the cruiser *Sheffield* to shadow *Bismarck* and ordered *Ark Royal* to launch a Swordfish strike armed with torpedoes. Sub-Lieutenant Alan Swanton RN, a Swordfish pilot:

At 14.50, fifteen Stringbags took off. The ship slowed to eight knots for the launch, but even so, there was a good 40 knots of wind over the deck, which was rising by more than 55 feet. After almost an hour of flight, the first aircraft moved in for the kill. One after another, torpedoes fell away from the bellies of the Swordfish. It was only after eleven had been dropped that the pilots began to realize that something had gone horribly wrong. Their target was not firing back at them. It was the wrong ship.

Lady Luck, however, was smiling on *Sheffield* that day. A new design of magnetic detonator was being used that day. Six of the eleven torpedoes exploded on impact with the sea, and *Sheffield* manoeuvred to avoid the remainder.

Sub-Lieutenant Kenneth Pattison was one of those who did not drop his torpedo. Only the leaders of each trio of aircraft carried observers on this sortie, and on his return to *Ark Royal*, weighed down with his torpedo, he was falling further and further behind. Worried that he would not find the carrier, and with no radio communications between aircraft, he attracted the leader in the only way he could:

I fired my forward gun past him. Once he realized, he signed me to jettison my torpedo. I would not have been able to land with an armed 'fish' on board.

Alan Swanton:

The debrief was animated.

Unfortunately the signal, transmitted by light, detaching *Sheffield* had not been repeated to *Ark Royal*, so she was unaware that the cruiser was shadowing *Bismarck*.

Kenneth Pattison:

We went and had a cup of tea, rearmed and refuelled and off again. The weather had deteriorated and conditions were appalling, snow showers and low cloud.

Alan Swanton:

Tim Coode, the CO of 818, was leading with our boss [Lieutenant-Commander J. A. Stewart-Moore RN, CO of 820 Squadron] as deputy. We launched at 19.10. In those waters at that time of year, it is still light, although the cloud base had fallen to below 1,000 feet. This time we had been instructed to find *Sheffield* and depart from her position.

This time all aircraft carried observers; Charles Friend:

I was observer in 2P, in the second sub-flight of the first squadron of the strike, piloted by Tony Beale, air gunner Leading Airman K. Pimlott. Making all of 50 knots with our full loads we rumbled off in the right direction. We had sighted *Sheffield* below us, before the sub-flight following Tim Coode's lead climbed into the low cloud. When we popped out through the top, there was not another aircraft in sight. Tony said: 'Where, I ask, is the *Bismarck*?'

'Don't know,' I replied, 'but I know where *Sheffield* is,' and gave him a course to steer.

Sure enough we reached the shadowing cruiser as we come down through cloud. We flew low past her, and I made 'where is target?' by Aldis lamp.

'Enemy bears 185, distant 10 miles.'

They headed on that bearing; Alan Swanton:

Then we saw *Bismarck*. We descended to 100 feet behind Stewart-Moore in a four-ship formation. There she was half a mile away, big, black and menacing. She had guns all over her, and they all seemed to be stabbing red flame in our direction. I levelled, heading for her amidships. Gerry just behind me was shouting his head off with the usual sort of Observer rubbish. I pushed the 'tit', the torpedo fell away, and the aircraft jumped into the air. Then it all went sour. There were a series of flashes, and flak ripped through the underside of the fuselage. 'Christ,' I yelled, 'look at this lot.' *Bismarck* was firing her main armament on a flat trajectory ahead of us. The shells were hitting the sea in front, pushing up

100 foot mountains of water. We continued low and fast until we were out of range. Gerry gave me the heading for home, and that 'Flash' Seager our TAG [air gunner] had been hit but was all right. It was then Gerry spotted the dark stain on my flying overalls.

'No problem,' I lied, 'I'm perfectly OK,' but added that it would be nice to get back to the ship. I formated on 'Scruffy' who had a radar.

I was glad to have Gerry with me that day. He told *Ark* what was going on, and requested an emergency landing. Twenty minutes later we arrived back on deck. It was a bit of a controlled crash, but I was able to walk away from it.

Kenneth Pattison:

During our run-in at 9,000 feet in cloud, I was hit by flak from *Bismarck* (she must have had AA radar). We started our dive and came out of cloud at 800 feet, there she was. We turned in, only two of us, Godfrey Fawcett and I; Tony Beale had got lost. I was on *Bismarck*'s beam, as we made our attack at 90 feet and 90 knots. I dropped my fish. As we turned away, my observer saw it running. I am sure that either my torpedo or Godfrey Fawcett's hit *Bismarck*.

Charles Friend's aircraft was the last to attack, having gone back to *Sheffield* to ask the way:

She [*Bismarck*] seemed to be in the middle of a slow turn to port, as Tony put us into a shallow dive. He aimed carefully and dropped at about 800 yards from her port side. He turned violently away as the whole ship exploded in a flash of guns firing at us. Watching her as best we could in the weaving and jinking Tony was performing, I saw a column of water rise midships on her side.

'You've hit her.'

Tony looked over his shoulder. Pimlott was firing his Vickers K at the now distant Germans. Great splashes spurted up around us. I said, 'You ought to steer towards the splashes, and then they'll overcorrect and miss us.'

'Bugger that,' Tony answered, and forged on at about 100 knots, and we were soon out of range, untouched. Returning to *Ark Royal*, we flew low past *Sheffield*, giving her a thumbs up.

At the debrief, we discovered we were not the only Stringbag to lose touch in the cloud. Our whole sub-flight had lost the leader. Tim Coode's leading sub-flight, with another aircraft from further back had attacked first. Next, the other two of our sub-flight attacked after obtaining a bearing by radar; both were hit by shrapnel. The rest attacked in quick succession. Several other aircraft were hit by *Bismarck*, but only two crew were wounded. The earlier crews had observed one other hit aft on *Bismarck*'s starboard side, and noticed her swing to port.

The hit aft was decisive, hitting the steering rooms containing the machinery operating the rudders. *Bismarck* had been turning hard aport taking evading action. Her twin rudders jammed in that position. After completing two circles, working parties managed to centre one rudder. But the other remained jammed. Despite all efforts to steer using her propellers, *Bismarck* persisted in turning head to wind, straight for her hunters.

Captain Philip Vian, in *Cossack*, commanding 4th Destroyer Flotilla, and protecting a troop convoy, had been ordered to join Tovey, who had detached his own escorts to refuel. On hearing the Catalina's report, he acted on his own initiative and steered to close the *Bismarck*. All night Vian's five destroyers, *Cossack*, *Maori*, *Zulu*, *Sikh* and the Polish *Piorun*, ringed *Bismarck*, and closed to launch torpedoes. *Maori*, *Cossack* and *Sikh* scored hits, but none were mortal. The next morning *King George V*, *Rodney*, *Dorsetshire* and *Norfolk* closed in. Wake-Walker:

At 08.49 *King George V* and *Rodney* opened fire, and *Bismarck* replied. *Norfolk* opened fire four minutes later, and continued firing and flank marking for the battleships. The enemy's fire was ragged, and it was soon apparent that the fire from our battleships was taking effect. *Bismarck* appeared to be altering course aimlessly and not to be under control.

At 09.06 *Norfolk* fired four torpedoes at 16,000 yards. No hits were observed.

Dorsetshire opened fire on *Bismarck* at 09.40.

Gunfire had to be checked, and torpedo fire was withheld until 10.10, when four torpedoes were fired at 4,000 yards. Two possible hits were observed.

At 10.24 the Commander-in-Chief's signal was received saying that *King George V* and *Rodney* had to break off the action for fuel. At 10.22, as *Bismarck* showed no signs of sinking, I had ordered *Dorsetshire* to torpedo her at close range. My signal reporting this

Captain Philip Vian RN on the bridge of his destroyer *Cossack*. (A1595)

to the Commander-in-Chief crossed his ordering any ship with torpedoes to use them on *Bismarck*.

At 10.33, I signalled my intention to proceed to Scapa to fuel.

By now *Bismarck* was a battered wreck, but still floating after taking hits from hundreds of 16-inch, 14-inch, 8-inch, 6-inch and 5.25-inch shells, just how many will never be known, a total of 2,878 were fired, but not all can have hit.

At 12.05, the following signal was received from *Dorsetshire*:

'I torpedoed *Bismarck* both sides before she sank. She had ceased firing but her colours were still flying.'

There were 110 survivors. Lütjens, Lindemann and 2,090 of her ship's company perished. Curiously aircraft were not used to finish her off, although the air-minded Somerville had ordered a strike of Swordfish into the attack. Midshipman Friend records that they arrived to find *Bismarck* under heavy fire from the battleships and cruisers, and wanting to avoid being hit:

The strike flew towards *King George V* to ask for the ships to cease firing. They were shot at for their pains, although how anyone could mistake single-engined biplanes flying four hundred miles from land for enemy aircraft escapes my understanding.

The Admiralty signalled:

Their Lordships congratulate C.-in-C. Home Fleet, Force H and all concerned in the unrelenting pursuit and successful destruction of the enemy's most powerful warship. The loss of HMS *Hood* and her company, which is so deeply regretted, has thus been avenged, and the Atlantic made more secure for our trade and that of our allies.

From the information at present available to their Lordships, there can be no doubt that had it not been for the gallantry, skill and devotion to duty of the Fleet Air Arm in both *Victorious* and *Ark Royal* our object might not have been achieved.

On which one can only comment, that without the Fleet Air Arm it most certainly would not have been achieved. But perhaps the Admiralty could not bring themselves to say it.

Prinz Eugen, having developed engine trouble, returned to Brest on 1 June 1941. Lütjens' sortie was the last by major units of the German surface fleet into the Atlantic for the rest of the war. However the threat was to remain and be the cause of considerable trouble until 1944. Doenitz's star now gained the ascendancy in Hitler's favours, and henceforth the U-boat would be the major weapon of the German Naval effort.

SWORDFISH OPERATIONS

Nicknamed the 'Stringbag', the Swordfish was a biplane torpedo bomber of 1934 vintage. It could also carry bombs, rockets and depth-charges. Its crew of three – pilot, observer and air gunner/wireless operator – sat in open cockpits.

Midshipman Charles Friend RN was a Swordfish observer:

For an observer the journey down the deck was always hazardous. A small range of two or three aircraft was easier to approach than a big search or strike, but even then the aircraft were placed as far aft as they could be, and very close together. Very often it was necessary to duck under the wings of another aircraft to reach one's own – and to be careful not to duck into an invisible whirling propeller. The strong wind over the deck and the erratic slipstreams made things even more difficult. On my earliest flights, I used to take my chartboard under my arm to the Air Intelligence Office, but after having several times charged towards the assembled aircraft on an uncontrolled port or starboard tack, the eighteen-inch-square chartboard being a very efficient sail, I usually left it in my cockpit. The rest of the observer's load of Course and Speed Calculator, stop-watch, notebook,

A Swordfish Mark I. The observer sat behind the pilot, and behind him the Telegraphist Air Gunner (TAG), a rating qualified in sending and receiving Morse over the wireless (radio). There was no facility for voice transmission. In addition he manned the rearward facing machine-gun. (A3820)

signal pad, code book, coding machine, several sharp pencils, dividers and so on, was quite heavy and unwieldy if not contained. I had the sailmaker produce a canvas holdall, with shoulder strap to my specification. I had both hands free to pick myself up if I tripped on a ringbolt, to hold on to a wing if the slipstream threatened to blow me away, and to use climbing up the side of the Stringbag.

The best of air gunners were of great help in getting the observer into the 'office'. My parachute straps would be laid over my shoulders, and he knew exactly how I hung my holdall on the side of the cockpit. A quick check that my harness was clipped securely to the 'monkey chain' safety strap to the floor, and I was ready to go. By that time *Ark* had usually turned into wind, the steam plume forward was playing straight down the centre line of the deck, and off we went, one by one, in obedience to the green flag of the Deck Control Officer.

Off into the sky over the sea, mostly on air searches or anti-submarine patrols, more rarely on strikes with torpedoes or bombs. Air searches or reconnaissances (reccos) were carefully designed so that a number of Swordfish flew on parallel tracks, twice the visibility distance apart, to cover an area of ocean. Later, when our aircraft were fitted with radar, we needed fewer to cover an area, and we could look for surface vessels even in low visibility. But early on we depended on daylight, clear weather and our eyesight. I was responsible for guiding the Stringbag out from and back to the moving spot in the ocean which was *Ark Royal*. The outward journey had to conform to the recco orders, the inward one accurate enough to get us back at the appointed time. Ideally, I would

A Swordfish Telegraphist Air Gunner's view of another Swordfish astern. The round ammunition pan and barrel of the Vickers K Gun is bottom right of the picture. (Ad No 3319)

'find the wind' about every half hour by dropping a smoke float and taking bearings of it. It was then usually necessary to make minor alterations of heading to ensure we kept as close to the ordered track of the search as possible. I took great pride in dead reckoning navigation, and I was never lost by my own carelessness or inaccuracy, but once or twice I suffered drivers who were not all that skilled at courses steering or speedkeeping or whose performance went to pieces if the oil temperature of the engine rose, and then of course I needed help.

Fortunately for us, such help was automatically given by the Naval Beacon with which all aircraft carriers were fitted by the beginning of the war. In *Ark Royal*, it was housed in a dustbin shaped container at the top of her mainmast. It transmitted a narrow beam of radio signal rotating through 360 degrees once each minute. This gave me my bearing from the ship, when I was within range, which varied with our height and weather conditions. We could never pick it up at more than seventy miles, and we usually went out to 150 miles on recco. So we could only use it for a homing correction within about fifty miles of the ship on our way back.

Anti-submarine patrols were more simply arranged. One or two aircraft would fly across the line of advance of the fleet, at something less than visibility distance from the leading ship, searching ahead by eye, assisted by binoculars, looking for submarines or their periscopes. I did many patrols without ever sighting a submarine, although I did report by Aldis signal lamp the odd floating mine, empty boat or shadowing aircraft which had not been seen from the ships.

Usually we saw very little, except sea and sky for hours and hundreds of miles on end. The oceans are very, very big, and very, very empty. Recco in a single-engined machine over deep seas was a monotonous and lonely experience. There was not another aircraft in sight for most of the time we spent in the air, and we in the crew were absorbed in our separate tasks. The pilot, while watching the sea and sky, was conscious of every flicker of the instruments. The observer, also watching sea and sky, was busy keeping track of his whereabouts. The air gunner, watching sea and sky, was listening on his wireless.

In the clearest of Arctic weather the visibility was so good I could sometimes see for fifty miles. In less clear and calm weather, I flew over choppy grey-green water flecked with white horses, with lowering clouds above my head.

On reccos we were usually armed only with smoke floats for windfinding, and .303 ammunition for front and rear guns. On anti-submarine patrols, at first we had bombs, but later we had depth-charges.

Whenever *Ark* hove in sight at the end of a flight, however weather stained she looked, I felt not just relief that she was still there to take us aboard, but a distinct feeling of affection that I was home again.

Alan Swanton, a Fleet Air Arm pilot who eventually commanded a squadron of American Avengers, also flew Swordfish:

The forward firing gun in the Swordfish was strictly World War One stuff, firing .303-inch bullets through the rotating blades of the propeller. It was an ingenious invention in its day, but something of a quaint antique by 1943. The torpedo sight consisted of a metal tube fixed to the airframe in the pilot's line of sight, and at right angles to the flight path.

**A Swordfish Mark II
with rocket rails fitted.**
(A23783)

From this tube sprouted a line of small light bulbs. Before carrying out a torpedo attack on an enemy ship, the pilot would first estimate its speed by observing the length of the wake in relation to the vessel. Having decided the speed, the appropriate setting was made in the cockpit, and the sight switched on. This illuminated two bulbs, one of which was to Port of the line of flight, and the other to Starboard. In theory, and of course presupposing the torpedo was dropped while flying straight and level, at the right height and speed, using the appropriate bulb to aim for a point ahead of the ship and the enemy vessel maintained a straight course at the estimated speed, a hit should be scored.

It really says something for the skill of the Fleet Air Arm pilots [and navigators], flying these outdated old machines, largely at night, that a greater tonnage of shipping was sunk by Swordfish than any other aircraft during the course of the war.

No wonder the first verse of a favourite Fleet Air Arm song went:

> They say in the Air Force the landing's OK
> If the pilot gets out and can still walk away –
> But in the Fleet Air Arm the prospects are grim
> If the landing's piss-poor and the pilot can't swim.

5
Triumph and Disaster in the Mediterranean: 1941

Previous page: HMS *Valiant,*
HMS *Warspite* and HMS
Barham. **All three were at the
Battle of Matapan.** (HU2296)

Commander Manley Power RN, on Admiral Sir Andrew Cunningham's staff, wrote to his wife:

Warspite 1.4.41

My Darling Rabbit

I had to cut my last letter pretty short as we were just off to sea. I had an idea when I wrote it that we were going to have a scrap and it turned out well. We had a most terrific show about 22.30 on the 28th. We had been working up to them all day after our cruisers got contact early in the forenoon and were not far astern as night came down. The old man [Cunningham] was grand – he just pressed on in the dark regardless and we suddenly bumped into this party of 8-inch cruisers. It was a wonderful sight. The destroyer ahead of us put a searchlight on them. There one of them was, a lovely graceful ship all silvery in the searchlight. We let drive a broadside and in thirty seconds she was a blazing wreck going off like a Catherine wheel. Then we switched into another and shot her up the same and the other battleships did too. I think there was a third there too, who got clocked by the *Barham*, but I was looking at a destroyer by then who was firing torpedoes at us close on the port bow.

We shot her up too and turned away from the torpedoes while old Hec Waller in the *Stuart* led the destroyers in to finish the party.

The rest of the night we were just padding along waiting for daylight and listening to the destroyers' signals. They were all over the shop fighting like wasps all night. We knew we sank three big cruisers and some destroyers – probably another cruiser or so and certainly shook seven bells out of the whole gang. Judging by what was going on the Wops shot each other up quite a bit too. I don't know what happened to the *Vittorio Veneto*. She was heavily hit with torpedoes before dusk and the aircraft had another lap at her when it was too dark to see results. We could not find her in the morning. We went back over the scene of the action in the morning to pick up the birds, and collected 900 or so until some German aircraft started fooling about, so we had to leave the rest and poked off home to celebrate the Battle of Matapan (named by me).

The battle, named by Manley Power after the Cape of that name on the southern tip of Greece, was fought to protect convoys taking British and Dominion troops to that country. To bale out their Italian allies, the Germans had begun several moves in early 1941 which were to have dire consequences for the Royal Navy in the Mediterranean.

The Luftwaffe moved some ninety bombers and twenty-five fighters of Fliegercorps X to airfields in Sicily and southern Italy. On 12 February Major-General Erwin Rommel landed in Tripoli with the advance party of his Afrika Korps. The Germans made preparations to invade Greece through the Balkans. All these actions were known to the British thanks to Ultra decrypts.

For the first time the Mediterranean Fleet found itself under Stuka attack. Attacks by Italian bombers had been bad enough, but this was infinitely worse. The first casualty was the carrier *Illustrious* of Taranto fame. On 10 January 1941 while escorting a convoy she was engaged by no fewer than thirty German aircraft, while ten attacked the other ships. The aircraft dived from 12,000 feet, releasing their bombs at 800 feet and following up with gun attacks. *Illustrious* was hit by six 1,000-lb bombs. Although she survived with heavy casualties, and, after calling at Malta, eventually made Alexandria, she had to be withdrawn from the Mediterranean. She was repaired in the United States, but was not operational until the following year. Until the carrier *Formidable*, some weeks' steaming away, arrived via the Suez Canal, the Germans would have a free hand in the air in the eastern Mediterranean. To add to Cunningham's difficulties, the Germans had sown the Canal with air-dropped magnetic mines.

Rommel's arrival coincided with General Wavell, the C.-in-C. Middle East, being ordered to move troops to Greece against the expected German invasion. To do this, he had to strip Lieutenant-General O'Connor's Western Desert Force of his best formations. As a consequence, the British were pushed by Rommel

HMS *Illustrious* under air attack while undergoing repairs in Grand Harbour, Malta, after being damaged on 10 January 1941 in the first appearance of the Luftwaffe in the Mediterranean. Her flight deck and island are visible under the jib of the right-hand crane. (MH4625)

from the positions so brilliantly won by O'Connor back to the Egyptian border, and Tobruk, which the Germans besieged. At the same time, the German invasion of Greece, with overwhelming air support, against the hastily prepared, and in some cases non-existent, defences, resulted in the total collapse of the Greek Army. British and Dominion troops were evacuated, some being taken to Crete.

The German invasion of Greece was still in the offing when, thanks to Ultra, Cunningham received warnings that the Italians might be about to mount an attack against convoys between Egypt and Greece. He ordered Vice-Admiral Pridham-Wippell, the Vice-Admiral Light Forces (VALF), with four cruisers – *Orion* (flag), *Ajax*, HMAS *Perth* and *Gloucester* – and three destroyers, to be off Gavdo Island, south of Crete, by dawn on 28 March. At midday on 27 March, RAF reconnaissance reported three Italian cruisers 300 miles west of Crete. That night, Cunningham took the Fleet to sea, consisting of the battleships *Warspite* (flag), *Barham* and *Valiant*, the carrier *Formidable* (now arrived) and nine destroyers.

At first light on 28 March, air reconnaissance reported a strong enemy force of 8-inch cruisers nearing Pridham-Wippell's much lighter group of 6-inch cruisers. Cunningham turned the battle fleet towards Pridham-Wippell. HMS *Gloucester*, one of Pridham-Wippell's cruisers, had propeller shaft problems.

Captain Sir Philip Bowyer-Smyth of HMAS *Perth* writing to Admiral Crace:

I imagine VALF was about to detach *Gloucester* when we sighted masts; I reported them as 8-inch cruisers. By this time they had opened fire, we were turning away, and they towards. I derived much comfort from the old saying, 'those you hear, don't hurt you'. They were outranging us by about 4,000 yards. *Gloucester* was a great anxiety. VALF first increased to 24 knots, and she held on, to 26, to 28, and to our delight she still held it. We were leading them towards the battle-fleet. C.-in-C. was 90 miles ESE of us, coming towards at 20 knots. [The maximum the battle-fleet could make, because, to Cunningham's rage, his flagship had ingested some mud through her boiler room water intakes when she touched a mud bank leaving Alexandria, and her speed was reduced to 20 knots.]

Suddenly someone on the bridge said, 'Crikey what's that?' Over to the north a ship came fast over the horizon, obviously enemy. Brrrrrp went her broadside. 'That's not 8-inch,' said someone. We all turned, anticipating VALF's signal. Halfway through the turn the salvo fell. It was terrific. I'd no idea 15-inch splashes looked so big when they meant business. The second salvo was all around *Orion*. By this time our smoke was starting. We were doing a good 30 knots. Three or more salvos all round *Orion* before the smoke covered her. Up to 32 knots by now, *Gloucester* going to beat the band.

I had no idea the Italians could shoot like that. The range was now 29,000 yards [16.5 miles], and practically every salvo straddled for line and range. One hit and *Orion* was bound to fall out. Then what did he [VALF] do? Leave her, or turn and tackle a heavily armed and armoured ship with the only four cruisers C.-in-C. had? Besides there was *Gloucester*. She had a half-inch clearance between A bracket and shaft and a propeller might drop off at any moment. Also the three 8-inch cruisers were doubtless returning to the fray, C.-in-C. was 80 miles away. If VALF in *Orion* went it was up to McCarthy in *Ajax*. If he went it was up to me – but sufficient unto the day.

When *Orion* was covered with smoke, the enemy shifted his fire to *Gloucester*. Having got her range they pounded the sea all round her. Again it was terrific. They had aircraft spotting. I told the engine room to strike a balance between keeping a thick smoke screen and giving us all the speed they could, but for the love of Mike, not to clog the boilers. They were magnificent, responding with a smoke screen that completely hid *Ajax* and gave us 17,000 horses above the designed maximum. *Gloucester* was still winning the boat race amidst a foaming fury of splashes.

After half an hour or so, *Gloucester* signalled that the range was opening. The enemy appeared to have been attacked by aircraft. VALF ordered smoke to stop. When it cleared there was no enemy in sight.

The battleship was the *Vittorio Veneto*. Cunningham picked up Pridham-Wippell's signals to his own force to make smoke, realized he was in trouble, and ordered *Formidable* to launch a strike, to give him time to arrive at the scene. Six Albacores attacked *Vittorio Veneto*, all six torpedoes missed, but the Italians turned tail. A second strike was more successful. A torpedo from an Albacore flown by Lieutenant-Commander Dalyell-Stead hit *Vittorio Veneto* aft causing massive damage and slowing her down. But she could still steam fast enough to stay ahead of Cunningham until dark. Dalyell-Stead crashed into the

One of three Italian cruisers under attack by *Formidable*'s aircraft. One aircraft can be seen turning away from the cruiser having dropped its torpedo. (A9801)

sea and was lost with his crew. A third strike by *Formidable*'s aircraft hit and stopped the cruiser *Pola*. Bowyer-Smyth:

We joined the battlefleet about noon, and mightily reassuring they looked. About 3.30 news came that *Littorio* was damaged ahead [*Vittorio Veneto* was a battleship of the *Littorio* class]. VALF was to take his cruisers to locate her.

As darkness approached, Cunningham was faced with a momentous decision. Against the advice of his staff, who cautioned against a night action, he pressed on. Fortunately he held one card the Italians did not: some of his ships were equipped with radar. Nevertheless, to charge at high speed at night against an unknown number of enemy warships, particularly if information about their position was not absolutely certain, and especially if they included destroyers, was a bold decision, and against the current doctrine in the Royal Navy laid down in the Fighting Instructions. Although he hoped to catch the *Vittorio Veneto*, he met heavy cruisers sent to help the stricken *Pola*.

Lieutenant Alec Dennis, the First Lieutenant of the destroyer HMS *Griffin*, in her director tower:

We were steaming into a black night at 20 knots, peering into the darkness through our binoculars. Suddenly we received an emergency signal to clear the screen and take station on the starboard side. Increasing to full speed, we received another signal from *Warspite*: 'Get out of our way damn you.' At this moment I spotted a dark shape ahead, and got all guns on to it. It was obviously a large ship, and one felt a little naked up there in front. Moments later *Greyhound* ahead of us switched on her searchlight and in its silvery-blue beam was revealed a 10,000 ton cruiser heading towards us, quite close, and looking magnificent in her light grey standing out starkly in the beam. I gave an estimated range and opened fire. Ting-ting, went the firing bell. All hell broke lose. The enemy ship virtually disintegrated in an appalling series of explosions, flinging one of her turrets high in the air. 'My God did I do that?' was my first reaction, forgetting there were twenty-four 15-inch guns in the battleships behind.

A few seconds later a couple of Italian destroyers appeared, and we went off after them. I got a few salvos off, but they had the legs of us, although another pair were sunk by *Stuart* and *Havoc*.

The next morning, after Cunningham had ordered the fleet to disengage, *Griffin* picked up some of *Pola*'s survivors. Dennis:

Their morale was shot to ribbons. Many were drunk. Our ship's company formed a poor opinion of those who complained about the food. Next morning the Coxswain represented to me that our sailors wanted to throw them back. This request had to be refused.

The *Vittorio Veneto* escaped, but Cunningham had gained a great victory, with three enemy cruisers and two destroyers sunk, and one battleship damaged. Bowyer-Smyth:

Opposite: Albacores in formation. Ordered in 1937 as a successor to the Swordfish, and obsolescent when it came into service in 1941, the Alabacore did not last out the War, whereas the faithful 'Stringbag' was in service to the end. (HU66786)

We rejoined the battle-fleet at 07.30 next morning, a magnificent sight drawn up in good order behind their screen. Counting heads, there wasn't a destroyer missing, nor a scar to be seen on a battleship as we passed close by to our position. It seemed incredible.

The good fortune attending the Mediterranean Fleet was about to change.

Alexandria, as the Fleet base, could be pretty lively when the ships were in. The diary of Able Seaman Charles Hutchinson in the anti-aircraft cruiser *Carlisle*:

Wednesday 9.4.41

After the scrap with the Italian fleet there were no casualties, but there were a few after they all got ashore. It was *Warspite* and *Valiant* that hit the headlines on the wireless and newspapers and when the lads had had a bottle or two, some of the crowd off *Warspite* had started 'blowing', and the fellows off the destroyers and cruisers that do all the sea time didn't like it, and told them they hardly ever went to sea. One thing led to another and it finished up in a glorious scrap. The Fleet Club was closed and beer stopped at a lot of the bars.

He then had a good 'drip' about life:

Everybody on board is fed up to the back teeth, and now I've got to know him, I don't think much of the skipper or any officer on here for that matter. They get their comfort and gins anytime, and some of the lads haven't half been lashed up to some punishments and stoppage of leave for coming off a few hours adrift. There was all night leave last night, but myself and a lot more could not have it as I had been adrift previously, regardless of having been punished for the offence with one day's pay and one day's leave stopped.

In just over a week the fighting was more serious. The British and Dominion force sent to Greece was evacuated. A month later, part of the same force was evacuated from Crete, together with troops already there. Only a year had passed since the Norway and France evacuations. Again the Royal Navy had to face days of constant air attack, and both Greece and Crete, like Norway, were far from British air bases and close to German ones. Most of the evacuations from Greece and Crete were from beaches, and at night. But about half of the long haul back to Egypt was usually steamed in daylight.

Lieutenant Dennis in *Griffin*:

Air raid warning Yellow, followed by Red seemed to be the order of the day, so our solitary 3-inch AA gun was continuously manned by day.

After collecting the survivors of a badly damaged liner, *Griffin* returned to Suda Bay in Crete, before setting out with a convoy of three converted liners, *Glenearn*, *Ulster Prince* and *Slamat*, and the destroyers *Diamond*, *Wryneck* and *Hotspur*, for Nauplia and Tolon.

All day we plodded northwards watching the sun climb to its meridian, and sink; much too slowly. Just when we were beginning to feel that we might get through the day, an attack by JU87s was well carried out. A large bomb hit *Glenearn*, wrecking her steering gear, and filling her with 7,000 tons of water. She was a valuable ship fitted with landing craft and sent to the Mediterranean to invade Rhodes, in happier times, weeks earlier. Now she must be saved. When we were detailed to tow her back to Crete, our hearts sank a little. There were still a couple of hours' daylight left. The prospect of being sitting ducks at slow speed for the next wave of bombers did not please. But the job of getting the monster in tow fully occupied my thoughts.

Eventually after great difficulty because at first *Glenearn*'s rudder was jammed, and tows parted, *Griffin* got her into Kissamo Bay in Crete.

As soon as we were free, it was into Suda Bay, but only for twenty minutes. Nothing had been heard of *Diamond* or *Wryneck*, and it was almost certain they had been sunk. So back we went at 25 knots towards Nauplia. We now knew that we had been lucky to stay with *Glenearn*.

Ulster Prince had been bombed and set on fire, becoming a beacon for other attacks. Because the other liners could not get in, destroyers ferried troops out. These and other delays meant that daylight found the convoy only a few miles out. *Slamat* was sunk. *Diamond* and *Wryneck* picked up hundreds of soldiers. Steaming south, heavily loaded, they were bombed and sunk.

As we hurried northward during the rest of the night, we received orders to search for survivors, but not to linger after dawn. At 02.00 we heard shouts and found two Carley floats with a few survivors from *Wryneck*. Knowing that *Diamond* could not have been very far away when she was sunk, we searched around until just before dawn. It was high time to leave. Just before 06.00 we sighted two more floats with oil-covered men. They had been exhausted when sunk, and were now in the last stages. Each time we got a few inboard and were ready to depart, we came upon a few more; pathetic little groups of those who had lasted the day and night. Johnny [the Captain] now had a difficult decision: should we disobey instructions and risk losing ourselves and the survivors, or should we search further in the hopes of finding a few more. We stayed on another hour, biting our fingernails until there really appeared to be no hope of finding any more. We turned and fled for the comparative safety of Suda Bay. To me the saddest thing was the loss of my term-mate, John Marshall, my opposite number in *Diamond*. We had picked up less than 50 men out of about 900 in the three ships.

After four hours in harbour *Griffin* was on her way to Monemvasia to evacuate some more troops.

We arrived after dark having, on the way, carried out a burial service for some who did not survive the last rescue. I read the service at dusk, and committed the dead to the deep under the White Ensign. It was only a little later, to my horror, that the Chief Boatswain's

Mate found one more hidden under a pile of oily rags and clothing. I did not feel that I could get the ship's company out again and so, saying a quiet prayer, we sent him to join the others.

The lack of air support was a source of some bitterness. Able Seaman Charles Hutchinson:

Now we have one Hurricane with us and the blasted papers talk of air supremacy. I know it's probably not the Air Force's fault they couldn't be in Greece, as I don't think we have the planes, but if only the papers and wireless would not 'blow' so much about them.

Warships packed with men were often top heavy. Hutchinson:

Sunday 27.4.41
The total number of troops we had on board was thirteen hundred and ten [for one trip].

Able Seaman Turner in HMS *Hero*:

28.4.41
20.30 Arrived off Kalamata and could see tracer bullets going all over the place. We crept slowly into the harbour. Sent boat ashore to contact British Senior Officer. Contact was made and a signal sent to *Perth* that town was occupied by the Germans, but it was possible to evacuate from the beaches. Soon after the signal was made, an oil tank blew up ashore and a great sheet of flame shot into the air. *Perth* made the signal 'Retire on me

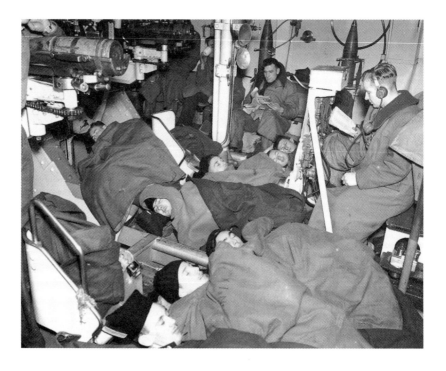

The Royal Marines crew of X Turret in HMS *Sheffield* stood down while at action stations. The woolly hats and overcoats indicate that this photo was probably taken in northern waters, rather than the Mediterranean. Crews in ships at the height of the war in the Mediterranean under air attack by day and in surface action at night had very little sleep. *Sheffield*, like many of the overworked cruisers in the Royal Navy had a busy war, serving in the Mediterranean, Atlantic and Barents Sea. The Royal Marines provided detachments in all ships from cruisers upwards.
(A6879)

operation abandoned'. Our captain decided to remain and take off what soldiers he could before daylight.

We took off 12 officers and 122 men. Several poor devils were drowned while attempting to swim to the ship. We left about 8,000 soldiers on the beach.

29.4.41

02.00 Hoisted boats and sailed for Suda Bay.

14.55 Attacked by 12 dive bombers. No damage.

16.00 Arrived Suda Bay and left 17.00 for Kalamata area to search for more soldiers.

The strain on ships' companies – short of sleep, under almost constant air attack or threat of attack, seeing ships bombed and sunk, and comrades and soldiers killed and wounded – inevitably took its toll on the nerves of those who took part in this evacuation. Most made light of it in letters home, a few did not, sometimes taking out their feelings on those to whom they wrote. Writing to his wife on 16 May 1941, Paymaster Lieutenant-Commander Jackie Jackson in HMS *Glenearn*, towed to Crete by HMS *Griffin*:

I am absolutely fed up with everything – the dirt and filth – the flies and heat, and more than anything, the fact that I am not hearing from you.

After telling her he has had no letters from her written in March and only one written in April,

the most depressing I have ever received in my life. Add to that a cable which more or less implied that the house had been wrecked and you can get a fair idea of how much I want to hear from you occasionally, and at the same time how I dread it, as I am probably going to have even worse news and more complaints.

After more in the same vein:

I've had a hideous time and I wonder why I'm alive at present.

The letters from his wife are not included in Jackson's papers, so it is impossible to judge just what he means by 'complaints'. What his letters do illustrate, is how important mail was to those away from home for extended periods.

Leading Seaman Fred Coombes also found himself in Crete after the evacuation from Greece. He was a member of the crew of an A lighter [a diesel powered, flat bottomed lighter] which was destroyed by bombing soon after their arrival on a remote beach in Crete. His party, under a Sub-Lieutenant, found a sunken boat, which they baled out and, using a stretcher for a sail, set off in an attempt to sail up the coast until they found a ship:

The Subby was only RNVR and had no idea how to sail a boat even without the handicap of having to use a canvas stretcher as a sail. After deciding to use one oar as a mast and the other as a rudder, we had just stepped the mast and were trying to find the best way of keeping it upright using our limited rope, when there was a shout and a much bigger sailing ship came round the headland. Hardly checking her speed, she came alongside, and threw us a rope to tow us abreast until we could scramble aboard her; a real smart bit of seamanship.

The Subby was about to take charge, when a scruffy Arab with a thin black beard took the wind out of his sails shouting in a typical pre-war naval officer's voice, 'Get those men below right away'. Whether it was because I was a scruff like him, or that I preferred to wear Arab sandals, I could not say, but I was the first to be told that he was Commander Cardinal-Ryan RN. If he had told me he was Jimmy Jesus I wouldn't have argued, there was no mistaking that RN officer's accent. His first instruction was to make myself handy with the wheel. Though I had never steered a boat by compass before, it only required a bit of practice to keep the boat on heading with as little wheel as possible by seeing the mast arching across a particular group of stars. The Arab with the RN accent told us to address him as Shereef. That spell of sailing that first night was a real treat. The Shereef squatted like an Arab going into great detail how to get the best out of the wind and sails.

The run south was a holiday, very little was seen and nothing to worry about if you forgot the Turkish ensign we wore, and kept near a hatch to jump down at the first sight of a plane [Coombes and his companions were in uniform, albeit ragged]. The Shereef taught me how to hold the foresail slightly against the wind by a strop hooked on a wheel spoke, while I left the wheel and adjusted a sheet. At one stage, the Commander showed he was not that behind the times, when he talked to a Sunderland flying boat by Aldis lamp.

On the sixth day we sailed into Sollum [North Africa], to be given a shower in the Army bath house, a good hot meal, and kip in a camp bed.

Some 50,700 soldiers were rescued from Greece, the majority from beaches. Fortunately the Germans had not bombed at night, and the Italian Navy was too cowed to attack. As at Dunkirk, the troops came away with small arms only, leaving tanks, guns and trucks behind. O'Connor's Western Desert Force had been stripped of its best to provide the troops for this disastrous expedition. His successors in the desert were to pay the price.

On 20 May, four days after Paymaster Lieutenant-Commander 'Jackie' Jackson wrote to his wife, the German airborne assault on Crete began. Some troops evacuated from Greece had been added to the existing garrison and British and Dominion forces on the island totalled some 22,000. After stiff fighting, when for a time the issue looked to be in the balance, German air supremacy and a ruthless determination to press home where small gains had been made decided the battle in their favour. They were not deterred by massive casualties among their parachute and glider troops, or by the loss of 4,000 men when three British cruisers and four destroyers utterly destroyed a troop convoy. Again, it was German air power, and the lack of such power on the British side, that caused the heavy casualties in ships and men. Thanks to the devotion of the Royal Navy, not one German soldier reached Crete by sea during the battle, and 16,000 British and Dominion troops were evacuated.

Lieutenant Alec Dennis in *Griffin*:

That night (20 May), we were formed into Force B with our sister *Greyhound* and the cruisers *Gloucester* and *Fiji*, and entered the Aegean past Antikithera to look for the German sea invasion forces. Clearly it was going to be a sticky night and day. Indeed, twenty-four hours later, we were the only ship in the force still afloat. I had the middle watch and turned in early to get some sleep, but it wouldn't come. This time I was really frightened and said a number of prayers. We found nothing.

But at dawn we were well inside the Aegean without air support of any kind. Sure enough a little after 06.00 the imperturbable AB Morgan, our best lookout, saw the first lot. The Stukas kept coming our way, climbing and eventually circling like hawks on a thermal. Then down in groups of three, one after the other, dividing their attentions among all four ships. It was a classic attack, technically interesting, physically terrifying, and actually ineffectual. Somehow they missed us all as we weaved at full speed and the cruisers put up plenty of flak. We pooped off with our 3-inch museum piece and our .5-inch machine guns did their best with their antediluvian control system.

At about 13.00 we were joined by yet another of the night forces [Force C], their experience had been worse than ours. *Carlisle* had been hit on the bridge and her captain killed. *Naiad* had thirty-six near misses in ten minutes.

Force D under Rear-Admiral Glennie had made contact, and sunk seventeen enemy transports. Rear-Admiral King's Force C had sighted another convoy, but not followed it up. Cunningham criticized him for not engaging. However, the convoy fled and landed no German troops. Force C was attacked without let-up.

Able Seaman Hutchinson in *Carlisle*:

Thursday 22.5.41
The bombers came and attacked us wave after wave. They seemed to single a ship out and deliver a mass attack on it, diving vertically and from all angles, bombing and machine-gunning.

A huge bomb exploded in the water beside the ship near our gun. Tons of water crashed down on us, tearing us away from the gun, and tossing us around like straw. I was certain we would be swept over the side. One thought flashed through my mind, 'My God, this is the end.' After what seemed an eternity, we picked ourselves up, blew up our lifebelts and kicked off our shoes, as I for one expected to abandon ship. But in a short time we were firing again, as we were still being attacked. Huge pieces of shrapnel lay around, one had chipped a piece out of the gun barrel. There was a huge column of black smoke amidships, and a direct hit on number two gun. There isn't a gun now, just a piece of charred metal; the ammunition lockers burnt out, the after funnel blown in, and the splinter shield flat. Nearly all the gun's crew were wiped out, most of the lads trapped underneath the gun or blown against the splinter shield. It was a ghastly sight. We've lived and slept all as a family for over a year and a half; laughed, quarrelled, joked, all gone ashore together, discussed our private lives, as we had no one else to confide in: poor Chas Enderly, married since the war began; Dak Walker, only twenty-one last week, and we gave him sips of our tots and got him drunk; and the Gunner's Mate. There are about twelve of our lads, and the rest badly burned and injured. It was a miracle anyone lived. Horspoole was blown out of the way, but badly burned. Poor old Bob Silvey is still under the gun – I've seen him, but it's impossible to get him out. I was ashore with him the night we sailed. Soon after we were attacked again, another stick of bombs exploded on our starboard side. We ducked as the plane machine-gunned us. The Captain was hit and we heard he had died.

Wherever you looked there seemed to be ships, and they all seemed to be getting bombed.

The *Gloucester* was hit and sunk. *Fiji* went to her assistance, and she too was sunk. Destroyers were despatched at dusk to search for survivors.

We've seen hundreds of planes during the whole day, and no sign of ours – it's been another case of the Silent Service takes the can back again.

Friday 23.5.41

We spent the night on the gun, cold, miserable and wet. We learned early this morning that the destroyers *Kelly* and *Kashmir* had been sunk, and that *Kipling* had struck a wreck and was sinking.

Saturday 24.5.41

Approaching Alex we had a few submarine scares, but got through all right. Our casualties are thirteen dead and twenty-seven wounded. The dead were all buried at sea except Bob Silvey, they got him when they lifted what was left of the gun by huge crane alongside.

The First Lieutenant now acting skipper has to go to hospital to have some shrapnel taken out of his shoulder. Whatever I've said about him he did his stuff all right when the time came. Before he went, he cleared lower deck and told us some things we didn't know. He said it had appeared to us all that it had been useless and seemed like suicide, but by our actions we had done our job well and he was proud of us. Many of the ships had sent messages to the ship congratulating us on our recovery. When we became visible through the smoke and water, our guns still firing, they said it was a marvellous sight.

Orion was very lucky. She had to do an emergency turn to avoid a torpedo from an enemy destroyer and she stopped a six-inch salvo from *Dido*, but only five killed. The destroyer was sunk.

One of the ships that came in had three Jerry soldiers stuck to her Paravane shoe on the bows.

Alec Dennis:

Greyhound was detached to sink a caique. Any one of us could have foretold her fate. On the way to rejoin, still alone, she was set upon, and sunk by eight JU87s. About a hundred men got away in rafts and a whaler. While in the water they were machine-gunned. Her First Lieutenant was killed, and Henry Trefusis, recently lent from us, was one of the survivors in the whaler, buried under a heap of dead. Poor old *Greyhound*, the last of our flotilla apart from ourselves. It could have easily been *Griffin*. After this performance we would not rescue the crews of downed German aircraft.

This was only the beginning. The evacuation of Crete began on the night 28/29 May and lasted until 1 June. The Royal Navy suffered terribly under the lash of the Luftwaffe. The *Orion*, earlier hit by what today we call 'friendly fire', had suffered five casualties. On 29 May, she was struck by a bomb killing 260 and wounding 280, the majority evacuated soldiers. Not all the dead could be retrieved while the ships were at sea, and committed to the deep. When ships arrived at Alexandria, their crews, and men sent over from other ships, too often had the ghastly job of clearing mess decks and other spaces of the remains of their shipmates; burned, pulverized by blast, and sliced by flying splinters of hot metal into lumps of meat. The bill for the defence and evacuation of Crete was: two battleships damaged; *Warspite* out of action for twenty-two weeks, *Barham* for six weeks; the carrier *Formidable* out of action for twenty weeks. Three cruisers had been sunk, and five were out of action from three to eleven weeks. Six destroyers had been sunk, and seven were damaged and out of action for between one and sixteen weeks. The Mediterranean Fleet now had two battleships, three cruisers and twenty-one destroyers fit to fight, until repairs could be made to the damaged ships.

Convoys to reinforce the British Army in the Western Desert and to supply the garrison in Tobruk also took their toll. Operation Tiger took place between the evacuations of Greece and Crete. It involved Somerville's Force H passing a convoy of ships carrying 295 cruiser tanks and 35 crated Hurricanes to Cunningham's Mediterranean Fleet. Somerville also planned to hand over the battleship *Queen Elizabeth* and the cruisers *Naiad* and *Fiji* to Cunningham.

Commander Jocelyn Salter in *Foresight* with Force H:

On 8th May we got to the exciting part of the journey when we reached the narrows between Sicily and North Africa. Bombing began at 13.30; an Italian was shot down in flames by a Fulmar. We were straddled by a stick of eight bombs but had no damage. Two of the convoy struck mines; *New Zealand Star* and *Empire Song*. The *New Zealand Star* went on, *Empire Song* caught fire and started dropping back. I being nearest destroyer stayed with her.

Empire Song, a brand new clan ship, had tanks, vehicles and explosives on board. Salter took off most of the crew, leaving the Master and a handful of others on board. Eventually the Master said he must abandon ship.

From outward appearance *Empire Song* looked as though the fire was not too bad, and might be extinguished with resolute action. I sent a message to the Master to come to the bridge as soon as he came on board. To my horror he was drunk and quite incapable of any useful action. I got hold of the Chief Officer to ask if he would be prepared to go back to his ship with some of his crew and some of mine to do their best to save the ship. He eventually agreed to go albeit rather reluctantly. We lowered a whaler and off it went with a mixture of *Empire Song* and *Foresight* men. They had almost got to the ship when the sides opened out like a flower, there was a tremendous 'whoof', a lurid red glow, and the *Empire Song* blew up. We were stupendously lucky. In the whaler one of my stokers was killed, and one man had a foot blown off, but otherwise there were no serious casualties. In *Foresight* the only fatality was my gunner T [torpedo gunner]. A large steel plate hit him and he was killed outright; but otherwise no serious casualties. The three of us on the bridge, the Yeoman of Signals and Midshipman McKaig, stuck our heads inside the wooden chart table with our backsides sticking out. Pieces of metal of varying sizes fell on the bridge deck, and twelve pieces went right through to the deck below. The cylinder block of an internal combustion engine was found in the Wardroom having gone through the steel deck.

Foresight landed her casualties at Malta and was patched up in the dockyard. After leaving,

going out in the mine infested entrance of Grand Harbour in half light is no fun.

She was increasing to 30 knots for passage back to Gibraltar, when she ran a pinion bearing. Salter perforce had to return to Malta. He went to sea on two nights to avoid the air raids.

Each time we came back, we had to wait outside until the entrance had been swept, and on both occasions, a mine went off in the entrance. After these two nights we were mined in. Mercifully we were not hit or damaged in any of the air raids, and there were three or four every day, and some most nights. Malta was not much fun those days and I was glad not to be living there.

After eleven days, Salter was sent back to Force H.

Next morning we embarked six officers, 15 soldiers, 14 sailors, one and a half million pounds in notes, and the mail for Gibraltar. We pottered about to the west of Malta all day to give the impression of a day patrol. This was wise because Vice-Admiral Malta signalled that we had been reported by air reconnaissance. The trip from Malta westwards was somewhat hazardous, so single ships did not often make the passage. I made as if to return to Grand Harbour, and when darkness fell turned and made for Gibraltar at high speed. We passed Pantellaria soon after midnight, and were sent a report of three Italian cruisers and seven destroyers not far from us. I reckoned it was unwise to seek them out, and cleared the area without meeting them.

We had been closed up at action stations all night, and the next forenoon until after we were clear of the area where attack by aircraft was likely. It was good to get my head down the second night. We arrived at Gibraltar at 11.30 on Friday 23rd [May] and were given a most encouraging welcome from all sides. The Admiral [Somerville] was kind enough to come over as soon as we were in, to welcome us.

The *Empire Song* was the only ship in the Tiger convoy to be sunk. Churchill persisted in calling the tanks 'Tiger Cubs', and bombarded Wavell with nagging signals urging him to employ them almost as soon as they arrived. Operation Battleaxe failed to achieve any of its objectives, including relieving Tobruk.

Cartoon of the Tobruk Run.
(Papers of Commander J. A. J. Dennis RN 95/5/1 negative number DOC523. Reproduced by kind permission of the artist, Captain M. A. J. Hennell RN)

The burden of supplying the beleaguered garrison of Tobruk fell on the hard-pressed Mediterranean Fleet. Although on 22 June 1941 Hitler invaded Russia, this major shift in German attentions did nothing to ease the strain on warships fighting in the Mediterranean. If anything it had the reverse effect; the requirement to find escorts for convoys carrying warlike supplies to Murmansk stretched the Royal Navy's resources even tighter, and every theatre of war had to bear the strain. Commander Jocelyn Salter:

Since I joined the ship in January, up to the end of July, we had spent 130 days at sea and steamed 41,661 miles.

Tobruk lay some 400 miles west of Alexandria. All the destroyers and fast minelayers that could be spared were employed on what was known as the 'Bread Run' or 'Beef and Spud Run' from Alexandria to Tobruk. There were also some supply runs from the small port of Mersa Matruh which lay about halfway between the two. After loading, the hazardous trip began.

Lieutenant Alec Dennis in Griffin:

A group, normally one fast minelayer and four destroyers, would leave Alexandria, timed so that you were still under fighter cover (we had some in the desert by now) until dark.

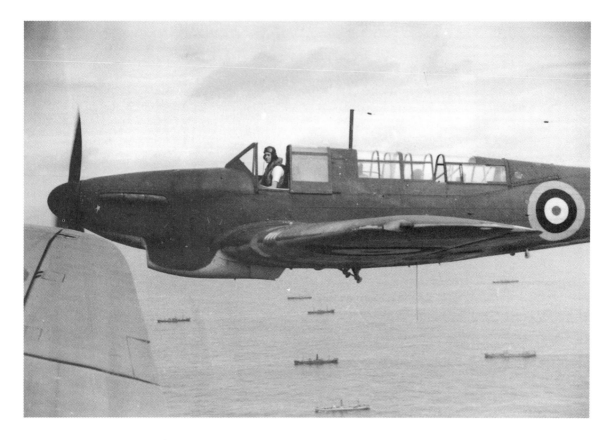

**A Fulmar over a convoy in
the Mediterranean.** (A3793)

Then it was full speed, zig-zagging to avoid U-boats, until about 23.30 when you turned towards the coast, trying to find the entrance. It was heavily mined, and a channel was kept open by some very brave sweepers who hid alongside the many wrecks by day. The channel was marked by a green light which didn't show up very clearly. Once you spotted it, you could steam in on a line of bearing, hoping the Germans hadn't set up their own green light leading you to the minefields. You then made your way into the harbour, which was littered with wrecks, some of which could be used to unload stores on to.

You had an absolute maximum of 45 minutes to get all 50 tons of stuff offloaded down wooden chutes, cast off and get out at full speed to be under the fighter umbrella at dawn. If you got caught it was probably curtains. To add to the incentive [to get away], a big gun called Bardia Bill would lob shells into the harbour from outside the perimeter.

At Mersa Matruh the Royal Naval presence included a fleet of A lighters and tugs which also supplied Tobruk. One of the tugs, commissioned as HMS *Vaillant*, was commanded by Johnny Carter, now promoted to Sub-Lieutenant RNR. He wrote to his parents, about a fellow officer:

He sailed this evening in an A lighter for Tobruk, George going too as navigator. I hope they are not attacked by anything; the feeling George is going through just now is, I am certain, the same that I experience every time I leave Matruh, 'I shan't be happy until I cross this boom again'. Or, 'I wish it was this time tomorrow night'. The day going up there is far the worst, the nervous strain simply grows and grows until you have to exert all your will-power to stop yourself from appearing jittery or nervous. That is courage – the quality of being able to keep from showing your fear in the face of nervous strain: not being able to press a trigger and keep the sights on what appears to be an enormous aircraft diving into your face, bomb hurtling towards you, and the ping and splintering crunches as his bullets tear through the wood and steel around you. Enduring that behind a gun of some sort is nothing in the heat of battle. Courage is behaving calmly and normally through the period before such an attack; during the six long hours which never seem to end, where time seems to stop, and that sudden deadly attack may develop in a moment. Then on top of that, the not-so-deadly anxiety one has of not finding Tobruk by daylight, and through you, three valuable lighters and their cargoes being lost.

Humour was, as ever, a great healer. Johnny Carter sent home the following poem:

In Lighter Mood

There's a famous seaside town called Mersa,
Which is noted for heaven knows what,
But C-in-C Med as he pored over charts
Said 'Ee that's exactly the spot'.

'We'll send the A lighters to Mersa Matruh,'
Said C-in-C Med to his staff,
'So arrange everything for their comfort, my boys;
Get them feather beds, beer and a bath.'

So straightway staff left Sir Andrew,
To do what their admiral had said,
But one old commander said, 'all this can wait,
Let's have a few pinkers instead.'

From Maxim's they went to the Union,
From the Union to Pastroudi's Grill
And as nobody's seen them from that day to this,
I expect that they're boozing there still.

So when the A Lighters arrived at Matruh,
In response to C-in-C's call,
There were no feather beds, no beer, and no bath,
In fact there was nothing at all.

Now poor officer chap who's in charge of t'base,
Has sent signals by sea, air and land,

> But C-in-C answers, 'It's all been arranged,
> My staff have the matter in hand.'
>
> But staff, as we know are still on the gin,
> And it's useless to grumble and shout,
> 'Cause there won't be no comforts at Mersa Matruh,
> 'Till the pinkers in Alex runs out.

In another letter home:

Roll on the end of this bloody war, and peace and sanity, and you people again!

Johnny Carter died of wounds the following year, serving in HMS *Kingston* at the second Battle of Sirte, and was mentioned in despatches for bravery.

Although convoys to Malta were no longer being run from the eastern Mediterranean, the island continued to be supplied from Gibraltar, but at considerable expense in ships. Operation Substance was the code name for a convoy in July 1941 consisting of six fast merchantmen loaded with troops and supplies escorted by Force X commanded by Vice-Admiral Syfret in the cruiser *Edinburgh*, with the cruisers *Manchester* and *Arethusa*, and the fast minelayer *Manxman*. Force H provided the cover. Jack Thwaite was a boy signalman in the *Edinburgh*:

The troops we were carrying were spread about the upper deck with their Bren guns to keep them occupied during the action, but eventually had to be stood down as they tended to follow the aircraft down with consequent danger to other ships and our own ship's company. Life in the mess decks was very uncomfortable with each mess doubled up with soldiers, and food and water heavily rationed. Sunday July 23rd started peacefully enough, so peaceful that HMS *Manchester* was seen to be holding Divisions and Church Service while the rest of us were closed up at action stations. It was not long before concentrated air attacks from high level and torpedo bombers commenced.

The Captain of HMS *Edinburgh* (Captain Hugh Faulkener) inspired great confidence in the bridge personnel, as he lay back in his chair on the bridge and with binoculars to his eyes, conned the ship between sticks of bombs.

HMS *Manchester* was hit by a torpedo and had to turn back to Gibraltar. The destroyer *Fearless* was also hit, and eventually sunk by our own forces. The plane that attacked her was blown up by its own bomb. The destroyer's signalman stood on the iron deck, semaphored the signal [from the Captain], 'I am abandoning the ship apart from a volunteer fire-fighting party. Good luck and safe journey', before giving a wave, throwing his semaphore flags over the side, and diving in after them.

Later we passed HMS *Firedrake* steaming back to Gibraltar with a great gash in her side from a near miss.

At dusk the air attacks ceased. Force H withdrew to the west, and Force X entered the straits of Pantellaria, steaming north-west towards the coast of Sicily with the aim of giving the slip to the E-boats off Pantellaria. It was a dark moonless night. I had the

Deck hockey on a carrier deck during a lull in operations. A game played in the Royal Navy to this day, with minimal rules. (A7654)

middle watch, keeping lookout in the port wing of the Flag Deck. I saw the splash and running track of what turned out to be two torpedoes from an Italian E-boat. As I yelled out a warning to the bridge, they saw the enemy at the same time, as we turned towards, and the Oerlikons and pom-poms opened up. Pandemonium, until the cease-fire bells rang, and 'Enemy E-boat sunk' came over the Tannoy.

The torpedoes hit the *Melbourne Star* (carrying the Convoy Commodore), and par- tially crippled her, although she managed to make Malta under her own power.

Later that morning, HMS *Edinburgh*, with her Royal Marine Band playing 'The British Grenadiers', entered Grand Harbour to the cheers of the crews of the transports and crowds lining the breakwaters and vantage points on the shore.

That afternoon, Force X sailed to rendezvous with Force H and returned to Gibraltar.

While we were alongside at Gibraltar, the Governor of Algeciras, who was paying a visit to the Governor of Gibraltar, passed the ship in his barge, and was given the ceremonial salute of Guard and Band. On the hangar top, in full view of the barge, one of our hostilities only signalmen, attired in his underpants was hanging out his dhobi, oblivious to the pipes and bugles on board the ship. The face of the Yeoman of the Watch was ashen with horror when he saw him.

Lieutenant-Commander George Blundell, now the First Lieutenant and Torpedo Officer of the battleship *Nelson*:

Thursday 25th September
The operation we are in is entitled Halberd; it is nothing more than getting another convoy through to Malta. Group 1 is *Nelson, Ark Royal, Hermione, Cossack, Zulu, Foresight,*

Skuas of 800 Squadron
waiting to launch from
HMS *Ark Royal* in 1941. To
modern eyes it is strange to
see at least two members of
the ship's company smoking
pipes near the flight deck
during flying stations.
(A3782)

Forester, Laforey and *Lightning*. Our group goes straight down the middle of the Mediterranean, well ahead of Group 2 as if we were the normal Force H out on a club run. Group 2 consists of *Prince of Wales, Rodney*, the convoy, *Sheffield, Kenya, Edinburgh, Euryalus*, and the rest of the destroyers. [There was a total of eighteen destroyers on this operation.] They follow behind us taking a more northerly route.

On the second day, all the cruisers in both groups, with nine destroyers, formed into Force X under Rear-Admiral Burrough, who took the convoy on to Malta, while Somerville with the remainder, including three battleships and the carrier *Ark Royal*, waited for them to return with an empty homeward convoy.

Saturday 27th September

The day has been exciting, but tragic for us in 'Nellie'. At 12.01 a big attack by torpedo bombers developed. One machine dropped its torpedo away from us, but a second came on and the ship was turned towards. When it was about 20 degrees on our starboard bow and 800 yards off, it dropped its torpedo. We couldn't see any track, it seemed to have run deep. But to our horror, the track suddenly appeared not more than 200 yards ahead, coming straight for us. There was nothing we could do.

Blundell thought that the torpedo might miss or run deep again:

Just as I was breathing again, there was a horrid underwater thud, the whole bow rose and quivered, and the ship shook itself like a mighty animal. But the splash was amazingly small, only as if a small sea had slopped over the side.

Another plane dropped a torpedo on our starboard bow, and we turned towards this, and it ran harmlessly down our starboard side. The plane came so close, one felt one could knock it down with one's fist. We hit it and it came down. I saw no more, although there were more attacks after this, because I rushed forward below to ginger up the repair parties.

With his accustomed drive, George Blundell stopped the flooding and shored up damaged bulkheads, so that *Nelson* could still steam and fight.

The bow has gone down 6 feet, and the ship looks most peculiar, as if she was plunging downhill. Quite a lot has been flooded: all the food stores forrard, all the cold rooms containing meat, cheese and butter, the flour stores, the main naval store, the huge provision room, and my torpedo body room are all flooded. I felt heartbroken about my 10 lb Cape Town cheese, husbanded all these months in the cold room, waiting for the day I go on leave.

Nelson still steamed on until:

At dusk all battleships, with nine destroyers and *Ark Royal*, turned west and left the convoy to go on through the dangerous Sicilian Channel. I always feel such a cad when we turn round, leaving the forlorn little party steaming east into the night and its unknown fate.

The convoy made Malta except for *Imperial Star*. On 28 September, *Nelson* was detached for Gibraltar, while the remainder of Force H waited for the return of Force X. Inspection of *Nelson* in Gibraltar dockyard revealed that she had shipped 4,000 tons of water through a forty-foot-long hole in her side. Blundell's first sight of the torpedo body room, where torpedoes were stored, but without their detonating pistols:

I had expected to see all the torpedoes snugly in their racks, but not a torpedo was in place and there was indescribable wreckage, tails torn off, engines smashed, heads disintegrated, and one torpedo round the other way. How thankful we must be there was no one down there at the time. Much of the damage must have been caused by the after bodies of the torpedoes being torn off which would break the pipes from the air vessel. The very high pressure of the escaping air would cause the torpedoes to whip round like scalded cats.

Malta was vital as a base from which submarines and aircraft mounted attacks on Axis convoys to Tripoli supplying the Italian and German forces in North Africa. In October, surface ships based in Malta joined the assault on Axis shipping so that less than 40 per cent of any convoy arrived at Tripoli.

Encouraging as this was, November and December were disastrous months for the British in the Mediterranean.

On 13 November, Able Seaman Eric Smith in the destroyer *Legion*:

At about 15.30, almost within sight of Gibraltar, the *Ark Royal* was hit amidships by a torpedo. I had been leaning against B gunshield watching *Ark* manoeuvring and saw the track of the torpedo as it passed beneath *Legion*, to hit the carrier square on.

Charles Friend in *Ark Royal*:

There was a very loud bang below me. I was the deck duty officer of 812 Squadron, waiting for some Swordfish to land. I was just forward of the island waiting to park the Stringbags. The explosion blew a great cloud of dust up from various hatchways, including the bomb lift doors close to me, preventing me from seeing what was going on. As the dust cleared, I saw Swordfish which had already been parked with their wings folded hopping down the list to starboard, their oleo legs flexing in and out, for all the world like giant grasshoppers dancing. One had jumped all the way to the edge of the deck, and teetered, one wheel in the nets, before plunging sixty feet into the sea. I ran forward and ropes were put round the aircraft to secure them to the deck.

Eric Smith:

Legion was ordered to close *Ark Royal* and take off her 1,487 officers and men, leaving only a skeleton staff of Engine Room and Damage Control parties, on board with her Captain.

Surgeon Lieutenant William Scott RNVR, the assistant medical officer of *Ark Royal*:

I had already heard the broadcast, 'All hands up from below the main deck', and after an interval, 'Hands prepare to abandon ship', followed by, 'the embarking destroyer is alongside'. I am confident of this order and the exact wording. No absolute order was given to abandon ship, but this seemed to be clearly implied by the final broadcast. This vagueness had unfortunate consequences, as many of the officers and ratings still required for the attempt at salvage, however vain, had interpreted the last two broadcasts as applying to the whole crew, which had not been intended. What was required was, 'Hands abandon ship, stand fast fire and repair parties'.

Close to me on the quarterdeck was the Captain's secretary, surveying the destroyer below, and wondering how it could be reached. I was given the answer by a young midshipman. He uncoiled a hose and threw the end of it down to the destroyer, over the gap of twenty foot or so. Holding onto this, he paid himself down backwards, keeping his balance with his hands. Without his example, I would never have believed that this balancing act was possible. To my surprise, I found that the hose held me securely by the groin, and I was never in any danger of overbalancing into the sea.

I saw no one following my route from the quarter deck, and very few were still on

ropes dangling from various decks. Those from the flight deck were about ten feet short, the final drop caused many fractured heel bones.

Ark Royal listing with the destroyer *Legion* by her stern, 13 November 1941. (A6332)

Eric Smith:

We were ordered to Gib, *Laforey* taking our place alongside *Ark Royal* to render what assistance she could. With this many passengers on board, every available bit of space was crammed, and no one could hardly move [sic]. We landed them safely and prepared to put to sea to give what further assistance we could to *Ark Royal*. Sorting out the mess decks later, we found our passengers had taken every bit of edible food from our storages. The Wardroom fared no better, being left only one bad tomato.

The struggle to keep *Ark Royal* afloat lasted for fourteen hours, and despite Surgeon Lieutenant Scott's comments above, not all her crew abandoned her. Damage repair parties under Captain Maund RN did all that was humanly possible to save their ship. Design faults were the principal cause of her end. She capsized and sank, at 06.13 the next morning. Only one rating was killed,

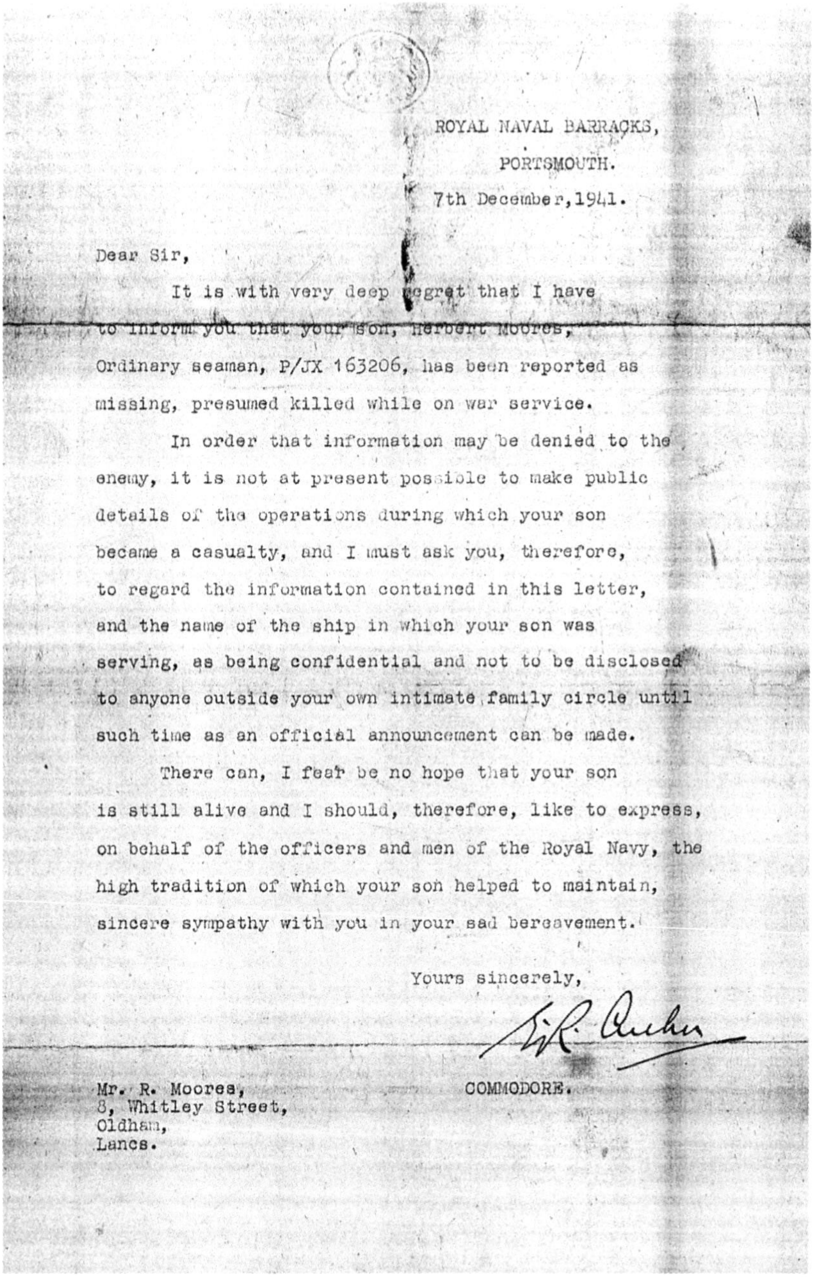

ROYAL NAVAL BARRACKS,

PORTSMOUTH.

7th December, 1941.

Dear Sir,

It is with very deep regret that I have
to inform you that your son, Herbert Moores,
Ordinary seaman, P/JX 163206, has been reported as
missing, presumed killed while on war service.

In order that information may be denied to the
enemy, it is not at present possible to make public
details of the operations during which your son
became a casualty, and I must ask you, therefore,
to regard the information contained in this letter,
and the name of the ship in which your son was
serving, as being confidential and not to be disclosed
to anyone outside your own intimate family circle until
such time as an official announcement can be made.

There can, I fear be no hope that your son
is still alive and I should, therefore, like to express,
on behalf of the officers and men of the Royal Navy, the
high tradition of which your son helped to maintain,
sincere sympathy with you in your sad bereavement.

Yours sincerely,

COMMODORE.

Mr. R. Moores,
8, Whitley Street,
Oldham,
Lancs.

Letter received by the father of Ordinary Seaman (Boy First Class) Herbert Moores who was lost in HMS *Barham* sunk by U-331 off Sidi Barrani. She blew up in less than five minutes, taking 862 men with her. There were 450 survivors of the massive explosion. (Misc2721)

the oldest in the ship, who had been on duty at the electrical switchboard where the torpedo struck.

On 24 November, Lieutenant Dennis:

We sailed from Alex. It was another club run, with eight destroyers escorting *Queen Elizabeth*, flying ABC's flag [another nickname for Cunningham], *Barham* and *Valiant*.

The cruisers were well ahead hoping to intercept an enemy convoy heading for Benghazi. We were in support in case the heavy Italian ships came out.

At about 16.30 the following day there was a heavy explosion, I ran up to the director to see *Barham* listing well over. She leaned over very rapidly, lying for a moment on her beam ends, then with a tremendous explosion her magazine blew up. One could hardly believe anyone would survive, but *Hotspur* and others picked up several hundred, including Vice-Admiral Pridham-Wippell with whom we had been through so much.

Barham took her Captain, 55 officers and 806 men to the bottom. She was sunk by a U-boat, one of seventeen transferred from the Atlantic to the Mediterranean in an attempt to stem the British destruction of Axis shipping in that theatre.

Lieutenant-Commander John Mosse was in Alexandria, champing at the bit to get back to sea after his time on the staff in Western Approaches headquarters in Liverpool, and now in the shore-side office of the staff of the Mediterranean Fleet:

Photo of HMS *Barham* exploding. Given to Commander Dennis after the war by Von Teisenhausen, the commander of U-331 that sank her. (Papers of Commander J. A. J. Dennis RN 95/5/1 negative number DOC524)

December 19th was a very black day indeed. Admiral Vian with the 15th Cruiser Squadron and destroyers had sailed to intercept an enemy convoy off Tripoli and ran into a minefield. *Neptune* struck four mines and sank with only one survivor. *Aurora* and *Penelope* also struck mines but were able to reach Malta with two of the destroyers.

Kandahar, the ship I was so angry not to be in, tried to go to the rescue of *Neptune*, and

herself struck a mine which blew her stern off. She drifted clear of the minefield and stayed afloat long enough for her company to be rescued by *Jaguar*.

But that was not all. Early that same morning, I was sleeping peacefully when the telephone rang and I was summoned immediately. Two Italian frogmen had been caught sitting on the bow buoy of *Valiant*, and had been sent across from the other side of the harbour for interrogation. We wanted to know:

(1). Had they completed their mission?

(2). Were they alone?

(3). How did they get into the harbour?

They denied the first two questions, and said they had got into difficulties outside the harbour and had to abandon their equipment and swim.

I did not believe them. I rang the battleships and suggested that they should drag chain bottom lines to try to dislodge any limpets. They were already doing this. C.-in-C. ordered that they [the frogmen] be returned to *Valiant* and put on the lowest deck in the fore part of the ship.

At about 6 a.m. there was a violent explosion under the stern of the tanker *Sagona*. The two Italians in *Valiant* then asked if they could come up now, because it was all over. But they were kept below, and soon showed signs of stress. They asked to see the Captain and advised him to clear the lower decks because there was about to be a big explosion. The Captain acted promptly and the Italians too were brought up. Some minutes later there was a huge explosion, which caused considerable damage.

Within minutes there was another great explosion which caused severe damage to *Queen Elizabeth*.

Three pairs of Italians wearing diving gear had been released from an Italian submarine outside the harbour. Each pair was riding astride a submerged 'chariot', a torpedo-shaped vehicle containing a large explosive charge. They also had tackles for lifting the bottom of the defence net, but by good luck they timed their entry when the gate was opened to admit some destroyers. All six Italians were eventually caught, having accomplished what was probably the greatest feat of the war by either side. They had immobilised the only two battleships left in the Mediterranean Fleet, and put them out of action for many months. Both ships went to America to complete repairs. There were no casualties.

Nineteen forty-one had been a disastrous year for the Royal Navy in the Mediterranean, despite the fighting qualities of ships' companies. On land, the Western Desert Force, now called the 8th Army, was back where O'Connor had been twelve months earlier. On 7 December, twelve days before the Italian attack on Alexandria, the Japanese had struck in the Pacific and Far East. Britain was now at war with Germany, Italy and Japan. But, at least, and at last, the United States, with its vast resources of manpower and *matériel*, was in the war on the side of Britain and Russia.

6
Japan Strikes: 1941

Previous page: When this photograph was released in November 1941 it read; 'The striking power of Singapore Island has been formidably reinforced in recent months and heavy artillery is now concentrated there for any eventuality.' One of the coastal guns in Singapore. (K758)

The Japanese went to war in 1941 to secure the resources of South-East Asia for their industry. The attack on the United States Fleet in Pearl Harbor was intended to shield the eastern flank of the Japanese drive south, while a neutrality treaty with the Soviet Union and strong forces in Manchuria were to keep the Japanese northern flank secure. Thus the Japanese hoped for the minimum of interference while heading for their main objectives: Malaya, the Netherlands East Indies and Burma. For here were the raw materials, oil, rubber and tin, which were totally lacking in Japan. By pushing out to the Philippines, New Guinea, the Bismarck Archipelago and the Marshall and Gilbert Islands, the Japanese would gain a perimeter of bases from which to defend their newly won prize.

The Japanese plans contained two fatal flaws and a miscalculation. There were no contingency plans for continuing with the offensive if it succeeded, or withdrawal if it failed. This was because the Japanese were gambling on a short war, which would end when they reached the limit of their planned conquests. They banked on the United States and Britain gracefully bowing out of the contest on the grounds that the alternative, fighting on, was too difficult. They might reasonably calculate that Britain, after nearly two and a half years of war and now at full stretch in the Atlantic and Mediterranean, might come to some accommodation with Japan. They also reasoned that the United States would not go to war to restore British and Dutch colonies to their former masters. But the treacherous manner in which they attacked Pearl Harbor scuppered for ever the prospects of the United States standing idly by, while the Japanese gobbled up territory in South-East Asia and the South-West Pacific. The Japanese compounded the error by including the Philippines in their initial strike. There were sound operational reasons for this; to gain naval and air bases for their assault on the Netherlands East Indies. But strategically it was an error, because such an attack involved the United States army, naval and air forces stationed in the Philippines and, in American eyes, served to reinforce the infamy of the attack on Pearl Harbor.

For some years, the British had been aware that the Japanese might attack their possessions in Malaya and hence threaten Australia and New Zealand for whose defence they were morally responsible. This possibility had been made more likely by the British decision not to renew the Anglo-Japanese Naval Treaty. The plan to meet this threat, conceived before the outbreak of war in 1939, called for a large battle-fleet to be sent to the Far East should a Japanese invasion look likely. The ships would be made available by leaving the Mediterranean entirely to the care of the French Navy. Now this plan was in ruins, thanks to the defeat of France, and huge losses suffered by the Royal Navy, mainly, but not exclusively, in the Mediterranean, over the past eighteen months.

A further ingredient of the plan involved the basing of this battle-fleet at Singapore. The military status of Singapore had been open to misunderstanding since well before 1941. For example, Churchill frequently referred to it as a 'fortress'. In fact the island was no such thing. It was not a Gibraltar, a Malta, or even Tobruk. The fleet base, in the Johore Strait, faced the mainland of Malaya. The threat was originally perceived to be the arrival of the Japanese fleet off Singapore before the British battle-fleet. So guns with flat trajectories, firing armour-piercing shells, designed to sink ships, were installed facing out to sea. Considerable nonsense has been talked and written on the obtuseness of those siting these guns, because they could not fire on to the Malay Peninsula. In fact, many were so capable, but lacking high explosive ammunition were poor substitutes for land artillery. Anyway no threat was perceived from that direction, that is until 1937 when the Chiefs of Staff produced a paper which assessed that an invasion of Malaya, followed by the seizure of Singapore within two months, from across the narrow Johore Strait was perfectly possible. As indeed it certainly is, as anyone who has looked at the ground with a professional eye could testify. This made nonsense of the choice for the fleet base, unless proper land artillery was immediately installed on both sides of the Johore Strait, and other measures, including adequate air defence, were put in hand. Nothing was done, and the myth persisted for years after the fall of Singapore, assiduously promoted by Churchill for obvious reasons, that the cunning Japanese had come through the back door, which no one had thought of before. In fact, they had actually followed the approach and the timetable forecast in the Chiefs of Staff's paper of four years before almost exactly.

Thanks to Marshal Pétain, the Premier of Vichy France, the Japanese had been allowed to station forces in French Indo-China, including airfields from which they could dominate the South China Sea. The approaches to Singapore and Malaya were now within reach of land-based enemy aircraft.

As the Japanese became more belligerent through 1941, the British tried to win support from the Americans for a joint defence plan in South-East Asia. The Americans not only refused to play, but triggered the onset of war by giving the Japanese an ultimatum: withdraw from their conquests in China or face an oil embargo. The Japanese kept up negotiations with the Americans as a smoke screen behind which they made their preparations to go to war.

In an attempt to deter the Japanese, Churchill proposed despatching the battleship *Prince of Wales* to the Far East. In a letter to Stalin on 4 November 1941:

With the object of keeping Japan quiet we are sending our latest battleship *Prince of Wales*, which can catch and kill any Japanese ship, into the Indian Ocean, and are building up a powerful battle squadron there.[1]

1. Churchill, *The Second World War*, Volume 3, Cassell, London, 1950, p. 469.

He deluded himself that the presence of a single battleship would have the same effect on the Japanese that *Tirpitz*, lurking in the Norwegian Fjords had, on the British Home Fleet; it would keep several capital ships from being available for anything other than waiting for her to sortie. In a note to the First Sea Lord on 29 August 1941:

Tirpitz is doing to us exactly what a *KGV* in the Indian Ocean would do to the Japanese Navy. It exercises a vague general fear and menaces all points at once. It appears, and disappears, causing immediate reactions and perturbations on the other side.

Although he was aware of:

. . . the fact that the Admiralty consider that three *KGV*s must be used to contain *Tirpitz*[2]

2. Churchill, *The Second World War*, Volume 3, Cassell, London, 1950, p. 773.

he seemed unwilling to face the fact that *Tirpitz* was more than a match for any one of the latest British battleships, and none of the latter were a match for the latest Japanese battleship, the giant 18-inch-gun *Yamato*. Furthermore, the Japanese carriers and naval shore-based air arm had a far greater number of more modern aircraft than those launched by the Royal Navy against *Bismarck*.

Eventually, after much deliberation, it was decided to send *Prince of Wales* and the battle-cruiser *Repulse* to Singapore. In charge of this squadron, not battle-fleet, was the newly appointed C.-in-C. Eastern Fleet, Admiral Sir Tom Phillips, lately Vice Chief of Naval Staff, elevated through two ranks, and picking up a knighthood on the way. He was a curious choice. There were several Flag Officers in the Royal Navy who had considerable practice of fighting when the odds were stacked against them, whereas Phillips, a brilliant staff officer, had no experience of fleet command in this war, and especially of operating under an adverse air situation. The First Sea Lord and Churchill held him in high regard, and that was enough.

Ordinary Seaman James Cockburn in *Prince of Wales*:

We were told that the purpose of the visit to Singapore was to discourage Japanese aggression. We thought it would be a cushy number, with no war. We believed the Japanese were not in our class when it came to fighting.

On 2 December, *Prince of Wales*, *Repulse* and the destroyers *Electra*, *Tenedos*, *Express* and HMAS *Vampire*, arrived at Singapore.

James Cockburn:

We had visited Cape Town on the way out. The English-speaking South African white population had been very friendly. In Singapore it was different. The British did not welcome the ratings at all. Only the natives spoke to the sailors.

On 6 December, two large Japanese convoys were sighted off southern Indo-China on a western course, apparently heading for Malaya. Early on 8 December the first of many Japanese air raids hit Singapore. The Japanese also

Admiral Sir Tom Phillips,
Commander-in-Chief
Eastern Fleet, with his
Chief of Staff, Rear-Admiral
Arthur Palliser. (FE486)

struck Pearl Harbor, sinking four battleships and damaging four, two of them
very badly. Fortunately the two carriers based at Pearl Harbor were at sea.

James Cockburn:

We didn't think this would change anything. We were remote from Japan.

The same morning Japanese troops landed at Kota Bharu on the east coast
of Malaya and Singora on the Kra Isthmus in Siam (Thailand).

Phillips judged that his task must be to destroy the convoys landing troops,
despite his force of two battleships and four destroyers being outnumbered.
He did not appreciate how outnumbered he was in surface ships. Protecting
the convoys, the Japanese had eight cruisers, fourteen destroyers and twelve
submarines, with two battleships, two cruisers and ten destroyers in a layback
position. The British were even more uncertain about Japanese air capability.
Based on experience in the Mediterranean, the landings at Singora were
deemed to be well outside the range of land-based aircraft, and there was no
sign of any Japanese carriers in the South China Sea. Phillips plumped for a
high speed attack on Singora, relying on surprise to even the odds against him.

In the evening of 8 December, Force Z, consisting of *Prince of Wales* and *Repulse,* cleared from Singapore Naval Base and, with four destroyers, headed out to sea.

Early on 9 December Phillips was told by signal from his Chief of Staff ashore in Singapore that the Royal Air Force would not be able to provide air cover, because all the airfields in northern Malaya were being evacuated. Nevertheless he elected to press on. Lack of experience, his belief, despite the evidence of over two years of war, in the invincibility of the capital ship, and his own temperament led to this unwise decision.

At about midday on 9 December a Japanese submarine in the piquet line off the east coast of Malaya sighted Force Z. A Japanese strike took off from Saigon, 300 miles away, but failed to spot Phillips's Force. But Japanese reconnaissance aircraft launched from cruisers picked up Force Z and shadowed until dark. Phillips, realizing he had lost surprise, turned south. Had he held on at full speed all night, he might have got away. Early on 10 December, Force Z was sighted by another submarine which fired five torpedoes; all missed. But Phillips's position, course and speed were again compromised. Before dawn another Japanese strike took off, consisting of 85 twin-engined bombers with a radius of action [distance out from base, with a guarantee of getting back] of 1,300 miles. By now Phillips had reports from his Chief of Staff of another landing at Kuantan, well south of Kota Bharu, and outflanking the British positions in north Malaya. He decided to steer south-west to attack the landing here, instead of holding on to his southerly heading. Kuantan was after all

HMS *Prince of Wales* leaves Singapore, 8 December 1941. The last picture of her before she was attacked by Japanese aircraft. (A29068)

some 400 miles from Japanese airfields, and he was unaware that the Japanese aircraft were capable of operating out to three times that distance.

Just after first light on 10 December, a Japanese aircraft was sighted, but Phillips held on, without asking for cover from the Royal Air Force based in Singapore, which was now well within range. By 07.00 it became clear that the reports of the landing at Kuantan were false. Now was the last chance for Phillips to make a run for it. But he steered north-east to investigate a sighting of a steamer towing landing barges. At 10.00, the *Tenedos*, detached earlier, reported being attacked by Japanese aircraft, some 150 miles south of where Phillips was fruitlessly searching for a minor target. At last, he made a run south-west at increased speed. At 11.13, the first wave of Japanese aircraft attacked Force Z. The first attack, with bombs, caused some damage to *Repulse*.

Surgeon Lieutenant-Commander S. G. Hamilton RNVR was assistant medical officer of the *Repulse*. His report, although couched in formal language, gives a flavour of what it must have been like to have been far below decks at his action station, under an armoured hatch, which could only be fully opened slowly with a winch. Here he and his party sweated in the steel compartment, shouting above the noises caused by the ship vibrating at high speed and the hum of machinery and fans, and gunfire overhead; staggering as the deck heeled with every twist and turn; suppressing the uncertainty and fear; guessing what the explosions meant; blind to what was going on overhead, totally reliant on the fragmentary information passed over the Tannoy broadcast.

HMS *Repulse* leaves Singapore 8 December 1941. The last picture of her before she was attacked by Japanese aircraft. (A29069)

Very soon a loud explosion was heard. As we were over Y magazine and smoke was beginning to enter the space from the deck above, I ordered the armoured hatch to be closed. Loudspeakers then announced that a bomb had fallen through the catapult and Marines' mess deck, exploded and caused a fire.

Tapping was heard on the armoured hatch, and we opened it to find five casualties. The first was dead from severe head injuries, so was removed. The others who were all frightened, consisted of a man with a lacerated wound of the forearm, a boy with a large haematoma [bruise] of the buttock caused by his being thrown to the deck by a bomb exploding near him, and two severe cases of burns. The two former were given first aid treatment, and the two cases of burns given morphia and retained below.

Hamilton tended more casualties at various places round the ship, within his area of responsibility.

The next strike, by torpedo bombers, hit *Prince of Wales* with two 24-inch torpedoes, each with 1,210-lb warheads. She lost electrical power, and with her rudder jammed, seawater poured in as she steamed in a circle.

James Cockburn:

These torpedoes were on the port side, near my action station, the port after high angle control position, which was five decks down, below the water line. We lost our primary lighting, and the secondary lighting was very dim. The two 5.25-inch gun turrets we controlled were out of action. The midshipman in charge received permission to evacuate the action station.

The Japanese now turned their attention back to *Repulse*. Hamilton:

A loud explosion shook the ship, so I ordered the armoured hatch to be closed, thinking that bombs were again falling. Actually it was a torpedo somewhere amidships.

But she still kept steaming and fighting. Her Captain immediately sent an emergency signal asking for air support.

An attack on *Prince of Wales* followed, and she was hit by two more torpedoes. *Repulse* came under attack again. Hamilton:

A few minutes later another bigger explosion occurred. The ship shook violently and the lights momentarily went out. About one and a half minutes later a still greater explosion occurred. One or two of the lights went out. The ship began to list. So I ordered the armoured hatch to be opened by means of the winch. Water started to pour down, so I ordered the hatch to be opened at full speed, and everybody out. Unfortunately it was out of the question to move the badly burned casualties because it was only just possible to climb the vertical ladder against the fall of water.

Repulse was hit by four torpedoes, and began to roll over. Captain Tennant RN gave the order to abandon ship.

Hamilton:

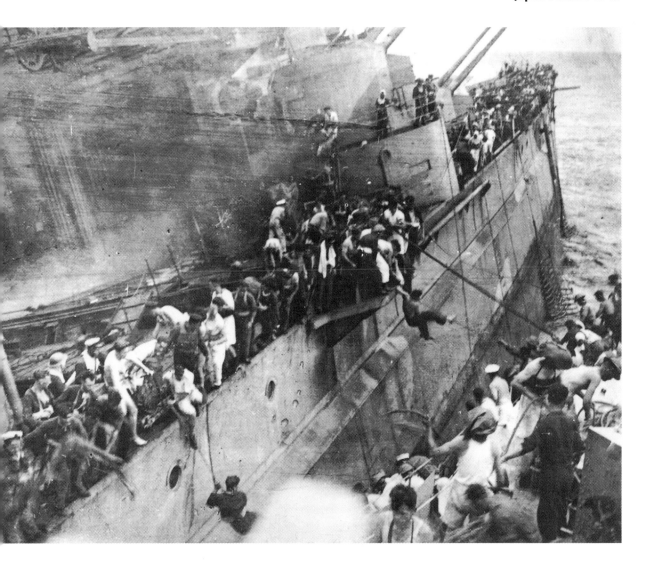

We proceeded to the quarterdeck which was listing heavily to port, to such an extent that it was difficult to reach the starboard rails. Many men had already jumped into the sea.

The ship's company of *Prince of Wales* being taken off by a destroyer. (HU2675)

Electra and *Vampire* picked up 796 out of *Repulse*'s ship's company of 1,306, including Tennant. Meanwhile the Japanese finished off *Prince of Wales*. Captain Leach RN gave the order to abandon ship at 13.10, and she turned turtle and sank at 13.20. Captain Leach and Phillips went with her. James Cockburn had jumped from *Prince of Wales*'s quarterdeck on to HMS *Express* when she came alongside before the battleship turned over:

As *Prince of Wales* turned over to port, her side caught under *Express*, and tilted her to starboard, before the destroyer righted herself and drifted away. Men swam to *Express* through the slowly widening gap of oily water full of flotsam. They all made it. As the gap increased, people were still coming up on *Prince of Wales*'s deck. She was listing so much, they had to slide down her side. Once committed they couldn't stop. Some people slid into torpedo holes on the ship's side, which were now out of the water. I don't know if they got out again.

Again the number rescued was surprisingly high: 1,285 out of her company of 1,612. The Japanese lost eight aircraft. The high numbers rescued probably owe their survival to the appearance of a handful of ancient RAF Brewster Buffalo fighters, which caused the Japanese to flee. Had they arrived earlier, the story might have been different. But Phillips had not asked for them. They had been on standby in Singapore, and had scrambled within a few minutes of the receipt of Tennant's signal in the Air Force operations room.

The Royal Marine detachments of *Repulse* and *Prince of Wales* were sent to join the 2nd Battalion Argyll & Sutherland Highlanders in the final phase of the battle for Malaya and Singapore. As both detachments came from Plymouth Division, the resulting composite battalion was called the 'Plymouth Argylls', after the football team of that name. The Royal Marines were fortunate in that the Argylls was one of the few well-trained British battalions in Malaya – possibly the only one. Those members of the Royal Marine detachments who were not killed became prisoners when Singapore fell.

Singapore surrendered on 15 February 1942, not before it had been fruitlessly reinforced at Churchill's insistence, so that the latest arrivals went almost straight into the bag. The Japanese invaded Burma, and overran the Dutch East Indies, the Philippines, Wake Island, most of New Guinea, and the Solomon Islands. In a desperate attempt to stem the tide, HMS *Exeter* and the destroyers *Encounter* and *Pope*, as part of an Anglo-Dutch squadron, were sunk in an encounter with the Japanese in the Battle of the Java Sea on the night of 27/28 February. By mid 1942, the Japanese held a wide arc from the eastern border of India, south through the Dutch East Indies, New Guinea and the Solomons, north to the Marshalls and Wake Island, and on to the southern Aleutians, and west to Manchuria, Korea and eastern China, including Peking, Hong Kong and Canton.

In those dark days of early 1942, it would not have been apparent but the period of the heaviest losses for the Royal Navy in the Second World War was over, although there was much fighting to come, and some desperate times ahead.

7
The Turning Point in the Atlantic
1942–1943

Previous page: HMS *Sheffield* in huge seas screening Convoy JW53 February/March 1943. 'Hove to south of Iceland, there was a colossal crash, the whole of the top of A Turret, armour plate, just curled back, and was swept into the sea,' recorded Sub-Lieutenant Geoffrey Tibbs RNVR. This a slight exaggeration. *Sheffield*'s log for 1942–43 shows that only one third of the turret roof was 'peeled away'. This is bad enough. (A14892)

If the war against Germany was to be won, a new front in Europe had to be opened from across the sea. Control of the sea had been critical for the survival of Britain, and would remain so. But in order to bring across the materials to conduct operations on any new front, as well as in existing ones, such as the Western Desert, sea control was vital. The vast resources of men and *matériel* of the United States, essential to winning the war, could not be brought to bear in Europe, or anywhere else, if the Allies lost the War at Sea.

It became clear to the Germans at the end of 1941, when their offensive in Russia did not end in a quick victory, that they must hold off the Americans and the British while they finished off the Russians. This meant hindering the Allied build-up in the west by attacking shipping in the Atlantic, as well as preventing them from supplying the Soviet Union. The principal weapon continued to be the U-boat. The heavy units of the German surface fleet were mainly stationed in the Baltic and Norwegian waters. Here they were positioned to protect German convoys from Scandinavia and, at the same time, threaten Allied shipping in the North Atlantic and the Arctic convoy routes to Russia. German coastal forces attacked shipping in the English Channel and North Sea. Over-arching all three methods of prosecuting their maritime strategy, the Germans employed land-based aircraft for attack and surveillance. The most effective aircraft in both roles was the FW Condor-200 C-3 reconnaissance bomber, with a range of 2,210 miles. By flying from Bordeaux in a wide arc from the west of Ireland to Stavanger, and returning after refuelling, a Condor could cover a huge area of the Atlantic. Fortunately, Goering was always reluctant to deploy Luftwaffe aircraft to maritime tasks, the one exception being Norway. From here, German aircraft were particularly well placed to attack the Arctic convoys to Russia.

The Royal Navy had its own problems with the Royal Air Force. Space does not allow a full discussion of what the First Sea Lord called 'The Battle of the Air', fought between the dark and light blue. In a nutshell: on one side stood the Air Staff and the 'bomber barons', who believed that the war could be won by bombing Germany into submission, that no Second Front was needed, and that anything that diverted effort from the bombing offensive was wasted. They begrudged providing any assistance to fighting the Battle of the Atlantic, although without the fuel, raw materials, spare parts and components carried in the hulls of ships, not only would the bomber offensive splutter out, but the war itself would be lost. On the other side stood the Royal Navy, stoutly supported by the airmen of Coastal Command, whose senior commanders risked their careers by questioning the gospel of Trenchard and his disciples: the supremacy of the heavy bomber. The maritime view was that effort put into

Leigh Light fitted to Coastal Command Liberator at RAF Station St Eval in Cornwall. It was first tried out at night on 4 May 1941 against a British submarine. Squadron Leader H. de V. Leigh RAF fitted a 24-inch searchlight to a radar-equipped Wellington. The aircraft located the submarine on the surface by radar and after illuminating it, attacked down the beam. It was judged that the attack would have been successful. It was not to come into service until June 1942. In July 1942, the first U-boat kill was made by an aircraft fitted with a Leigh Light. British and US shore-based aircraft of all types accounted for nearly as many U-boats as did ships. (CH13998)

long-range aircraft such as the B-24 Liberator to provide air cover over the whole Atlantic, the fitting of aircraft radar to locate U-boats on the surface at long range in darkness and all weathers, and other equipment such as the Leigh Light were far more effective than anything Bomber Command could do to destroy U-boats. The Bomber Command view was articulated by Air Chief Marshal Sir Arthur Harris:

At no distant date the Admiralty will recognise that U-boats can be effectively dealt with only by attacking the sources of their manufacture. . . . If it [the bomber offensive] is reduced by further diversions of large numbers of bomber aircraft for seagoing defensive duties, it will fail in its object. . . . This in my opinion would be a greater disaster than the sinking of a few extra merchant ships each week.[1]

1. Gretton, *Convoy Escort Commander*, Cassell, 1964, p. 22.

In fact, despite the efforts of Bomber Command, U-boat production steadily increased throughout the war. In 1940 an average of 4.1 U-boats were produced each month, at a time when a mere 2,656 tons of bombs were dropped on U-boat production centres. By March 1945 production had risen to 26 per month, under a deluge of 28,632 tons of bombs. This is not to imply that Bomber Command's efforts were wasted. But for their attentions, many more of the newer types of U-boat would have been in service earlier. The

Before the arrival of the escort carriers, often the only means of attacking enemy shadowing aircraft on Atlantic and Arctic convoys was provided by Hurricanes catapulted from converted merchant ships. This was a one-way trip, because the merchant ship had no means of recovering the Hurrricane once launched. The pilot ditched in the sea, hoping to be picked up before he died of exposure. This is a posed photogrpaph, as the ship is at anchor.
(A9422)

overriding priority allocated to fighter production to defend Germany against the day and night bomber offensive, precluded the manufacture of long-range reconnaissance aircraft which formed such a vital part of Doenitz's control of his boats. However, all this was well in the future, and much of it was only revealed after the war. When Harris made his pronouncement the U-boat offensive was in full swing, and Bomber Command were not in a position to do much about stopping it.

The bombing of the U-boat pens, with their sixteen-feet-thick concrete roofs, was fruitless, as even Harris agreed:

When bombs exploded on the roofs of these shelters they made no more than a slight indentation in the surface.[2]

2. Webster and Frankland, *The Strategic Air Offensive Against Germany*, Volume ii, HMSO, 1961, p. 137.

To be fair to Harris, the bombing of the pens was requested by the Admiralty, which did not help their case in 'The Battle of the Air'.

One effect of the entry of the United States into the war was the U-boat assault on shipping off the coast of North America. Losses, often within sight of American waterfronts, far exceeded those in the North Atlantic and Western Approaches. U-boat commanders, gazing unbelievingly through their periscopes at processions of individual ships starkly silhouetted against the bright lights of coastal towns and resorts [blackout was not introduced until April 1942], called the period the 'Second Happy Time'; the first being the autumn of 1940. Not until mid May were convoys instituted along the coast of the United States. Ships sunk off the American coasts were not just American, but British and those of other allies and neutrals trading across the Atlantic. Despite being given access to complete information on British anti-submarine warfare techniques from 1939 onwards, the United States Navy did not perform really effectively against U-boats until 1943. Between January and September 1942, Allied and neutral shipping losses averaged 650,000 tons a month, just below Doenitz's target of 700,000 tons of shipping a month, and calculated to bring the Allies to their knees. The number of operational U-boats rose from 95 on 1 January 1942 to 175 at the end of June. The morale of U-boat crews soared.

The crews and passengers in merchant ships sunk by U-boats were rarely picked up by the enemy, who could not risk stopping for long enough or clutter up their boats with survivors. Sometimes rescue ships or escorts with the convoy collected them, some were spotted by aircraft who directed ships to the scene, and some were picked up by chance. Some floated in their boats and rafts until they died. Mrs Marjoribanks-Egerton, evacuated from Malta, was travelling in the 20,000-ton liner *Duchess* from Cape Town to England with her husband Phil, a captain in the Royal Irish Fusiliers, and their six-year-old daughter Anne. *Duchess* was unescorted south-east of Ascension Island in mid-Atlantic on 10 October 1942:

At 6.30 a.m. *Duchess* was hit by a torpedo. I got out of bed and tried to dress quickly, but a numbness seemed to bind my limbs and make my fingers like wool. I was at last dressed, but had forgotten the most important part of female dress in my hurry – my bra. I was to regret it bitterly for the next weeks. A tap at the door, and Smith looked in, 'No need for alarm. Torpedo, Sir. I will leave this lamp in the corridor. No electricity.' He was gone. We joined the throng moving up to the boat decks. No panic. We might have been on our way to breakfast instead of taking to the boats. We stood by our lifeboats awaiting orders. I found I had left my wrist watch behind and in a selfish moment told Phil. He was given leave to go, but at his own risk. Time seemed to pass deadly slowly, I pictured the ship sinking with Phil trapped below. I felt sick. 'Couldn't find the watch, darling, but brought these', he held out my lipsticks bought in Cape Town.

A shudder ran through the ship, we swayed. 'Another torpedo, keep calm.' Whistles went. 'Lower the boats.'

She, her husband and Anne were in the same lifeboat. *Duchess* was sunk by the third torpedo.

Not far off surfaced the enemy, the captain of the U-boat was looking for our captain. A machine-gun was trained on each boat in turn as the search was made. The Hun submarine hung around like some large dark hound. The men in our boat took off their caps and hid the badges. Moments passed and to our relief the submarine dived. We were alone.

After two days, an aircraft from Ascension spotted them, and they were rescued by HMS *Corinthian*, an armed merchant cruiser. In Freetown they were transferred to the *Nea Hellas* with the survivors of several other torpedoed ships, including friends:

Just before we left Freetown, the last party of survivors came on board, from the *Oronsay*. It was a dreadful shock to fail to recognise them. Exposure from nearly two weeks in open boats had altered their faces, eyes were sunken, and lips so swollen speech was difficult. Walking was an effort. We soon realised our episode had been a very mild affair.

The weather grew colder as we neared England. Most of us had only cotton dresses, few had coats. Luckily I had clung on to my fur coat. I had but one cotton dress, and one under garment, but such are the vagaries of war.

On arrival at Greenock at the end of October, her first sight of Britain since 1938:

Everything was pitch dark, save for a few lamps skilfully shaded close to the ship. We were assembled on the quayside, shivering in our inadequate garments. It was not until 11 p.m. [3 hours later] we were given orders to proceed, so on numbed feet we tottered off, small children crying from sheer weariness; we picked our way over the railway lines in the blackness. We came to a halt on mid line and discovered we were alongside a train. 'Climb in and get settled', was the order from the Military Policeman. The train was dimly lit, and unheated, and we were warned we would not get to London until noon next day. No food or drink were provided. No good complaining.

Having arrived home with no belongings, only the clothes we stood up in, Anne and

I were fitted out by the American Red Cross. Philip was given uniform by the Government, and after one month's survivor's leave, went out to Italy [*sic*] for two years.

Mrs Marjoribanks-Egerton's stoic account of her arrival in Britain gives an inkling to our spoonfed age of what life was like for many families after two and a half years of war. The halfway point had yet to be reached.

The Battle of the Atlantic was unremitting and exhausting. The weather was often atrocious; sometimes months would pass without action for the crews of the escorts. On other occasions, running fights lasted night after night, as packs of U-boats moved in like a pride of lions on a herd of buffalo; attacking on the surface, or submerged by day, from all points of the compass. Lieutenant-Commander Evelyn Chavasse RN, in the ex-United States four-funnel destroyer *Broadway*, was an escort group commander:

The average North American convoy consisted of roughly 50 ships (though at one time they rose to 100 or more), ordinary cargo ships of from 3,000 to 7,000 tons, oil tankers etc., and capable of speeds in fair weather of 8 to 10 knots. Each eventually had a single gun. They were formed up in perhaps twelve columns, with about four ships in each column. The front of a convoy covered some five to six sea miles, and the depth from front to rear might be anything up to two and a half miles. You had an area of ocean as big as a fair sized city, 15 square miles, populated by 50 ships. The four sides of the convoy, some 15 to 20 linear miles, had to be screened from submarine attack by a group of about eight escorts. A clever U-boat might easily, and often did, dodge through a gap and loose off a number of torpedoes from close to the convoy, or even right in the middle of it. The first thing to do: find the U-boat, keep it down, and if possible sink it. If you did not, it might go deep, wait until night, surface and dash ahead at twice the speed of the convoy, dive again and lie in wait for another attack the following day.

Rescue work on torpedoed ships, though important, was a secondary concern, the safety of the convoy being always of paramount importance. The primary job of the escort was to keep the U-boat down, and kill it if possible. If Asdic detection was not made quite soon, back to your station around the convoy, for we might well have bumped into a U-boat pack. As well as Asdic for underwater detection, we had radar, and High Frequency Detection Finding (HF/DF) [or 'Huff-Duff'], which gave the bearing of a U-boat if she were careless enough to chatter on her wireless.

Sometimes U-boats attacked by night on the surface, when they could move much faster, and dash away at high speed. That is where fast ships like *Broadway*, fitted with superb radar, were especially useful. With any luck, we could detect a U-boat on radar, dash out to meet it, and force it to dive in the dark before it could get near the convoy.

I usually chose a station directly ahead of the centre of the convoy. The Commodore, sometimes a retired admiral or senior and experienced Merchant Navy captain, always had his ship stationed at the head of the centre column, and therefore close to me. The convoy was his baby; the escort mine. He alone was responsible for the navigation and discipline of the merchant ships. What splendid men they were; always co-operative, always ready to sink the pride of their seniority and experience to take orders from an upstart Lieutenant-Commander.

Convoy conference. Merchant Navy masters (captains) attended in uniform or mufti, whichever took their fancy. (A4551)

Before we sailed, the Commodore had been given a route to follow. If for any reason I wanted to diverge from the route more than a prescribed distance, I had first to obtain the C.-in-C.'s [C.-in-C. Western Approaches] approval, before informing the Commodore. Within those limits I was entirely free, and in the face of the enemy, the tactical handling of the convoy was completely at my discretion.

Convoys were briefed at conferences, usually at Liverpool, attended by every ship's master and the commodore. Escort commanders did not always attend, as they might be based at Londonderry, as Chavasse was, or in the Clyde:

A day or two before our departure, with butterflies fluttering wildly in my stomach, we would slip down the River Foyle from Londonderry, and go to sea to spend the intervening time on strenuous day and night exercises in the Irish Sea, carrying out dummy attacks on our own submarines, gunnery etc. On the last day we would fill up our fuel tanks, leave our last bag of mail in the tanker, and have a quiet night in bed. Early next morning, we would slip out of harbour and steam to the dawn rendezvous with the convoy, six miles west of Oversay on the Island of Mull. The convoy had been brought there by local escorts of trawlers, after being collected from various ports in the Irish Sea and the Clyde. It was now up to us.

Then started the long business of forming the convoy into ten or a dozen columns, for which there had been no room in the narrow waters of the North Channel; collecting the convoy papers which had come up in the Local Escort from the conference at Liverpool, making them up into packets, and shooting them by line to each ship of the escort, so that all my ships should know the exact position of every other ship, what her cargo was, and many other domestic details. I signalled to the commodore, or shouted to him by loud-hailer, giving him my policy, dispositions for the night, up-to-the-minute U-boat intelligence, and a dozen other details. When we had finally got his ships into their proper places, and all my butterflies had flown, we settled down to our long slog across the Atlantic.

On perhaps our tenth day at sea, or sometimes much later if we had made a slow passage, somewhere to the west of Newfoundland, at the Western Ocean Meeting Point (WESTOMP), we would meet a Canadian escort group, and hand over to them.

Since the autumn of 1941, and before the entry of the United States into the war, their Navy had taken on the escort of convoys to and from WESTOMP, which had lightened the burden being borne by the Royal Navy and Royal Canadian Navy. But the experience gained in the months running up to December 1941 was clearly not as well used to hone up the US Navy's anti-submarine procedures as it might have been. Eventually, the Royal Navy and Royal Canadian Navy assumed responsibility for the whole North Atlantic escort task, the Royal Canadian Navy becoming in the process the third biggest in the Western World; a far cry from their minute fleet today.

Now desperately short of fuel, we would thankfully make our way to St John's, New-foundland, for a few days' rest. In the summer it wasn't always easy to find in the fog and icebergs drifting down from the Arctic. As often as not we had been stumbling along for the last two or three days in dense fog, with never a sight of stars or sun to fix our position; and to find the harbour entrance, which is a narrow crack a few score yards across in a cliff, was sometimes a tricky business.

Unlike these days of global position satellite systems which provide the most bumbling weekend yachtsman with his position to within a yard, day or night, navigation then depended solely on star and sun sights, and good dead reckoning.

Chavasse's remark about fuel is a reminder that the Royal Navy lacked an effective resupply-at-sea system, so the endurance of escorts was limited by the capacity of their fuel tanks. At times, particularly in the early days of the Battle of the Atlantic, escorts had to turn for home to refuel, before their task was done, leaving the convoy to the mercy of the U-boats. Throughout the Second World War, considerations of refuelling shaped all naval operations in a way quite unknown today. Ships were effectively tied by a string to the nearest refuelling base.

Life at sea in escorts was far from comfortable, and sometimes dangerous without any interference from the enemy. Signalman Richard Butler, on joining the destroyer *Matchless*:

I looked round the mess deck, no bigger than a large living room, where twenty-two of us had to eat, sleep and live with no privacy at all. Two wooden tables each side of the mess deck occupied much of the deck space, which was further reduced by a gun hoist in one corner, and some machinery in another. The mess deck being in the bows, the forward end curved inwards reducing the space yet again. Just above my head, the deckhead was a mass of pipes, cables, ducts and hammock bars. Fitted in both port and starboard sides were a few small portholes. At sea they were closed with dead-lights down. Personal hammock positions were zealously guarded, and in a beam sea, I found out why no one had taken the one allocated to me. Instead of being rocked, I was knocked to sleep as my hammock bumped on the ship's side. I contemplated sleeping on the locker tops, but after seeing others being rolled off on to the deck, which at times was awash with sea water seeping through loose rivets and oil spillage from the gun hoist in the corner, I decided to stay in my hammock. I learned that the air duct over my head was used by the ship's rats as a means of visiting other mess decks.

Coastal waters could be as unpleasant as the open sea:

By mid-morning a gale was raging and orders were piped that no one was allowed on the open deck which was being continually swept over the waists amidships by solid green seas, the ship lying deep, having almost full oil tanks. Down on the mess decks it was chaotic. A rope was strung the full length of our mess to cling to and stop us being flung around by the motion of the ship.

Butler had the afternoon watch on the bridge, which unlike those on warships today, was open:

Three destroyers in a gale: *Matchless, Musketeer* and *Mahratta*. (A20448)

At first I couldn't see anything for the swirling spray. The wind shrieked through the rigging and superstructure. It looked as though we were sailing through boiling water as the wind whipped the wave tops into horizontal spume, white and fuming, which stung my eyes and face. I could hardly breathe. Now and again, I caught a glimpse of one of the big merchant ships being rolled on its beam ends by the huge swells sweeping up under rain-laden skies.

Later the Captain decided to heave-to, stern to the wind. But slowly the convoy began to separate. *Matchless* stayed with one ship.

We received a message from the freighter in our care; 'Have twelve-foot split in upper deck, cannot cope with weather, will have to return to harbour when convenient.' A member of the bridge party remarked, 'I hope she doesn't split apart. God knows how we could possibly save any of her crew in these bloody awful conditions.' The chances of saving anybody if it became necessary grew more remote when the Captain was informed that our motorboat had been washed overboard, along with the port side guardrails.

A few minutes later a man was washed overboard.

Just for a moment the Captain hesitated, then dashed over to the wheel-house voice pipe and shouted, 'Full speed ahead, hard aport.' Hearing this, I thought, 'The Captain's gone crazy, he's going to risk the lives of two hundred men to look for some silly bastard that hadn't the sense to keep off the upper deck.' As the ship began to turn, she caught the full force of wind and seas and rolled alarmingly. We hung on, fearing she would turn right over. After what seemed an eternity, the bows came round and plugged the monstrous waves, and the Captain ordered reduced speed. It was impossible to see anything, as whipped-up spindrift covered the surface. No one could live for more than a few minutes in seas such as these. The search was abandoned, and the ship was turned about, which gave us some anxious moments, but soon, to everyone's relief, *Matchless* was riding stern to wind and sea.

Later after a roll-call to establish who had been washed overboard:

I was stunned to hear it was one of my best messmates, 'Snowy' Snowden. I was saddened and shocked, and filled with remorse about my selfish attitude when the Captain did his best to save him. 'Snowy' was well liked and had the reputation of being a 'gannet', someone who never stopped eating. Never again would we hear him ask cheerfully at mealtimes, 'Any gash left?'

Matchless had a reputation among her ship's company for being unstable:

After sub-hunting in the Southern Approaches, we sailed round the west coast of Ireland to return to our Scapa base. But something very frightening happened which prevented us from arriving there. To say it put the shits up us is an understatement. We were steaming along at 23 knots with a brisk following sea. The day was pleasant and sunny, with a stiff breeze that whipped up a high stern sea and big swells. Following seas had a tendency to push the stern round. As we stood watching, we gasped in amazement as a monster wave crept up to the stern and slowly engulfed it. The quarterdeck was submerged under tons of green water, gradually the after end was pushed round and *Matchless* laid over on her side. Spume and spray scudded round as the ship lay on her starboard side with clouds of steam billowing from her horizontal funnel. The ship came to a stop. Those of us on the flagdeck heard things crashing around, and yells and screams coming from below deck. The burly PO on the flagdeck shouted, 'It's all right lads, it'll come back, it's got to.' I didn't share his confidence, and had already inflated my lifebelt and had my leg over the guardrail ready to slide into the sea. I hung on waiting to see if the ship would right itself. After what seemed a long time, but must have been only seconds, *Matchless* shuddered and came slowly upright. After a big roll to the other side, she settled on an even keel, wallowing with engines stopped in the swells.

Ashen faced men came up from below. Some were injured, but none seriously. Ratings said that when the ship reached its maximum roll, they had actually stood on the bulkheads. Tin hats and ditty boxes started flying about. One man got hit in the face by a helmet, lost his grip on the table he was clinging to, and ended up wrapped around the iron ladder with messmates falling on top of him. His oppo extracted him from beneath the pile of bodies, led him to the upper deck and lit a fag for him. It took us a long time to get over the fright.

The destroyer a mile astern caught up. Those on her bridge thought that *Matchless* had foundered when we suddenly disappeared from view. They sent a visual signal: 'The sight of your delicate pink bottom is most becoming.' The Captain instructed the duty signalman to make back: 'We are always on heat in the Springtime.'

Matchless went into Londonderry to repair the damage.

Until early 1942, the threat from heavy surface units of the German Navy was possible from two directions: the battleship *Tirpitz* (sister ship to *Bismarck*), the pocket battleship *Scheer* and heavy cruiser *Hipper* in Norwegian waters, and the battle-cruisers *Scharnhorst*, *Gneisenau* and heavy cruiser *Prinz Eugen* from Brest. In January 1942, Hitler decided that the three ships in Brest should be transferred to the Baltic where they would be on hand should the Allies invade Norway; this was always an obsession with Hitler and was used to advantage in the deception plans for the Normandy invasion two years later. Norway was not the only matter on Hitler's mind: he feared that the ships in Brest might be destroyed by bombing. Several bombing attacks had been inflicted on them since March 1941, and some had succeeded in causing severe damage. Although the route the ships would have to take, up the English Channel and well within range of land-based aircraft, was highly risky, Hitler saw it in terms of use them or lose them.

A year before, the Admiralty and the Royal Air Force had prepared contingency plans to meet the possibility of a German break-out from Brest and passage up Channel. Thanks to Ultra decrypts, the Admiralty were aware that a move was imminent. The two things they did not know were date and time. Vice-Admiral Dover, Ramsay, was responsible for the operation in the Dover

Command area for dealing with any attempt by German heavy units to pass through the Straits. The naval forces available to Ramsay were six destroyers based at Harwich, six Swordfish at Manston and eight MTBs split between Dover and Ramsgate. With these sparse resources Ramsay hardly had enough force to stop German heavy units running up Channel. The major part in the operation fell to the Royal Air Force: three squadrons of Beaufort torpedo bombers of Coastal Command, 300 bombers of Bomber Command, and six squadrons of Spitfires of Fighter Command. Each Command controlled its own aircraft, and there was no overall Royal Air Force co-ordinating headquarters. The Royal Air Force part in operations in Ramsay's area was under the control of AOC 11 Group.

Air reconnaissance patrols were intensified over Brest and Boulogne and it was hoped these would give warning of a break-out. British plans were based on the reasonable assumption that the Germans would pass through the Straits of Dover at night; however, as so often happens in war, the enemy does not do what appears to be logical by one's own calculation. The Germans considered that the absence of the three ships in Brest must be concealed for as long as possible. By doing so, they hoped that by the time it was discovered the quarry had bolted, it would be too late to move the battleships of the Home Fleet from Scapa to intercept them off the German coast. This meant leaving Brest soon after last light, when visual air reconnaissance would be ineffective, and passing through the narrowest part of the Channel in broad daylight.

Scharnhorst (flag Vice-Admiral Ciliax), *Gneisenau* and *Prinz Eugen*, with six destroyers, left Brest at 22.45 on 11 February. At daybreak the Luftwaffe was to provide a combat air patrol (CAP) of sixteen fighters, with more on standby.

Admiral Ciliax addressing crews of German warships in Brest, before the 'Channel dash'. (HU2228)

Three E-boat flotillas and three T-boat flotillas were to screen them through the Straits. There were no radio transmissions by the Germans to give the game away to Ultra. The German ships remained undetected until 10.42 the next morning, thanks to a number of equipment and human failures, and one piece of bad luck. A French dockyard worker, who was actually an agent, saw the ships preparing to leave, but could not get to where his radio was hidden because of a cordon round the dockyard. The submarine acting as piquet off Brest withdrew from her patrol position to recharge batteries. The radars on aircraft patrolling the area during the night broke down on two occasions. Ramsay was not informed of either of these breakdowns. Fog the next morning caused the withdrawal of air patrols that might have seen the ships. Air patrols off Boulogne had intense interference on their radars. The final piece of misfortune was heavy snow at Leuchars, preventing fourteen Royal Air Force Beaufort torpedo bombers from taking off to re-position further south. Thus arguably some key members of the cast were missing when the curtain went up on the drama about to be played out. At 10.35 two Spitfires had sighted the battle-cruisers, but failed to report this immediately, because they had orders not to break radio silence, and waited until landing at 11.09 before reporting. At 11.25, nearly an hour after the first sighting, the Admiralty informed Ramsay that the battle-cruiser group was one hour's steaming from the Dover Straits.

From the British Admiralty Battle Summary dated 1948:

The Force rounded Cap Gris Nez at 11.56, and Vice Admiral Ciliax ordered the E-boats to lay a smokescreen to port between him and the English coast. Some twenty minutes later

Scharnhorst, Gneisenau and *Prinz Eugen* **during their dash up the English Channel. German photograph.** (HU2216)

he received the first indication that the presence of *Scharnhorst* and *Gneisenau* at sea was no longer a secret, when at 12.18 the first shells fired at them by the British coastal batteries were observed.

Unfortunately neither these nor any other shells from coastal batteries hit. Ramsay, in accordance with his contingency plan, ordered an attack by MTBs from Dover and six Fleet Air Arm Swordfish from Manston. Ramsay asked 11 Group to provide fighter air cover for both attacks, but the Royal Air Force failed to provide it in time for the MTB attack. This attack failed, thanks to engine breakdowns, torpedo misfires, and the efforts of the E-boat screen supported by two *Narvik* class destroyers. Admiralty Battle Summary:

At about 12.45, almost concurrently with the attacks of the last MTBs, the attack by six Swordfish developed. By what Vice Admiral Ramsay describes as a 'major tragedy', the plan to escort these aircraft miscarried and only 10 fighters effected the rendezvous with them over Manston. With this meagre escort, the Swordfish started off, steering for a point 23 miles from Ramsgate, in which position the interception was expected to take place. The first sub flight was led by Lieutenant-Commander Esmonde; the second by Lieutenant Thompson.

Lieutenant-Commander Eugene Esmonde DSO RN, a gallant Southern Irishman who had led the first Swordfish attack on *Bismarck*, realized that if he waited for the full escort of Spitfires promised by the Royal Air Force, the German ships would have passed beyond the range of his squadron. He decided to wait no longer. Extracts from the report of the Intelligence Officer Manston, on interrogation of survivors from 825 Squadron:

The following report has been taken from Sub-Lieutenant Lee, one of the survivors of the attack, after he had interviewed the four other survivors. The following aircraft took off at 12.20 hours:

First Sub-Flight

A/C letter	H	G	L
Pilot	Lt-Cdr Esmonde	Sub-Lt Rose	Sub-Lt Kingsmil
Observer	Lt Williams	Sub-Lt Lee	Sub-Lt Samples
Air Gunner	PO Clinton	L/A Johnson	L/A Bunce

Second Sub-Flight

A/C letter	F	K	M
Pilot	Lt Thompson	Sub-Lt Wood	Sub-Lt Bligh
Observer	Sub-Lt Wright	Sub-Lt Parkinson	Sub-Lt Benyon
Air Gunner	L/A Tapping	L/A Wheeler	L/A Smith

The formation was escorted by about 10 Spitfires flying at about 1,000 feet. The Spitfires had to weave very widely owing to the slow speed of the Swordfish. About 10 miles

. . .

from Ramsgate, the Swordfish were attacked by about 15 enemy aircraft, ME109s and FW190s both being seen. The enemy aircraft seemed to dive out of the clouds on to the tail of the Swordfish, and all three of the first sub-flight, and probably some of the second, sustained damage. The Spitfire escort became involved in the general dogfight. For the next 7 or 8 minutes, the Swordfish were subjected to incessant fighter attacks, the FW190s appearing to be the more dangerous opponents. The Swordfish were slowed down by the need for constant evasive action.

The leader then saw the enemy ships and altered course towards them. There was some flak from the screening vessels, but this was restricted by the presence of enemy aircraft. As the Swordfish passed over the screening vessels it was seen that the lower port main plane of the leader's aircraft [Esmonde] was practically shot away. The pilot nearly lost control, but recovered and kept closing the enemy ships. When about 3,000 yards away he was hit again, it is believed by fire from an enemy fighter, and he crashed into the sea, the crew of the following aircraft having the impression from the behaviour of the aeroplane that the pilot was killed. It cannot be said whether the torpedo had been dropped. The bodies of the observer and air gunner from this machine were subsequently recovered.

The other two pilots continued to close. Just after passing over the destroyer screen, the air gunner in the second aircraft (G) had been killed by machine-gun fire. The observer Sub-Lt Lee tried to take over the gun, but could not move the gunner's body.

At about the same time the third aircraft (L) was badly hit by cannon shells. The pilot Sub-Lt Kingsmill and observer Sub-Lt Samples were wounded, the top two cylinders of the engine were shot away, and the engine and upper port wing caught fire. The air gunner continued to engage the attacking fighters, and saw one crash in the sea, he thinks as a result of his fire. The pilot managed to keep control of his aircraft long enough to aim his torpedo in the direction of the second large ship from under 3,000 yards; he then turned with difficulty and tried to land near some vessels which turned out to be E-boats and which opened fire on him. He kept flying until the engine finally cut and the aircraft crashed into the water a few hundred yards from British MTBs [motor torpedo boats] which rescued the crew, (who had taken to the water, the dinghy having been destroyed by fire), after about 10 minutes.

While this was happening, the second aircraft was again attacked and the pilot Sub-Lt Rose severely wounded in the back. Nevertheless he held to his course, although he must have been in great pain. A further attack resulted in a burst petrol tank, and both pilot and observer were affected by the fumes. The pilot decided he must drop his torpedo as the engine was faltering. He aimed it from about 2,000 yards range at the second large ship, and it was seen to be running well. He then turned and passed outside the destroyer screen, crashing on the sea about 500 yards away. Sub-Lt Lee assisted Sub-Lt Rose out of the aircraft and after a struggle in the water was able to get him safely into the dinghy. He then tried to release the body of the gunner, but was unable to do so before the aircraft sank. He returned to the dinghy and after waiting until the enemy surface vessels were well out of the way, fired two distress signals which were seen by MTBs, which picked up the two survivors after they had been about one and a half hours in the dinghy.

The three Swordfish in the second sub-flight were last seen passing into the attack, crossing the destroyer screen as Sub-Lt Rose's aircraft came out. They were taking violent evasive action, but were steadily proceeding towards the large ships.

None of the Swordfish in the second sub-flight were ever seen again. No torpedoes hit. The Admiralty Battle Summary:

The Vice Admiral Dover describes the sortie of these six Swordfish as 'one of the finest exhibitions of self-sacrifice and devotion to duty this war has yet witnessed'. In recognition of this gallant attack, HM the King subsequently approved the award of the VC to Lieutenant-Commander E. Esmonde, the award of the DSO to each surviving officer [Sub-Lieutenants B. W. Rose, E. F. Lee, C. M. Kingsmill and R. M. Samples], and the CGM to the only other survivor, Leading Airman Bunce. Each of the other twelve officers and men who did not survive was posthumously mentioned in despatches.

As Ciliax's force cleared Dover Command's area, responsibility for the battle now passed from Ramsay to C.-in-C. Nore. Between 14.45 and 17.00 a series of attacks by 242 aircraft of Bomber Command and 28 Beauforts of Coastal Command was carried out using bombs and torpedoes. Some 398 fighters escorted these strikes. No hits were obtained.

The final attack was launched by destroyers based at Harwich under Captain Mark Pizey RN in HMS *Campbell*, with *Vivacious*, *Worcester*, *Mackay*, *Whitshed* and *Walpole*. Each was armed with four or five 4.7-inch or 4-inch guns, and six 21-inch torpedo tubes. Pizey, whose force had been at five minutes' notice for the operation for the last three weeks, was carrying out firing exercises in the swept channel off Harwich:

The plan was to proceed at speed and set course for the Hinder buoy, skirting the British minefield [off Harwich] and sailing through the narrow swept channel in single line. On arrival, the pre-arranged plan was to station half the destroyers one side of the anticipated route of the German ships and the other on the other side – all this under the cover of darkness. So much for the PLAN.

At about noon, I received a signal from C.-in-C. Nore: 'Enemy cruisers passing Boulogne, speed about 20 knots. Proceed in execution of previous orders.' I ordered all destroyers to join me at full speed and shaped course for the swept channel. With the German ships going 20 knots I estimated that we could just reach our RV in time. Subsequent reports gave a much greater speed, and it was not long before I realised that I hadn't a hope of intercepting them.

The only possible way was to cut across eastwards and try and head them off close to the Hook [of Holland]. But this meant skilful navigation through a minefield which had a narrow passage clear of mines and marked by buoys. Could we be sure to sight the buoys in the bad visibility? I decided to take the risk.

To our intense relief, the first buoy was soon reported in sight and we made the 15 miles through the mine barrier successfully. Not knowing exactly the enemy position, I altered more to the NE to make doubly sure of getting ahead of them, rather than dropping astern and thereby not getting in a torpedo attack.

This proved a wise move. Shortly after we were bombed by a JU88 and later by a Hampden who mistook us for the enemy – no bombs found their mark, although one or two perilously close. At 15.17 when we were beginning to give up hope, our RDF [radar] reported two large echoes slightly before the beam, and then smaller echoes came up. There was then no doubt about what they were. We were in an ideal position closing the enemy on a steady bearing.

As we approached at full speed, great numbers of aircraft, friendly and hostile, were sighted. Low down a large number of ME109s and an occasional Beaufort. Higher up were Hampdens, Dorniers and ME110s, while still higher a few Halifaxes, Spitfires and Wellingtons were also sighted.

Many of the enemy aircraft obviously thought we were friendly, and fired their recognition signal. Many of the British aircraft took us for hostile. We on the other hand hadn't time to find out who was friendly and who was hostile, as we had other things to think about.

During this mêlée, we were closing fast, being engaged by the main armament of the battle-cruisers. Shells of all calibres fell very close. We had closed in to 3,500 yards and when I saw a large shell which failed to explode or ricochet, dive under the ship like a porpoise, I felt this was the time to turn and fire torpedoes. By this time the battle-cruisers were turning away and thus avoided any torpedo hits.

Having fired our torpedoes, we could do no more, and course was set for Harwich, sad but fortunate to be alive.

From the Admiralty After Battle Summary:

Throughout the operations all the destroyers were greatly hampered by the weather conditions as regards both gunnery and torpedo attacks. Seas were breaking green fore and aft, and there was continuous spray over the bridges. Guns' crews were at times knee-deep in water, and difficulty was experienced in training the torpedo tubes, especially in the second division, which was beam to the sea in its approach.

HMS *Worcester* went in closest and 'caught a packet'. She was hit several times by 11-inch, 5.9-inch and 5.1-inch shells. From the report by her Captain, Lieutenant-Commander E. C. Coates:

From the time torpedoes were fired hits were received continuously. Almost immediately numbers 1 and 2 boiler rooms received hits, and the ship stopped, swung on past the retiring course towards the second battle-cruiser, then back beam to wind with the port side exposed to the close range fire of both battle-cruisers for about ten minutes.

When four salvos running had scored hits, I gave the order to 'prepare to abandon ship', meaning to knock off the slips on the life-saving gear. Unfortunately all communications were broken and everyone was deafened. The order reached some parts of the ship as 'abandon ship'. Many wounded were put into floats, and others went with them. Owing to the strong wind drifting the ship, I could not get them back on board. At last salvos became erratic, then ceased altogether.

The ship had settled but was afloat. The fires in the paint shop and elsewhere were put out by buckets of water. The fore peak, fore boiler room, wardroom, after magazine, and shell room and after stores were flooded. The ship was in this condition, when Captain (D) 21 in *Campbell* and *Vivacious* appeared to our great relief, and picked up those in the water.

No torpedoes hit. The Admiralty Battle Summary:

With nightfall, Admiral Ciliax must have felt well satisfied with the day's work, as he entered the last lap of the race for home, but at 19.55 north of Vlieland *Gneisenau* hit a mine. The damage proved to be slight, and after a short time she was able to proceed at 25 knots, arriving with *Prinz Eugen* off the mouth of the Elbe at 07.00 on 13th February.

More serious damage was sustained by *Scharnhorst* which hit a second mine at 21.34, not far from the spot where *Gneisenau* had been mined. With engines stopped and both steering motors out of action, the ship drifted to starboard; the fire control system and echo sounding system were also temporarily broken. It was not until 22.23 that the centre and starboard engines were again working and *Scharnhorst* was able to proceed at 12 knots. She had shipped 1,000 tons of water, the port engine was out of action, and the turret training gear was no longer working; in this condition she limped slowly into Wilhelmshaven.

The mines had been laid earlier by Bomber Command, the only useful contribution they made to the battle. The rage and frustration felt in Britain is well summed up by *The Times* in a leading article on 14 February:

Vice-Admiral Ciliax has succeeded where the Duke of Sidonia failed . . . nothing more mortifying to the pride of sea power has happened in Home Waters since the 17th century.

Although the Admiralty Battle Summary states that the subsequent Board of Inquiry 'found there was no lack of co-ordination of plans between the Admiralty and the Air Ministry and the Commands concerned', this misses the point. There was grave lack of co-ordination when it came to putting the plans into action. But, more fundamentally this sorry affair highlighted the folly of allowing the Royal Naval Air Service to be swallowed up by the Royal Air Force in 1918, with all that flowed from this decision, which has been covered in Chapter One.

Bomber Command made up for their lack of success during the passage of Ciliax's ships through the North Sea by hitting *Gneisenau* in dock in Kiel, and damaging her bows. Despite this, *Scharnhorst* and even more so *Tirpitz* were a constant menace to the Arctic shipping route to Russia. Their whereabouts and intentions had always to be taken into account in the routing and protection of every convoy. *Tirpitz* was attacked several times from the air, and on one occasion by midget submarines. All the attacks, except one, were carried out while she was in Norwegian fjords. The only attack on her at sea was in early March 1942, and Charles Friend took part, being the only commissioned aircrew to have attacked both *Bismarck* and *Tirpitz* at sea.

By now, Charles Friend was in *Victorious*, which he found an unhappy ship after *Ark Royal*. He had also converted to the Albacore, 'a first class version of the Swordfish' according to him, but still obsolete by Second World War standards before it came into service:

It had a more powerful engine and was more aerodynamically efficient, but it was still a fixed undercarriage biplane. It could reach about one hundred and fifty knots in level flight. It did have a 'greenhouse', all three of us being in enclosed cockpits. The pilot was just in front of the upper mainplane, and between him and the observer was a long petrol tank. In the Stringbag, if the pilot had forgotten to plug in his Gosport tube, one simply reached over and banged him on the head to attract his attention. But in Albacores we all carried a long garden cane to reach forward past the tank to tap him on the shoulder. The ultimate refinement was an empty Very cartridge tied on the end, in which to place a written note to the pilot. The wireless was for communicating in Morse code with other aircraft and the ship. It was only used to report enemy or in dire emergency. The Aldis lamp was [usually] used to speak with other aircraft and ships. In formation flying we resorted to making Morse with a swung forearm; called 'zogging'.

Victorious, in company with two battleships and a battle-cruiser, was in the vicinity of Jan Mayen Island covering two Russian convoys. On 8 March 1942, she received a signal informing her that *Tirpitz* would be off the Vestfjord the next morning. Although those on board *Victorious* did not know it, this information was based on Ultra. The next morning Albacore reconnaissance found her. The reconnaissance was followed by twelve Albacores carrying torpedoes. The leading two sub-flights in the strike were led, as was customary in the Home Fleet, according to Friend, by the most senior not the most experienced:

The first disheartening experience was of flying at ninety knots against a thirty-five knot wind, to a target which was steaming directly away upwind at twenty-five knots. Our closing speed was therefore thirty knots. We sighted *Tirpitz*, with one destroyer, and from our low approach height we climbed to begin the attack. Ice began to form on our wings in the climb, which took us into cloud cover. The huge ship seemed to be there for hours as we crawled towards her. The first sub-flight were to port of her, the remainder on her other side. The theory of torpedo attack then was that all aircraft should get down to dropping level of fifty to a hundred feet as nearly together as possible, to drop their torpedoes in a fan-shaped pattern across her bows to make it as difficult as possible for her to 'comb the tracks'. Then, all turning away at once, preferably downwind, we all jinked to present a maximum number of elusive targets for the defending gunners. The greatest danger to us occurred during the few seconds of aiming and firing, when the pilots were flying straight and level, very low and slow. The optimum range for dropping was between eight hundred and a thousand yards, and the training of our pilots and setting of the torpedo sight was based on that.

The attack by the first six aircraft was badly co-ordinated, and the torpedoes dropped too far away. No aircraft were hit:

The other two sub-flights, Sugden leading [Lieutenant-Commander P. Sugden DSC RN], had by now cut the corner, and he was able to head a co-ordinated attack, albeit at too long range, but not so far from *Tirpitz* as the first six [with an inexperienced leader]. These six Albacores did fire together a proper pattern across her bows. She was already turning to starboard, and the torpedoes all missed astern. These two sub-flights lost an aircraft each to flak.

The debriefing and dissection of the fiasco ended in the surviving crews being mustered on the quarterdeck of *Victorious* to be addressed by senior officers in a very recriminatory way. We received for our efforts and the loss of six men a very severe 'bottle'. I could not but compare what was happening with the mistakes which led to the attack on *Sheffield* instead of *Bismarck*. Then, Captain Maund [CO of *Ark Royal*] was so sympathetic as to make disappointed aircrews feel he was really with them in spirit when they flew, and Sir James Somerville was known to have shouldered most of the blame. In this *Tirpitz* operation, the main cause of the failure was again not of aircrew making, but the decision to let seniority not experience count. That was their [failure], not ours.

On 21 August 1941, a convoy of merchant ships had sailed from Iceland to Murmansk; the first of forty British convoys to make this hazardous journey

HMS *Belfast* off Iceland in February 1943, screening Convoy JW53. Now moored above Tower Bridge she is part of the Imperial War Museum. (A15530)

over the next three-and-a-half years. Nearly one in eight of the ships that travelled this route were lost to U-boats, aircraft or mines. The conditions on Arctic, or Russian, convoys were even worse than the North Atlantic. Often the spray froze, forming ice on upper decks, guns and superstructure. This had to be chipped away when it became so thick as to affect stability. The sea was so cold that two minutes' immersion was often enough to freeze to death anyone who fell in or had to abandon ship. In winter north of the Arctic circle, the sun did not appear above the horizon for months. In summer, it never set, and the perpetual daylight gave no respite from the attentions of shadowing and attacking German aircraft. Snow, gales sweeping down from the frozen wastes, ice and mountainous seas were commonplace. Friend:

I remember looking out from a furiously rolling and pitching *Victorious* to see *King George V*, nearly eight hundred feet long, climbing up the slope of a wave. Under ordinary conditions such big ships steamed along, and what waves there were undulated along their steadily level hulls. But these waves were moving mountains. We were climbing up one side and sliding down the other. There was plenty of slope both above and below the battleship, so the billows were a thousand feet from crest to trough. In those enormous seas, even *Victorious*'s high freeboard did not always prevent her from taking it green, the bow driving through the crest of a wave, which crashed down on her flight deck. We received some unexpected leave when one banged down so hard that the forward aircraft lift was put out of action by distortion. The sea had bent the four-inch armour of the deck.

There were also days of Arctic high pressure weather, bitterly cold, but clear with a long, glassy swell. But the cold is what most remember; Alec Dennis, now First Lieutenant in the destroyer *Savage*:

The other enemy, the weather was always with us, and I remember being unable to stay in my bunk for fear of being pitched out, and trying to nap on the deck. The other trouble was cold feet (both kinds). While one could keep one's body reasonably warm, even on an open bridge, I found it impossible to keep my feet warm, in spite of fur-lined boots. Working watch and watch, one would get off the bridge, say, a little after midnight with four hours off before the morning watch. The first hour of the four would give little sleep, as I can't sleep until my feet are warm. But, by putting an electric light bulb in each boot, I could at least start warm for the next watch. Of course one had to be called about twenty minutes before the next watch, so that one could pull on all the warm clothing again and clamber up the swaying ladders.

The conditions in the North Atlantic and on Russian convoys took their toll, particularly on the older men, in positions of responsibility:

For some time now Cosmo Gordon had been unwell. He had been at sea in command for many months and was, I suppose, in his mid-thirties – getting a bit old for this kind of battering. A relief had been asked for and duly arrived on board. I was sorry to lose Cosmo. I respected his outward imperturbability.

Winter 1941/42: ice on
a signal projector on
board HMS *Sheffield*
November 1941, with
Arctic Convoy PQ5.
(A6872)

The welcome for convoys arriving in Russia was usually cold both in climatic and human terms:

Our arrival in Kola Inlet was eerie. It was December and pretty dark. There were great swirls of fog, black water and white snow-covered ice. The bare rocks on either side of the inlet were menacing and the silence was broken only by constant sounding of mournful fog-horns of various pitches. Altogether it was a forbidding place. I felt that if Hell were to be cold, this would be a foretaste of it.

A run ashore in Polyarnoe:

For once the Russians were almost friendly and, suitably fortified with cherry brandy, we were bidden to an entertainment at the Red Navy Club. After the choir performance there was music and a dance floor around which sat some rather square-shaped women, some of whom danced with Russian officers. Naturally we approached the 'girls' to ask for a dance. The lady would look horrified and glance across to one of the commissar officers, who would give a little nod, and the unfortunate girl, terrified, would do a quick round of the floor and retreat rapidly to her bench again. The feeling of fear was palpable, and once again one wondered about a system like that. Next day Jon and I went skiing in death valley and wandered about the dreary streets, full of sentries and large women sweepers.

Life ashore in Kola for the ratings was even more dismal.

The baleful influence of the German heavy surface units, and *Tirpitz* in particular, was never more acutely felt than in the affair of Russian Convoy PQ17. At the end of June 1942 PQ17 sailed, consisting of thirty-six merchant ships loaded with aircraft, tanks, vehicles and thousands of tons of supplies for the sorely pressed Red Army. They followed the route normally followed by Russian convoys in summer: north of Iceland after the escorts had refuelled at Reykjavik, north of Bear Island in the Barents Sea, and into Kola. The close escort consisted of eleven destroyers and corvettes, and four trawlers. The 1st Cruiser Squadron consisting of four cruisers and three destroyers would cover the convoy as far as Bear Island. Admiral Tovey in HMS *Duke of York*, with the battleship USS *Washington*, the carrier *Victorious*, two cruisers and fourteen destroyers, would provide support standing off north-east of Jan Mayen Island.

A week after sailing, when the convoy was approaching Bear Island, an assessment based on incomplete signals intelligence received in the Admiralty convinced Pound, the First Sea Lord, that *Tirpitz* was at sea heading for PQ17. His staff disagreed with the assessment. Unfortunately, Pound overruled them and Tovey, the commander on the spot, and in a disastrous example of back-seat driving, ordered the convoy to scatter. The extracts from the diary of Captain Cecil Harcourt RN, commanding Tovey's flagship, the battleship *Duke of York*:

4th July

Late in the evening Admiralty ordered PQ17 to scatter & CS1 [1st Cruiser Squadron] to withdraw to the westward at high speed. The former order seems rather premature. During the latter part of the day, we had stood to the south-west but at 22.00, we stood

to the north-east again, so as to provide cover for CS1 to fall back on if engaged by heavy forces.

5th July

In the evening *Tirpitz* and *Hipper* were seen out to the north-west of North Cape.

Tirpitz was recalled that day, and the scattered convoy left to be torn to pieces by U-boats and the Luftwaffe. After *Bismarck's* demise, Hitler never allowed his heavy units to go to sea if the whereabouts of carriers was uncertain. Within hours, thanks to Ultra, *Tirpitz's* recall was known to the Admiralty; too late. Only eleven ships from PQ17 reached Kola. Sent to the bottom in the holds of twenty-five ships were 210 aircraft, 430 tanks, 3,350 trucks and 99,316 tons of spare parts and other supplies. Meanwhile the Red Army was reeling under the hammer blows of German Army Groups A and B, who by the end of July had reached the River Don, at one point only seventy-five miles from Stalingrad, and were set to go forward to the Volga and the Caucasus.

Russian convoys were to continue until May 1945. The frigate *Goodall* was torpedoed by U-968 off Kola on 29 April that year, the last ship torpedoed on this route, and last major loss to the Royal Navy in the Second World War.

The third strand of the German maritime strategy for prosecuting the war was attacks on east coast convoys in the Channel and North Sea, mainly by their coastal forces [all called E-boats by the British]. Against the German coastal forces were ranged the motor gun boats (MGBs) and motor torpedo boats (MTBs) of the Royal Navy's coastal forces based along the east coast. At first, in general terms, the MTBs were designed for anti-shipping strikes, and

Torpedoes being loaded on to MTBs at Felixstowe. (A12909)

Coastal forces captains coming ashore after a successful action off the Dutch coast in 1943.
Left to right:
Lieutenant W. Harrop RNVR, Lieutenant P. C. Wilkinson RNVR, Lieutenant-Commander Donald G. Bradford RNR (Flotilla Leader), Lieutenant D. G. Dowling RNVR, Lieutenant J. A. H. Whitby RNVR.
(A19264)

the MGBs for protecting the MTBs and also hitting the German E-boats. Later, the MTB became an all-rounder, as Commander, as he was to become, Donald Bradford RNVR explains:

The Fairmile designed C class MGB was a sturdy heavily constructed craft, possessing the great advantage of a low silhouette, and very great gunpower for its size. On the hull the following armament was carried: a two-pounder pom-pom forward, in a power-operated turret, two pairs of twin .303-inch machine-guns, two twin .5-inch Vickers machine-guns in power-operated turrets amidships (subsequently replaced by two twin Oerlikon cannon), one twin Oerlikon cannon abaft the .5 machine-gun turrets, and a 2-pounder pom-pom aft, plus depth charges, and sub-machine guns and hand grenades for close quarter fighting and boarding.

Unfortunately the C class MGB could not close with the enemy in a stern chase to bring this formidable array of guns to bear, because its maximum speed was 26 knots against the E-boats' 35 (increased to nearly 50 knots later in the War). The D type MTB, which came into service in mid 1942, was bigger and faster, although still around 20 knots slower than its adversary. Its gunpower was impressive, including a 6-pounder automatic forward, and one aft, as well as two twin .5-inch and two twin .303-inch machine-guns, a twin Oerlikon, and two rocket projectors. These boats also carried two 21-inch or four 18-inch torpedoes. The 6-pounder was a naval adaption of the Army's high velocity, flat trajectory anti-tank gun, with automatic feed added. Donald Bradford, a Marks & Spencer branch manager in peacetime, was one of the ace skippers and

Lieutenant G. C. Dickens RN (great-grandson of Charles Dickens) after leading an attack on German armed trawlers off the Dutch coast. *Left to right:* Sub-Lieutenant David Moore RNZVR, Sub-Lieutenant George Macdonald RNZVR, Lieutenant Dickens, Lieutenant A. C. Jensen RNVR, Sub-Lieutenant Gordon Fish RNVR. (A15978)

flotilla leaders of coastal forces. In March 1943, his boat and another were lying in wait for E-boats on a pitch black night:

Guns manned and engines ready to spring into life we had lain there for three hours, rocking and rolling on the long low swell. Suddenly I caught the faint murmur of engines carried down on the breeze. They had come. I pressed the buzzers for a 'crash start', and just before the roar of the three supercharged engines burst with shattering effect on our eardrums, I heard the slam of the breech of the forward pom-pom as the gunner settled himself in readiness. I cast a last hurried glance round the boat to reassure myself. There was no need of it, my gang of scallywags, as usual bursting for a fight, were set and ready.

Bradford and the other MGB intercepted five E-boats:

They made no effort to escape, and indeed gave no indication that they had seen us. I closed at speed, until at a range of about forty yards, I felt the moment had arrived, and ordered 'open fire'. At forty yards my guns couldn't miss. The E-boat shuddered and jerked as the gunners smothered it with high explosive. The opposition was feeble, a small squirt of light machine-gun fire from the E-boat. But it hit the magazine of an Oerlikon, and the remaining rounds burned and exploded. However there was nothing to be done about it in the thick of the action. I concentrated on a quick kill, and edged in closer. I could see large chunks flying off the E-boat's hull, and the deck lifting as our heavy stuff ripped into its side and exploded.

Frank was enjoying himself with the twin light machine-guns on the bridge just behind me. Squirting into the E-boat's bridge as fast as he could replace the empty pans,

Convoy PQ18 September
1942. The escort carrier
HMS *Avenger* with six
Hurricanes embarked. This
was the first Arctic convoy
to have an escort carrier.
(FL1268)

he was practically sawing it in half. The empty rounds rattled around our bridge, spattering my ears and down my collar in their hundreds.

We pressed in closer to twenty yards. The Oerlikon came back into action again. The crew had torn off the burning magazine, thrown it overboard, and put on another. With a belch of flame from the E-boat, her decks folded back as if hinged. She disintegrated and disappeared. I ducked as a deluge of wood and metal rattled down on our decks.

The leading E-boat was about fifty yards away, slightly ahead of us, firing at us. The other E-boats had vanished, as had my partner after them. I risked a depth charge from the leader, and cut across his wake, opening fire on him as I crossed. He was turning rapidly to get away, as I increased to full speed to overtake him, and drew up on his port side at about forty yards range. My guns were hitting him heavily, we had him cold, then the forward pom-pom jammed. I decided to ram, rather than risk his escape. Ringing the signal for 'ramming stations' on the alarm bells, I grabbed the wheel from the Coxswain, and spun it hard to starboard as we bore down on him. We hit, about twenty feet from the stern. The sharp bronze shoe on the bows of my boat bit into soft wood as she lifted and rode partly over the low after deck of the E-boat. I could feel her crunching her way through, deep into her vitals, as the E-boat broke. The stern came off and slid down my starboard side, and the remainder down the port side; we had bitten straight through.

Bradford pursued the other three boats, but they got away.

At daybreak we entered harbour to be met at the quayside by practically the whole Base staff. We received a tremendous welcome. It was the first time for many months that the E-boats had really been decisively defeated on our convoy route by a boat from Yarmouth.

By May 1943, Doenitz had lost the Battle of the Atlantic, but was to continue the U-boat war for two more years. Right up to May 1943, there were moments when it appeared that the Allies would lose. March 1943 was one of the worst months of the whole War for shipping losses, exceeded on only three other occasions. If the loss rate of March 1943 had been continued, there would have been no question of opening the Second Front the Russians were clamouring for, no question of further amphibious assaults in the Mediterranean, following the Torch landings in North Africa in November 1942, no question of winning the War. A number of measures turned the tide. Perhaps the most significant was the extension of air power to cover the whole of the Atlantic convoy routes, using land-based aircraft and escort carriers with the convoys. Many would argue that just as important were improved radar, support groups of hunter-killer sloops, frigates and destroyers, and 'hedgehog'. In a depth-charge attack, dustbin-like containers filled with explosives were dropped over the stern. The ship had to pass over the submerged U-boat, which as it heard the propellers overhead could crank on speed and evade, sure that it would not be picked up by Asdic in the turbulence of the attacker's wake and the noise of the explosions. It often took minutes, or even hours, for the escort to 'acquire' the U-boat again. Sometimes contact was never re-established. Hedgehog threw

Convoy PQ18, the ammunition ship *Mary Luckenback* exploding after being torpedoed in an air attack on 14 September 1942. Ten out of forty Merchant ships were lost on this convoy, but it marked a turning-point in north Russian convoys. (A12275)

a pattern of projectiles ahead of the attacking ship, so that loss of contact was far less frequent. There was one other vital factor: the codebreakers at Bletchley Park succeeded in breaking the cypher used in the radio messages tasking U-boats at sea. As U-boat losses mounted, so more inexperienced skippers and crews went to sea, and the losses spiralled. Most important, all the techno-logical measures, and the persistence, patience, ingenuity and fighting spirit of sailors and airmen, principally from Britain, Canada and the United States, combined to make May 1943 the turning point of the Second World War.

Before 1943 ended, one more drama was played out in the Arctic gales, ice and fog off north Norway. On Christmas day 1943, the German battle cruiser *Scharnhorst* (Captain Hintz, Flag Rear-Admiral Bey), escorted by five destroyers, sailed from Altenfjord in north Norway, heading for the Russian convoy routes in the Barents Sea. She still had Christmas decorations up in her mess decks. Thanks to Ultra, Admiral Sir Bruce Fraser, C.-in-C. Home Fleet in *Duke of York*, had been forewarned. Lieutenant Alec Dennis, in *Savage,* some days before Christmas:

Evidently something was in the wind, because all the way to Iceland we were engaged in a rather strenuous series of exercises, including a 'night encounter', which we didn't welcome at the time because it cut into our short ration of sleep, but which later proved its value.

After arrival in Iceland:

My evening was made by an invitation to dinner with Admiral Fraser in the Flagship. He asked the Captains, Executive Officers and Engineer Officers of the Group. After dinner

Vice-Admiral Sir Bruce Fraser inspects a Royal Marines guard of honour after taking command of the Home Fleet in May 1943. He was appointed second-in-command Home Fleet in 1942, C.-in-C. Home Fleet in the rank of Admiral from 1943 to 1944, C.-in-C. Eastern Fleet in August 1944, and C.-in-C. British Pacific Fleet from November 1944 to the end of the war against Japan. (A16486)

he told us what was up. He had good reason to believe that the next convoy would be attacked by *Scharnhorst*. At the time we assumed that this intelligence must have come from Norwegian sources. The C.-in-C. ran over his plan, which was to keep in the offing until the convoy was attacked and then get in between *Scharnhorst* and her base. He demonstrated his tactics with pepper-pots and said he planned for *Duke of York* to open fire at 12,000 yards, while we destroyers went in to attack with torpedoes.

Thus did Admiral Fraser, in the great tradition of Nelson, take his captains into his confidence, relying on their initiative to fight the battle according to his overall design, with the minimum of orders. Like Nelson's band of brothers they set out, confident of the outcome. Dennis:

He was so simple, cheerful and amiable that I felt it was rather like an exercise. Indeed we rehearsed the action next day, with *Jamaica* taking the part of the enemy.

On Christmas Day two convoys were at sea, RA55A homebound and almost out of danger, and JW55B, outbound. In midwinter in these northern latitudes the sun does not rise over the horizon at any time. At best, at midday, a steely

Ice and snow on HMS *Belfast*. She played a crucial role at the Battle of North Cape shadowing *Scharnhorst*. (A20687)

gloom is all the light available. In the vicinity of JW55B were the cruisers *Belfast* (flag), *Norfolk* and *Sheffield* of Vice-Admiral Burnett's 10th Cruiser Squadron (CS10).

Richard Butler in *Matchless*:

It was about ten degrees below zero on the open bridgedeck. It penetrated the thick Arctic clothing and cut right through us. At 00.00 hours, Christmas Day, the Admiralty transmitted, 'Merry Christmas All.' Some bloody Merry Christmas we were having. Shortly after receiving these cosy greetings, Captain D3 [3rd Destroyer Flotilla], instructed four destroyers *Musketeer*, *Matchless*, *Opportune* and *Virago* to leave the homeward bound convoy, and join the Russia bound JW55B. There were nineteen freighters and the escort strengthened to fourteen when our four joined.

Next day, Boxing Day, Lieutenant-Commander Graham Lumsden, now navigating officer of the *Sheffield*:

At 08.40 we made radar contact with an enemy heading south at high speed and 09.20 we in *Sheffield* sighted *Scharnhorst* now steering east, seven miles on our port beam.

She was alone, having detached her destroyers to search for the convoy. They never rejoined. Despite her two radars, *Scharnhorst* had been unaware of the approach of CS10 until she was illuminated by star shell, followed by a salvo of 8-inch shells from *Norfolk*, one of which burst on *Scharnhorst*'s foretop causing a number of casualties and destroying her forward radar.

Hintz increased to 30 knots, turning to circle round Burnett and attack the convoy. Burnett, whose cruisers could not match the battle-cruiser's speed in the heavy seas, decided to head straight for the convoy, and interpose between it and *Scharnhorst*. Meanwhile Fraser in *Duke of York*, with the cruiser *Jamaica* and four destroyers, was 200 miles away to the west steaming at best speed with a south-westerly gale under their tails, to get between *Scharnhorst* and her base. Lumsden:

As soon as we encountered the convoy, we took station ten miles to the east. We were soon joined by four destroyers from the convoy. On joining the senior officer signalled; 'Am awaiting your instructions to attack.'

Our Admiral replied, 'Attack what?'

'Anything that turns up.'

Richard Butler in *Matchless*:

A very strong south-westerly gale was blowing with flurries of snow and huge white-crested waves picking up our ship and flinging it around.

At midday CS10's radar again picked up *Scharnhorst* approaching from the east; Burnett had been right. Lumsden:

All three ships engaged with forward guns at a range of five and a half miles, reducing at a mile a minute. We plunged towards each other through rough seas at high speed. *Scharnhorst* first engaged *Norfolk*, as foreseen by her Captain in Iceland. [Of the three cruisers, *Norfolk* had 8-inch guns, the other two 6-inch.] She hit *Norfolk* twice with her second salvo; a huge pillar of flame shot up from her X turret, her cordite supply had caught fire, but the anti-flash arrangements saved her from exploding. She briefly reduced speed to fight the fire, but our Admiral ordered her to 'Keep up in case *Scharnhorst* should be too much encouraged.' I took up a strategic position behind the binnacle, which offered some psychological protection; others similarly fooled themselves that the front of the bridge offered some cover against 11-inch shells. All of our ships were using tracer shells of various colours. We could watch the groups of shells from our own ships flying through their arc right up to the point when they fell on the target. Her shells could only be seen from the moment they were fired until they dipped over towards us at the top of their trajectory. Having hit *Norfolk*, *Scharnhorst* switched to *Sheffield*. The first salvo landed with a tremendous crash close to our starboard side, raising huge dark splashes.

HMS *Savage* Pennant Number G20. (Papers of Commander J. A. J. Dennis RN 95/5/1 negative number DOC522)

Scharnhorst obtained no more hits on the cruisers weaving at high speed. Although the British inflicted no further damage either, Bey had had enough

and decided to turn for home. Earlier he had ordered his destroyers to close the convoy, whose position had been signalled by a U-boat. Luckily, the position given was incorrect, and before the destroyers could locate the convoy, Bey ordered them back to Norway. Richard Butler:

From then on, all through the afternoon, we sped south-south-east at 30 knots shadowing *Scharnhorst*. The weather conditions were appalling, accentuated by the high speed necessary to keep up the chase. Huge rolling grey swells swept up on the starboard bow, making the ship roll dangerously to each side for minutes at a time, before slowly coming upright again. All day we were closed up to Action Stations and feeding on soggy sandwiches. Those of us on the bridge were soaked through as the bows tore into the incoming waves, flinging sea water in a continual stream over fo'c's'le and bridge. We had to shout to be heard in the gale as we tried to keep our balance on the heaving decks, hanging grimly on. Now and again, through the spray, the phantom shapes of the other ships could be seen before being lost in the gloom.

Lumsden:

At 16.15, with *Scharnhorst* retiring some six miles ahead of us, we detected *Duke of York* on our radar, twenty miles away on our starboard bow, in a perfect position to intercept the enemy.

Fraser had ordered his four destroyers, *Savage*, *Saumarez*, *Scorpion* and *Stord*, out ahead of him, from where they could launch a torpedo attack when the time came. At 16.15, *Duke of York*'s radar picked up *Scharnhorst* at twenty-three miles. At 16.39, Fraser signalled Burnett, 'Prepare to fire star shell over enemy.' At 16.50, *Savage* signalled to C.-in-C. Home Fleet: 'Enemy in sight bearing 020.' At that moment, *Belfast* illuminated the target, and *Duke of York*'s and *Jamaica*'s first salvos crashed out. Both were deadly. *Duke of York*'s full broadside totalled 15,950 lb (seven tons) of shells, 9,290 lb heavier than *Scharnhorst*'s full broadside, although *Scharnhorst*'s 11-inch guns outranged *Duke of York*'s 14-inch guns by over 8,000 yards. *Duke of York* was pitching and rolling in the enormous waves, taking it green over her bow. But thanks to her high state of training and superb Type 284 gunnery radar, two shells from her first broadside hit, as did one of *Jamaica*'s. One of *Duke of York*'s 14-inch shells completely disabled *Scharnhorst*'s A turret, cutting her gunpower by a third. But she was by no means out of action, and was faster than *Duke of York* by over 3 knots. As the range opened in the running fight, eventually only *Duke of York* could hit *Scharnhorst*. Because of the appalling visibility and damage to *Scharnhorst*'s main radar, despite her range advantage, she scored no hits on *Duke of York*. Just as Fraser thought that *Scharnhorst* must escape, he heard that *Savage*, *Scorpion*, *Saumarez* and *Stord* were attacking with torpedoes. Unknown to the C.-in-C., *Duke of York* had hit *Scharnhorst* hard yet again. One shell had wrecked B turret, leaving her with only three guns of her main armament in action. The other, even more telling, had burst in the starboard boiler room, reducing her speed to 10 knots. Although damage control measures and devoted work by her engine room crew served to increase this to 22 knots, it was not good enough to outrun the pursuing destroyers. Dennis in *Savage*:

My position was on X gun deck aft, and well away from the bridge, in a position to take over command if the Captain were wiped out. We managed to work up to some 34 knots with a heavy swell on the quarter. It was hard to keep one's footing, and we hung on to guns and ammunition lockers for life. Orders came from the bridge to illuminate the enemy with star shell so we pooped off with X gun, using flashless cordite.

After a while *Scharnhorst* must have seen us, as they started to shoot with their secondary armament, 5.9-inch guns. To our astonishment, just as we felt we would never get into a good firing position, the battle-cruiser turned about, and came down in a cloud of smoke, placing us in a perfect position on her bow. It turned out that *Scorpion* and *Stord* had been hitherto unobserved, and had worked their way up *Scharnhorst*'s other side. She had turned to avoid their torpedoes, and was about to run into ours. She was a superb sight, massive yet elegant. She appeared to be a light grey colour in the light of the star shell falling eerily about her. We got off all eight torpedoes at very close range; about 3,000 yards.

Astern of us *Saumarez* went even closer, and rather unwisely, to my mind, opened fire with her 4.7-inch guns, which could have done little damage, but attracted a salvo or two from *Scharnhorst*, which killed or wounded about 20 men, and resulted in *Saumarez* being able to fire only four out of her eight torpedoes.

Stoker Kenneth Evans in *Saumarez*:

Ammunition supply to one of the 4.7-inch was my action station if not on watch in the engine room. There was a blinding flash, our gun was hit. Next thing I remember was another boy lying alongside me with his stomach hanging out. I couldn't feel my legs and thought they were blown off. Actually they had been cut across by shrapnel, and were doubled under me. An officer gave me a morphine injection. I came to on a stretcher below decks with a drip set up. Other stretchers were alongside, some with dead and dying.

Of the total of twenty-eight torpedoes fired by the four destroyers, three hit *Scharnhorst*. Two caused serious flooding aft, but the most deadly wrecked A boiler room, and bent a propeller shaft. The battle-cruiser's speed was again reduced to 10 knots. Alec Dennis:

As soon as we got rid of our 'fish', we hauled away into the darkness. Within minutes we were drinking hot cocoa, and blessing our lucky ship. No killed and only a few wounded. We lay off and kept an eye on the wounded *Saumarez*, while the rest of the Fleet moved in and started to pound the wretched *Scharnhorst* to pieces.

After a while, Fraser ordered *Belfast* and *Jamaica* to finish her with torpedoes. Each fired three, but *Scharnhorst* was masked in smoke, and all missed.

Reloading 4.7-inch guns in HMS *Eskimo*, a Tribal class destroyer, in February 1942.
(A7716)

Jamaica fired three more, two hit, and *Scharnhorst* stopped firing. *Belfast* was closing for the kill, when her target was masked by the destroyers *Opportune*, *Virago*, *Musketeer* and *Matchless* hurrying up to be in at the death. Butler in *Matchless*:

In the gloom I could see *Scharnhorst* listing to starboard with a dull red glow illuminating her through clouds of billowing smoke. We increased speed to the maximum; 36 knots. As we turned to port to fire our torpedoes from the starboard side, we headed into the incoming seas. Our speed caused the ship to bury its bows deep into the huge waves, sending solid water over the fo'c's'le and bridge. By the time we on the bridge had sorted ourselves out, the chance to fire our torpedoes had gone. We couldn't have fired them anyway, because the massive waves sweeping inboard amidships had sprained [*sic*] the torpedo tubes rendering them ineffective. The final minutes of the battle were like a scrimmage, as destroyers darted around from every quarter at fast speeds in the gloom. *Musketeer* bore down on us from dead ahead after her torpedo run, and we passed down her port side much too close for comfort.

Lumsden:

Eventually every ship with any remaining torpedoes closed in and fired them at the now helpless and hapless ship. As always, one had to admire their bravery.

At 19.45, *Scharnhorst* sank, taking almost 2,000 of her company with her. None of the thirteen 14-inch shells, and twelve or so 8-inch, plus several from destroyers' guns, had sunk her. It was the eleven torpedoes that finished her. That she could absorb such punishment was a tribute to her designers, builders, and gallant crew. To begin with there was some doubt about whether or not she had sunk, and some anxious signals followed:

20.14 To: *Scorpion* From: C.-in-C. HF
    Please confirm *Scharnhorst* sunk.
20.18 To: *Scorpion* From: C.-in-C. HF
    Has *Scharnhorst* sunk?
20.25 To: C.-in-C. HF From: CS10
    Survivors in *Matchless* say *Scharnhorst* sunk.
20.31 To: C.-in-C. HF From: CS10
    Satisfied *Scharnhorst* sunk. Where should I join you?

Finally:

20.55 To: Admiralty via Scapa W/T From: C.-in-C. HF
    Scharnhorst sunk.
21.36 To: C.-in-C. HF (R) CS10 From: Admiralty
    Grand Well Done.

Richard Butler:

It was uncannily quiet as the ship drifted in the swell on stopped engines. The seas still big didn't seem to be so menacing as we drifted in the snow flurries. The eerie silence was broken by a whistle blown on our port beam. The Captain ordered me to switch on our port twenty-inch lamp and use it as a searchlight. The first thing I saw illuminated was three German sailors clinging desperately to a small raft, gazing up at us with shellshocked faces before disappearing for ever as the ship drifted into the main area of wreckage. The carnage was horrifying. Mingled among the wreckage and fuel oil were lifeless bodies held afloat by life jackets. One, a few feet away, floated by; his upturned face just submerged below the water appeared to have a green halo around it as I shone the lamp on him. Around him were many dead bodies, and what could have been fragments of bodies among the flotsam and jetsam.

Scrambling nets and lines were thrown over the side. Some of our crew risked their lives by going part way down the ship's side to grab hold of the exhausted sailors. Not all who reached the ship's side were rescued. Several rolled under the hull. Others desperately tried to hang on to the life ropes, but in their weakened state, they gave up and slipped back into the sea. Nearly all were slick with fuel oil.

Our Captain shouted repeatedly down to the German sailors, 'Ist *Scharnhorst* gesunken?', but in the chaos there was no firm answer. A few hundred yards away to starboard, I saw the destroyer *Scorpion* with lights around her stern also, picking up survivors out of the icy water. Between the two of us we rescued 36 sailors, but no officers. I knew if we had stayed longer, many more would have been rescued, but the C.-in-C. gave orders by Fleet Wave radio to sail for Murmansk, 'My course 090 degrees, follow me.'

Our Captain said; 'Douse that light, Signalman, we don't want to give any false hopes.' To the deck he shouted, 'Cut those nets free, we're getting under way.'

The frantic shouts from German sailors still alive in the water on the darkened starboard side as the ship began to move, when they realised they were being left behind, will haunt me for the rest of my life. U-boats could have been in the vicinity, and we could have been at risk if we had stayed longer. Stoker PO Denis Wells saw several German seamen drawn into our propellers as we got under-way. AB Sandy Manson heard German sailors singing in the water.

Our six survivors were given hammocks to sleep in and kitted out with dry clothing. They were given rum to drink, as most had swallowed fuel oil and sea water.

The sinking of *Scharnhorst* marked the end of the attempts to attack the sea lanes by heavy units of the German fleet. Although *Tirpitz* remained skulking in the Norwegian fjords, she never emerged again.

On the way back from Murmansk to Scapa in filthy weather, Richard Butler was on duty, when a signal came in ordering *Matchless* to investigate a radar contact. He threw the message over the side:

for us to go and investigate by ourselves on this dark and stormy night could have been the end of *Matchless*. The only reason I acted so stupidly must have been the exacting events of the last few days and nights that affected my nerves.

The next day he was summoned to see the Captain.

'What happened to the signal during the night from the Flagship?'

'I thought it was for another destroyer, and only repeated to us, Sir.'

The CO very angrily told me that because of my stupidity, he had some explaining to do to the C.-in-C. I thought I would really get it in the neck, but surprisingly was dismissed without being punished. Our benign acting CO must have realised that this 'stupid young bugger', like most of the crew, was beginning to feel nervy and my liking for him grew.

As 1943 had seen the turning point in the Atlantic, so it had in the Mediterranean.

ONE U-BOAT BATTLE IN MAY 1943

An escort group commanded by Lieutenant-Commander Evelyn Chavasse RN, in the destroyer *Broadway*, fought one of the convoy battles at the turning point of the Battle of the Atlantic:

Convoy HX237 from Halifax to UK started in annoyance, chaos and complete frustration. My Escort Group consisted of the *Broadway*, the only destroyer, the River class frigate *Lagan*, the British corvette *Primrose*, the Canadian corvettes, *Morden*, *Drumheller* and *Chambly*, the trawler *Vizalma* and a tug. But, best of all, I was allotted for the first time a 'Woolworth Carrier', equipped with Swordfish aircraft, HMS *Biter*, and three splendid Home Fleet destroyers, *Opportune*, *Obdurate* and *Pathfinder*. All were senior to me, but I was senior officer of the escort and they played the game magnificently.

At what Chavasse calls a 'council of war', the 'four stripe' Captain of *Biter* refused to come inside the convoy and insisted on operating some fifty miles away, taking the three fleet destroyers to screen him. Nothing that Chavasse said would dissuade him.

The 8th May was still misty. *Biter* operated independently some 50 miles north of us. She sent out some air searches, but all of her aircraft failed to find the convoy, and were useless in detecting any U-boat in a threatening position. The following day, the weather deteriorated, and the *Biter* was unable to fly off aircraft. In the low visibility I took the opportunity of refuelling from a tanker in the centre of the convoy. We were still sucking greedily, when *Broadway* intercepted a wireless transmission from a U-boat close astern of the convoy. While we were disconnecting from the hose-pipe, I ordered *Primrose*, stationed astern, to search and attack. I told *Biter*, but she couldn't do anything useful, as she didn't know where we were. *Primrose* sighted the U-boat, but she dived, and Asdic contact was never made.

At that moment somebody in England must have had a brainwave. A signal was received from the Admiralty ordering *Biter* to join and enter the convoy. This was exactly what I had fought for at our 'council of war'. It paid dividends. *Biter* joined us next day, 10 May, and the Commodore made her a nice manoeuvre space bang in the middle, where she was safe and useful. We were now a co-ordinated team. *Biter*'s aircraft scoured the seas all round the convoy, her destroyers, with their 30 knots plus, streaking ferociously out to put the fear of God into any U-boat spotted by aircraft, forcing it to dive and go blind. My own little team, perhaps a little more experienced in these matters, provided the close protection of the convoy. Navy list seniority went to the four winds and everyone was keen to do what I asked.

As soon as the *Biter* boys joined us things began to happen thick and fast. *Primrose*'s U-boat had evidently spread the news about us, and we had received a few more HF/DF bearings of U-boat signals, but now they began pouring in from various directions. It was clear to me that a wolf pack was forming mainly to the north of us.

On each occasion I asked *Biter* to send out a search. Several U-boats were sighted. For the most part the U-boat stayed on the surface to fight it out with the contemptible Swordfish (one pilot was wounded) [Chavasse is not being critical of the aircrews, but of the policy that led to them having to fight in such an obsolete aircraft], but as soon as the destroyers came roaring up, they dived in some haste. These tactics prevented the U-boats from concentrating or even getting near the convoy. The Admiralty estimated there were six U-boats trying to close with us. As soon as we were within range of the Azores, shore-based aircraft were sent to operate under my direction.

Every night I expected surface attacks, as night flying from *Biter* was not possible. But Jerry couldn't face it and our nights were quiet, except for continuous U-boat chatter on HF.

Through the following days, it was a busy time in my operations room plotting U-boat reports, analysing them, and directing aircraft, ship and shore-based. Aircraft from shore and from *Biter* claimed to have damaged more than one U-boat with depth charges. But the destroyers, who were trained for surface battles, had no luck. It was terribly dull for *Lagan* and the corvettes whom I kept with myself round the convoy.

On 12 May, an aircraft from *Biter* reported a U-boat on the surface six miles dead ahead of the convoy. I told the Commodore to turn the convoy 90 degrees to starboard. I increased to 29 knots to attack, calling *Lagan* to follow. I handed command of the Escort to young Lieutenant Kitto in *Primrose*. Meanwhile the aircraft had attacked with depth charges, and possibly damaged the U-boat which had dived. The aircraft, short of fuel, dropped a smoke marker on the spot where the U-boat had dived, and returned to the convoy. Reducing speed, I almost immediately got a firm Asdic contact; the hunt was on.

My first attack by Hedgehog missed. *Lagan* came trundling up, obtained contact and likewise missed. There followed a prolonged hunt. The U-boat was a wily bird, had dived to about 400 feet, where she twisted and turned like a snake. *Lagan* and I shared the hunt, if one lost contact, the other regained it. Finally the lot happened to fall on *Broadway*. A salvo of bombs from our hedgehog soared into the air, splashed in a neat circle 250 yards ahead, and after the usual pause, we were rewarded with a lovely bang. We had hit her fair and square.

Early next morning, a Sunderland from home attacked another U-boat, which had managed to get uncomfortably close to the starboard side of the convoy. *Drumheller*, who was nearest, closed, obtained Asdic contact, and made a good depth-charge attack, which seems to have immobilised the U-boat. *Lagan*, whom I sent to help, strolled up and sank it.

And the battle was over. Just as we felt we were getting into our stride, *Biter* and her destroyers were withdrawn to assist another convoy in peril. Simultaneously, any survivors of 'our' wolf pack evidently decided to give it up as a bad job. An unearthly silence descended over our stretch of the Atlantic, which for the past five days had been almost deafening with German and British radio.

By the end of the month, all U-boats had been temporarily withdrawn from the North Atlantic. For us it was indeed a merry month of May.

8
The Mediterranean: 1942–1943

By the end of 1941, attacks by submarines, surface ships and aircraft on Axis convoys to North Africa had resulted in losses of 63 per cent. Hitler had earlier responded by sending four more U-boats to the Mediterranean, bringing the total number of [German] boats up to ten. It was one of the new arrivals that had sunk *Ark Royal* [Chapter Five], thus temporarily depriving the Royal Navy in all theatres of war of any modern carriers. Both *Illustrious* and *Formidable* were undergoing repair in the United States, and *Indomitable* had damaged herself running aground in the West Indies while working up her air group.

In early 1942 Hitler ordered Fliegerkorps II from Russia, where they were desperately needed, to Sicily and North Africa. In this and other ways, the British efforts in the Mediterranean had a considerable effect on the distant war in Russia. With Fliegerkorps X in the eastern Mediterranean, the new arrivals would form Luftflotte 2 under Field Marshal Kesselring. The Field Marshal had been ordered to obtain air and sea superiority between North Africa and Italy to ensure the safe passage of convoys to Axis forces in Libya and Cyrenaica. To do this, it was important to suppress Malta. In addition, he was to prevent Allied shipping passing through the Mediterranean, and particularly to stop the re-supply of Malta and Tobruk.

Malta was the linchpin of the British land and sea campaigns in the Mediterranean theatre of operations, and a thorn in the side of the enemy. From here submarines and aircraft sortied to sink Axis transports.

If the defences of the island could be crushed, or the garrison starved, the situation in this theatre might turn permanently in the favour of the Axis powers. Therefore it was vital for the British to keep Malta's air defences as strong as possible. Spitfires for air defence had been flown in from the ancient carriers *Argus* and *Eagle*, to augment the Hurricanes. But anti-shipping strike aircraft were also needed, if the island was to fulfil its function as a base for attacks on Axis convoys. In February 1942 it was decided that torpedo-carrying aircraft should be flown in from Egypt. Sub-Lieutenant Alan Swanton RN had been sent to Egypt with 821 Naval Air Squadron:

There weren't any Swordfish available, but the Fairey Aviation Company had brought out a successor, the Albacore, and some had been shipped out in packing cases to Fayid airfield near Suez. Although it was supposed to be a considerable advance on the Swordfish, I never felt the same confidence in the Albacore as I did for the trusty old 'Stringbag', for all its shortcomings.

Although not qualified to fly Albacores, he had once flown one illegally in England:

In Egypt at the sharp end, the fact that I had once flown an Albacore was the only confirmation the authorities needed of my competence. I had teamed up with an Irishman named Kevin Gibney, and for the next couple of weeks we did our best to learn as much as we could about our new aircraft in preparation for our night flight to Hal Far, the RN airfield at Malta. The plan was that a pair of aircraft should fly there from a forward landing ground near the coast [of that part of North Africa still in British hands]. Even so it entailed a long flight over the sea, so an extra fuel tank was installed in the rearmost cockpit, normally occupied by the telegraphist/air gunner. Before our arrival in Egypt, my total night flying experience amounted to 18 hours, and by the time we were due to leave for Malta, I had managed to notch up only a couple more hours.

The departure 'landing ground' (LG) for Malta was El Adem:

On this particular night the sole illumination was provided by the shaded lights of a vehicle on the far side of the LG. We lumbered off into the darkness with our extra load of fuel, while the accompanying aircraft maintained formation on my dimmed lights.

We reached the sea, when the second aircraft suddenly burst into flames. Kevin and I watched the fireball descending until it hit the sea and was extinguished. It seemed unlikely that it could have been the victim of a night fighter, we had seen no tracer, and only our aircraft had shown lights. For a while we felt utterly impotent and dejected, but there was nothing for it but to grit our teeth and press on. It was very evident from the expletives from the rear cockpit that all was not well with the W/T set and that Kevin was having no success in contacting Malta.

At last we spotted searchlights in the far distance, and altered course slightly towards them. As we drew nearer and saw flashes in the sky, it dawned on us that we were sharing the airspace with an unknown number of enemy aircraft, and with our unserviceable wireless, it wasn't going to be easy to establish our identity. Fortunately it was still dark, and we decided to bide our time and mingle inconspicuously with the other aircraft above Malta. I fervently hoped they would go away before it began to get light, or our fuel ran out. After a time the furore died down, we cautiously approached the airfield, and identified ourselves by flashing the letter of the day. The runway was illuminated, and we landed with a sigh of relief after an eventful six and a half hour flight.

Here they experienced life in Malta under siege in early 1942:

There were air raids practically every night, and on our second night, a bomb landed a bit too close for comfort. We decided to repair to the air raid shelter, but it was so full, we returned to our beds in the fond belief that lightning never strikes in the same place twice. Our attempts at sightseeing weren't a great success. No sooner had we disembarked from our transport at Valetta, than all hell broke loose. A dozen or so JU88s swept in and released a hail of bombs on the town and harbour. It was all over in a few minutes, but we seemed to lose our enthusiasm for exploring Malta's capital.

Our exodus from the island was aboard a Wellington bomber, en route for Cairo. It was a night flight, but we were so eager to get off, we didn't even give a thought to the fact that the young sergeant pilot was probably no more experienced than we were.

On 21 March, Cunningham decided to send in another convoy to Malta from Alexandria. It was to be met by the light cruiser *Penelope*, based in Malta, commanded by Captain Angus Nicholl RN:

Penelope and the destroyer *Legion* sailed from Malta to bring in our fifth convoy, *Breconshire*, *Clan Campbell*, *Pampas* and *Talabot*. The escort [from Alexandria] under Rear-Admiral Philip Vian consisted of 15th Cruiser Squadron, *Cleopatra*, *Euryalus* and *Dido*, the anti-aircraft [AA] cruiser *Carlisle* and fourteen destroyers. As *Penelope* joined we passed close to *Cleopatra*, and I could see Vian on the bridge greeting me by making a large V sign with his arms.

Our submarines off Italy had reported strong enemy forces leaving Taranto and Messina the previous night: the battleship *Littorio* with two heavy cruisers, one light cruiser and ten destroyers.

Vian, expecting an attack on a Malta convoy, had already rehearsed manoeuvres with the Alexandria forces, and issued written orders to meet such a situation. The cruisers were to engage the enemy while making smoke to hide the convoy; the AA cruiser and half the destroyers were to stay with the convoy to beat off air attacks; and the remaining destroyers were to make torpedo attacks on the enemy.

At 2.30 in the afternoon, *Euryalus* sighted smoke to the north-east, and hoisted the signal: 'Enemy in sight.'

Vian at once made the signal for: 'Carry out prearranged plan.'

The convoy and all the ships of the escort then began moving in various directions, but I had no knowledge of any prearranged plan. No copy of Vian's orders had reached *Penelope*. However there is a well tried course of action I had learned in destroyers, 'when in doubt, follow father'.

So I tacked on to Vian's cruisers and *Legion* joined up with the nearest destroyer division. Vian led us towards the enemy at high speed, all ships making smoke. The enemy turned out to be heavy cruisers, though in *Penelope* we could see nothing of them because of the smoke. *Cleopatra* and *Euryalus* began a long-range battle, and a number of shell splashes fell quite close to us. The smoke carried by a rising south-easterly wind was lying perfectly, completely screening the convoy from the enemy who turned away. Vian led us back to the convoy. Although I had no instructions, I had no difficulty in sensing what Vian wanted the cruisers to do.

However the Captain of *Dido* knew that *Penelope* should have been following him. He had also noticed that *Penelope*, though conforming to the movements of the other cruisers, was acting in a somewhat independent way. Not being quite certain who was in command of *Penelope*, he signalled:

'What is seniority of Captain?'

'June 1939,' I replied.

He was senior, and promptly hoisted the signal that means 'Take station astern'.

Now I knew *Penelope*'s position in the cruisers' battle formation. It was a great help.

During our absence the convoy had been under heavy air attack, but no ship had been hit. We had no sooner rejoined than once more the enemy came in sight to the north-west, this time led by the battleship *Littorio*, barring the way to Malta. Once more Vian led us straight at the enemy. For the next two and a half hours there was some very brisk fighting. Our cruisers, one after the other, darted out of the smoke, fired a few rounds at the enemy, or perhaps a torpedo, and dodged back into the smoke again whenever the enemy seemed to be getting our range. Each time we turned back towards the enemy through the smoke, I wondered if we would emerge to find ourselves at point-blank range from the Italian battleship. But *Littorio* held well away from the smoke, and the shortest range at which our guns fired was over six miles.

The Italian fleet would not close, despite their 15-inch, 8-inch and 6-inch armament far outgunning and outranging the 6-inch guns of the British light cruisers, and 4.7-inch and 4-inch of the destroyers. Able Seaman Eric Smith, in the destroyer *Legion*, takes up the story of the destroyer flotilla his ship had joined:

At about 18.15 destroyers were ordered to attack the enemy with torpedoes, using smoke-screen as cover. We were about eight miles from the enemy on parallel tracks. At 18.30 *Sikh* made a complete turn to lay a new smokescreen. We were now in a position to launch our attack. *Jervis*, *Kipling*, *Kingston* and *Legion* turned to bring our ships in line abreast. Speed was increased to 28 knots, and all destroyers opened fire together, we in *Legion*

Second Battle of Sirte, 22 March 1942, *Cleopatra* **making smoke, seen from** *Euryalus.* (A8166)

***Euryalus* fires her broadside.**
(A8168)

holding our fire until we were within 4,000 yards. Looking through my gunlayer's telescope, we seemed to be right alongside the battleship [*Littorio*].

Angus Nicholl in *Penelope*:

The destroyers *Havoc* and *Kingston* were hit by 15-inch shells as they closed the enemy, but survived and fired their torpedoes. *Littorio* had been hit by the cruisers' shell fire and one of the enemy cruisers was on fire aft. In fact none of our destroyers' torpedoes hit, but *Littorio* turned away. By 7.0 p.m. the enemy had had enough, and hauled away to the north-east.

Vian's daring tactics, at what became known as the Second Battle of Sirte, saved the convoy. By their timidity the Italians had missed an opportunity to destroy it, which they could easily have done by working round the smoke. The bold attack by the destroyers had probably been the move that tipped the scales. By then darkness was approaching, and the Italians, lacking radar, were aware of the risks of night-fighting. When the Italians turned and ran, Vian, as already planned, took his escort force back to Alexandria; for he could not re-fuel or re-ammunition in Malta. The damaged destroyers and the convoy

Convoy under Rear Admiral Vian fighting its way through to Malta 1942 *by Charles Pears.*

(LD2175)

Abandon ship on
Arctic convoy, 1942;
in the Barents Sea
by James Morris.
(LD4522(8))

Dawn, 22 April 1942;
Arctic convoy.
by James Morris.
(LD4522(7))

Allied convoy arriving in Murmansk in winter sunshine, 1943 *by James Morris.*

(LD3973)

**Troops embarking in invasion craft at Charlie Beach near Santa Theresa di Riva in Sicily for the invasion of Italy,
3 September 1943 by** *Edward Ardizzone.*

(LD3384)

Infantry landing craft disembarking troops at night 1943 *by Henry Carr.*
Possibly painted during a night rehearsal. The long trails are possibly from mortar illuminating bombs or star shells.
(LD3099)

HM Submarine X24 cutting through an anti-submarine net *by J Brooks.* X craft (midget submarines) were fitted with an escape hatch to allow a diver to exit while the boat was still submerged to cut through anti-submarine nets. The special net-cutting tool is still classified fifty years on. The painting depicts the scene in a way that would be virtually impossible to photograph. Unless the water was exceptionally clear, little or nothing would be visible in the murky waters of the average harbour or anchorage. (LD5508)

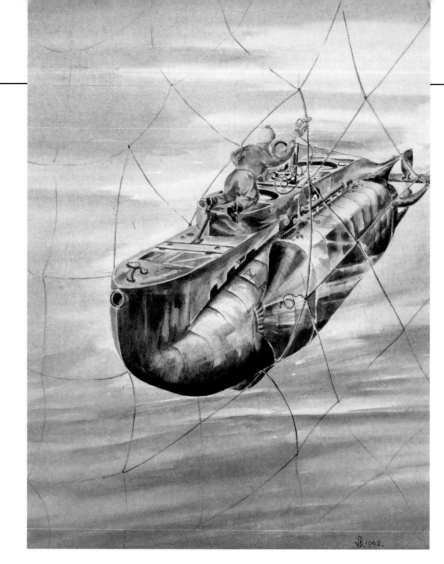

U-boat POWs landing from HMS *Starling,* **24 February 1944** *by Stephen Bone.* HMS *Starling* was commanded by Captain Frederic Walker CB DSO RN, the most outstanding escort group commander in the Second World War. Ships of his escort groups accounted for twenty U-boats. After his death from exhaustion in July 1944, his group, using tactics devised by him, sank eight more. (LD3877)

**The wreck of the *Tirpitz*,
June 1945** *by Stephen Bone.*
Tirpitz capsized and turned
turtle after the final attack
by 32 Lancasters of Bomber
Command on 12 November
1944. (LD5441)

**Boarding a German
U-boat at Loch Eriboll,
Sutherlandshire, 1945**
by Stephen Bone.
Loch Eriboll was the
rendezvous ordered for
many U-boats to
surrender. (LD5369)

HMS Chaser in Hong Kong *by James Morris.*

Painted in Hong Kong after the War. *Chaser* was an escort carrier. (LD1187)

were sent on to Malta, with *Carlisle*, *Penelope* and *Legion*. The next day they were subjected to continuous air attacks by Fliegerkorps II. *Talabot* and *Pampas* reached Grand Harbour to the cheers of thousands of the populace standing on the battlements. *Clan Campbell* was sunk twenty miles out. The oil tanker *Breconshire* was damaged and anchored outside Grand Harbour. Eventually, after many set-backs, she was towed to Marsaxlokk, a bay at the southern end of the island. Captain Nicholl was in charge of the operation with the tugs *Ancient* and *Robust*, with fifteen volunteers from *Penelope*.

It was with relief and satisfaction that I signalled to Vice Admiral Malta: '*Breconshire* secured to number two buoy Marsaxlokk.'

The next day, enemy dive-bombers found her, and the ship was holed by near misses. She rolled over on her side in the shallow water of the bay and lay with about fifteen feet of her hull out of the water:

A hole was cut in her side and into one of her oil tanks. All activities were confined to the hours of darkness. Before daybreak lighters full of oil pumped from her were towed back to Grand Harbour. The operation was repeated night after night, and hundreds of tons of

Kipling emerges from the smokescreen to fire her torpedoes at the Italian fleet. (A8176)

fuel oil were salvaged. Two weeks later some of this precious oil was supplied to *Penelope* for her dash to Gibraltar.

By then both *Talabot* and *Pampas* had been sunk at their berths in Grand Harbour. *Talabot* had been carrying bombs for the Royal Air Force, and was set on fire. Captain Nicholl decided that the only course was to sink her before the fire reached the bombs, and blew up causing massive damage in Floriana and Valetta. He took a demolition party across under Lieutenant Copperwheat, the *Penelope*'s torpedo officer. A depth-charge was slung over *Talabot*'s side and lowered just below the water line:

The electric leads for detonating it were led to the shore, but were not long enough to reach a sheltered position. While the rest of us left the scene or took cover behind a stone wall, Copperwheat gallantly stayed in the open by himself to press the plunger. There was a tremendous explosion and *Talabot* started to settle at once with flames dying down in great clouds of steam. Copperwheat was thrown up in the air, but was not seriously hurt. In due course he was awarded the George Cross for his bravery.

Penelope **tries to take** *Breconshire* **in tow.**
(AX112A)

Only about one fifth of the 26,000 tons of cargo that left Egypt were unloaded.

Legion after suffering damage earlier was also in Grand Harbour. Eric Smith:

We were hit in the forward magazine. There was a violent explosion. *Legion* quickly went down by her bows until her forefoot touched bottom. The order 'abandon ship' was given, but failed to reach one of the gun crews and they had to swim for it. We lost eight killed and a few wounded. One of our Asdic operators, Jock Warwick, who had been a boy with me at *Ganges*, was in a bad way and pinned by his legs. Commander Jessel, who had been wounded in the heel, endeavoured to reach and support him, but was unable to do so. The ship was slowly sinking by now, and Jock unfortunately drowned. Slowly the ship disappeared. Those of us who had survived stood around on the jetty, sad and forlorn, hardly able to realise that we had lost our 'home' of the past 17 months. *Legion* had been a happy and efficient ship. Commander Jessel, our Captain, was one of the finest officers I have ever served under, always cool and calm under fire, and an inspiration to all of us who watched him manoeuvring his ship from the bridge under attack.

Penelope was holed by a near miss and had to go into dock. The dockyard officials estimated it would take a month to repair, 'provided the raids got no worse'. The ship was damaged again by a bomb falling between the dock and the hull. She was so full of holes, the sailors started calling her HMS *Pepperpot*.

Talabot on fire in Grand Harbour, Malta. (A9327)

By Nicholl adding his own shipwrights to the dockyard workforce, the time for repairing *Penelope* was reduced to two weeks. Angus Nicholl:

It was now Good Friday, April 3. After an early morning raid, I sent for the padre and said:

'There are drinking songs and hunting songs. What we need is a shooting song. Can you compose a simple tune and simple words, as crude as you like?'

The padre took about an hour. I approved it and the bandmaster orchestrated it for the band [Royal Marines]. At dinnertime [noon], I ordered the Quartermaster to pipe: 'Hands lay aft to sing a song'.

I climbed to the top of the after turret, megaphone in hand and the words on a blackboard:

> Get them in your sights
> And shoot the buggers down
> Shoot the buggers up
> Shoot the buggers down
> As overhead they pass
> Just shoot them up the arse
> And - shoot - the - buggers - down.

The ship's company came doubling aft, grinning as they read the words on the blackboard. The band played, I sang the words through the megaphone, and then they all had

Captain A. D. Nicholl RN, HMS *Penelope*, with Commander J. W. Grant RN, the executive officer or commander (second-in-command) of *Penelope*. (A8682)

a go. The song went with a swing, and we felt like taking a bow when there was a hearty round of applause from several hundred dockyard workers, attracted by the sound of the band. This light-hearted interval seemed to cheer everybody up, and during the next few days, I heard snatches of the song with ribald variants of the words.

The bombing continued:

A bomb hit a hole in one of the port propellers and started a fire. All the after cabins were wrecked and the wardroom burnt out.

Penelope had two cases of men deserting their posts under fire; to one, a stoker, Nicholl said:

'You are a married man, with two children and you know that your family will suffer while you are in detention. Evidently your duty to your country and your shipmates is not enough to overcome your fears, but I hope that the thought of your wife and family will succeed in doing so. For their sakes I will suspend your sentence [of detention], but if you show any further sign of cowardice you will be sent straight to detention. Now, carry on with your work, and think of your wife and children.'

The stoker gave no more trouble. To the other:

I knew that he had been to a famous public school before his call-up. I sentenced him to thirty days' detention on shore, and spoke to him privately: 'The whole ship's company know your background, and they are intently watching this case. The very fact that you come from a public school, as I do, makes it impossible for me to show you leniency or to suspend your sentence.'

Penelope's repair while under attack, with new damage being inflicted before the old was patched up, is an epic. She wore out her gun barrels, changed just before going into dock. She fired over 5,000 rounds of 4-inch and over 75,000 rounds of smaller anti-aircraft ammunition. As her captain put it:

It had been a testing time for everybody in the ship and events had proved that a wee chap with a stout heart was worth ten of a brawny athlete with clay feet.

Penelope escaped from Malta on 8 April, and after some close shaves arrived in Gibraltar on 10 April 1942. Nicholl:

At the height of the excitement, the ship's cat gave birth to three kittens. She used the bunk in my sea cabin for her accouchement. The kittens were named Bomb, Blitz and Blast.

Among the signals received: '*Penelope* from Prime Minister. Bravo.'
Penelope was repaired in the United States.

In June, two more convoys set out from Malta: Harpoon from Gibraltar and Vigorous from Alexandria. Of the six merchantmen in the Harpoon convoy, two reached Malta with 15,000 tons of supplies, but two destroyers were sunk, and a cruiser, three destroyers and a minesweeper damaged. The Vigorous convoy never made it. Six hundred miles from Malta, low on ammunition and fuel, Vian ordered the convoy about. That such a doughty fighter should decide to withdraw speaks volumes for the savagery of the air attacks on the convoy and escorts. Vian's decision was backed by Admiral Sir Henry Harwood, of River Plate fame. He was now C.-in-C. Mediterranean, in the place of Cunningham, who was appointed Allied Naval Commander Expeditionary Force (ANCXF) to command the joint British/American naval force for the invasion of French North Africa, Operation Torch.

By mid July, the Eighth Army, back on the Alamein position, had repelled Rommel's attempt to break through to Alexandria and the delta. By August Rommel was complaining that, thanks to the efforts of British surface ships and submarines, he was receiving insufficient supplies to build up a reserve for another offensive. With the Eighth Army building up for its offensive in October under its new commander, Lieutenant-General Bernard Montgomery, and Operation Torch due in the November, it was important to maintain the pressure on the Axis in the Mediterranean. The key was Malta, which must be kept supplied.

Operation Pedestal was mounted from the western Mediterranean. With the

HMS *Penelope* (HMS *'Pepperpot'*) in Gibraltar after her escape from Malta. What look like corks bristling from her side are wooden plugs, each stopping a splinter hole from near misses.
(A8603)

Axis airfields stretched along the coast of north Africa to within a hundred miles of Alexandria, convoys from the eastern end were far too costly. Vice-Admiral E. N. Syfret commanded Operation Pedestal. The convoy comprised thirteen freighters and the tanker *Ohio*. The escort was massive, consisting of the battleships *Nelson* (Flag) and *Rodney*; three fleet carriers, *Victorious*, *Indomitable* and *Eagle*, the AA cruisers *Cairo*, *Phoebe*, *Sirius* and *Charybdis*, the cruisers *Nigeria*, *Kenya* and *Manchester*; and twenty-four destroyers. On the carriers were 46 Hurricanes, 16 Fulmars and 10 Martlets for air defence. In addition, and not part of the escort, the carrier *Furious*, accompanied by a further eight destroyers, had thirty-eight Spitfires to be flown off to Malta. These aircraft could not take part in air defence of the convoy, because *Furious* was to operate at some distance from the main body, and once launched, the Spitfires could not be recovered except in an emergency. *Nelson* sailed from Scapa on Sunday 2 August, George Blundell her executive officer:

The Chief [Commander Engineering] is his usual gloomy prophet, foretelling that we are going out in a huge fleet, joining up with the Yanks, and carrying out a life or death operation such as storming Italy.

Victorious, Indomitable and *Eagle* (nearest to camera). *Eagle* was sunk on this convoy on 11 August 1942 torpedoed by U-73. (A11155)

To the regular officers, the Royal Navy often resembled a large family:

Instead of a great fleet as I expected, only *Rodney* came with us and half a dozen

destroyers from the 6th Flotilla. 'Oily' Onslow is acting Captain D6. (R. G. Onslow DSO and bar, one of our most successful destroyer commanders in the war. He was in my term [at Dartmouth] and because of his long, sallow face we called him 'Oily'.)

At 10.00 on Monday 3rd August we rendezvoused with our convoy of 14 ships, some of them old friends; *Empire Hope, Dorset, Waimarama, Brisbane Star,* with the Commodore in *Port Chalmers, Almeria Lykers, Santa Maria, Wairanga, Rochester Castle,* the tanker *Ohio, Clan Ferguson,* and *Glenorchy. Nigeria* and *Kenya* are with them, *Nigeria* flies the flag of CS10, H. M. Burrough. *Kenya* is painted pink!

I read the orders for the operation. It makes me sweat reading the bit about poor convoy getting through the last bit. Otherwise it is just one of our usual club runs through the Med, leaving the poor blighters at the Skerki Channel.

The Skerki Channel lay between the Skerki Bank and Bizerta. Here the main body of the escorts would turn back, leaving the most dangerous part of the route to three cruisers and the AA cruiser *Cairo*, with twelve destroyers. Even sustaining Malta was not deemed worth the risk of exposing capital ships to the full fury of Luftflotte 2. The Royal Navy had well and truly learned the lessons of the past two years, including the loss of *Prince of Wales* and *Repulse*.

Sunday 9 August
At 23.00 I went to the flag deck. A perfectly clear sky, with the Milky Way banded across it and every star shining goodwill upon our enterprise. Cape Spartel light to starboard and Cape Trafalgar to port. [The western end of the Straits of Gibraltar.]

I felt indeed that some of our party were entering the narrow seas on a desperate venture and prayed to the Ruler of Destiny for his favour on our venture.

Tuesday 11th to Friday 14th and on to the 15th
What a tragic failure this convoy has been! Nine ships out of the fourteen [merchantmen] lost, and great damage and loss to warships. The first terrible happening occurred about 13.15 on Tuesday. A submarine got inside the screen, and the first anyone knew about it was to see *Eagle* listing over to starboard as far as her flight deck.

Lieutenant Lumsden, the navigator of the cruiser *Phoebe*:

She was struck by four torpedoes, and presented a terrible sight as she heeled over, turned bottom up and sank with horrible speed. Men and aircraft could be seen falling off her flight deck as she capsized.

George Blundell:

She had gone in eight minutes. It makes one tremble. If anyone took a good film of it, it should be shown throughout the country, and especially to the Director of Naval Construction and his department. I remember thinking of the trapped men. I saw Skinner, the constructor, looking like a man who'd seen a terrible nightmare. He was sweating and white, and I heard him say, 'They couldn't have had anything closed [watertight doors].'

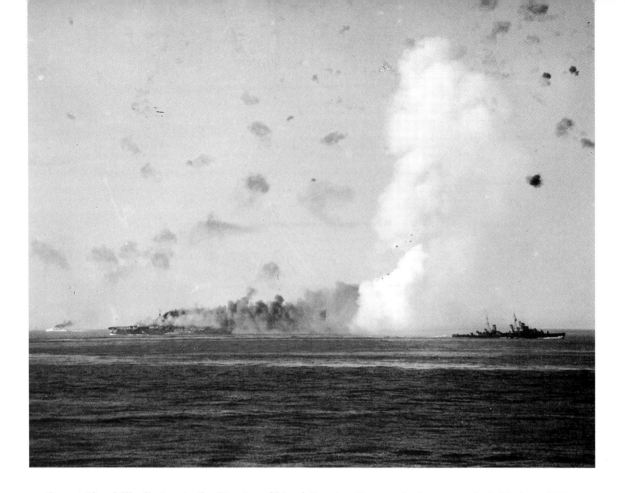

George Blundell's allusion to the Director of Naval Construction was in the context of his responsibility for ship design. Some of the fault can be placed at his door, but most of the blame for her speedy demise lies with policies in the 1920s and 1930s resulting in men being sent to fight in a ship laid down in 1914, and totally unfit to take part in war as fought in 1942.

That night I was planning to give a final pep talk to the ship's company, but it was not to be, for at 20.30 we sounded off, 'Alarm to Arms', followed by the alarm rattlers. Then followed two of the most exciting hours in my life. At about 21.00 we were missed by two torpedoes as near as any ship can ever have been; one passed for'ard, its bubble track actually went under us, and the other passed aft. It can hardly have missed us by more than a few feet. Bombs fell all over the place. When it got darkish, about 21.15, the barrage put up by the fleet and its screen was aesthetically one of the weirdest, most beautiful and wonderful I have ever seen: the purple sea, black sky, red in the west, pearls and rubies of the tracer necklaces, lurid bursts in the sky, and the dark little ships. People who had seen it all had a look on their faces as if they had seen a vision, the sort of expression a man would have on his face if he had looked on the Almighty.

On Wednesday we were closed up at 1st degree AA stations all day. These days, this includes the 16-inch turrets, because we fire 16-inch shell set to burst at 3,000 yards. Our 16-inch barrage was very effective against torpedo bombers appearing low over the horizon. It spread and threw up a curtain of spray through which the planes seemed loath

Indomitable **almost hidden by near misses, seen from** *Victorious* **on 12 August 1942, Malta Convoy Operation Pedestal.** (A15964)

Merchantman *Dorset* under bomb attack, Operation Pedestal. She was sunk on 13 August 1942. (A11173)

to fly. Our fighters were up and back the whole day, and broke up most of the enemy formations before they got to us. Those that got through got a good dusting from our destroyers. Nothing came near us all day, except three planes which got within fair range of our close-range weapons and were all shot down.

The *Deucalion* got a near miss and dropped astern. Poor *Deucalion*, who has had such former adventures in the Med, was ordered off to try to creep along inshore, but she was sighted by a U-boat who finished her off. We had three near misses on our port side from one bomb attack, and later on several fairly near the port bow. Just after 7 p.m. there was a fierce air attack. I counted about a dozen torpedo planes coming in on the starboard bow, but they were beaten off by our 16-inch barrage. Just after this, about 14 Stukas caught *Indomitable* just at the wrong angle, coming down on her out of the sun.

Indomitable disappeared, for all we saw of her for minutes was columns of spray. Finally the maelstrom subsided, and there was 'Indom', still there, but blazing both for'ard and aft of the island, with great columns of smoke pouring from her flight deck.

Nelson and *Rodney* were ordered to leave the convoy and turn back to shield her, as the Admiral feared that torpedo planes would try to finish her off. So we said goodbye to the convoy, and shortly after we left, they got beaten up badly.

We paddled away out of the area as usual at 20 knots with *Indomitable*, *Victorious*, *Rodney*, *Scylla*, *Phoebe* and destroyer screen. The convoy going through the Skerki Channel had a terrible time, submarines doing most of the damage. *Cairo* and *Manchester* were sunk, *Nigeria* and *Kenya* torpedoed, and eight of the surviving merchant ships were

destroyed. Only *Port Chalmers*, *Brisbane Star*, *Melbourne Star*, *Rochester Castle* and *Ohio* (although the latter was torpedoed) got into Malta. What a price to pay!

We got back to Gib about 19.00 on Saturday 15th August. Humphrey B [Jacomb] put the great ship alongside like a picket boat. He's a marvel and has been the whole operation; was ever a man more fortunate than to serve under such a Captain?

Sunday 16th August

All the commanding officers in the Fleet came on board for a conference. Most of us felt depressed by the party. Operation 'M' for Murder we call it. 'The Navy thrives on impossibilities,' said the BBC. Yes, but how long can it go on doing so?

The tanker *Ohio* enters Grand Harbour, 15 August 1942. (GM1480)

The passage of the Pedestal convoy to Malta is one of the epics of naval warfare. When the freighters arrived, the stricken *Ohio*, carrying her precious load of 10,000 tons of fuel oil, was still seventy miles away, under tow. Stukas and JU88s came roaring in to try to finish her off. Spitfires from Malta held most of them off, but a 1,000-lb bomb burst close alongside the *Ohio*, holing her again, and breaking the tow line. This was the last attack to get through the Spitfires. Now it was a race to get her in before she sank. With two small ships lashed on each side, and one towing, she crept along agonizingly slowly. Outstanding seamanship got her into Grand Harbour. The tide of fortune for the Allied cause in the tideless Mediterranean was on the turn.

On the night 23/24 October, the Eighth Army went on the offensive at El

Alamein. On 8 November, the Allies landed in French North Africa. The offensives from both ends of the African littoral were to expel the Axis from the southern shore of the Mediterranean for good. Both offensives were supported by sea power, and Torch began from the sea.

Operation Torch was the first of a series of great Allied joint operations. Much had been learned from the disastrous raid on Dieppe in August that year, but there were still a great many matters to be got right before the assault on the mainland of Europe, Overlord, at some, as yet undecided, date in the future. Fortunately in Cunningham, and especially Ramsay, his deputy for Torch, the Allies had the right commanders to see that the lessons were applied with energy. Admiral Sir Bertram Ramsay became without question one of the greatest 'amphibious' admirals in the history of the Royal Navy.

The assault areas for Torch were: Casablanca, to be the responsibility of the Americans mounted from the United States direct, designated the Western Task Force; Oran, to be assaulted by US forces mounted from the United Kingdom, designated the Centre Task Force; and the assault on Algiers by a combined British/United States task force, designated the Eastern Task Force. Airborne operations were also included in the plan. The planning for the operation was complicated by one special factor upon which much depended: the degree to which the French would resist the landings. Intelligence indicated that there was a chance that resistance would be light. Indeed it was possible that they might welcome the Anglo/US forces. But there was no certainty, and the Allies had to plan on the assumption that the landings would be opposed. To reduce the possibility of resistance, the leading troops to come ashore were to be American, even on beaches allocated to the British. It was felt that the French, still smarting after the destruction of their ships in 1940 by the Royal Navy in Oran and elsewhere, might allow their feelings of outrage to dictate their actions, if they encountered British troops in the first assault waves. As a deception the Eastern Task Force was routed as if it were a Malta convoy. Under the guiding hand of Ramsay, for Cunningham was never a man for detail, the staff work for Torch was a model of its kind. The initial assaults involved some 400 merchant ships and 170 escorts.

Fortunately, in most places, there was only slight opposition to the seaborne landings, because many elementary mistakes were made in the actual conduct of the amphibious operation. Troops landed on the wrong beaches, landing craft grounded offshore on sand bars, and the offload was chaotic in places.

Lieutenant-Commander George Grandage RNR, who had been a beachmaster at Dunkirk, was the beachmaster allocated to Beer Green Beach, one of the three allocated to the Eastern Task Force, whose objective was Algiers. The beaches here were A, B and C (Apple, Beer and Charlie in the phonetic alphabet of the time) and each beach was subdivided into sectors denoted by a colour. The task of a beachmaster in an amphibious assault was, and still is, to land behind the leading waves of assault troops, and set up a control organization on the beach. He calls in subsequent waves of craft, and despatches them back to their parent ships, and is generally responsible for the smooth running

North Africa landings,
Operation Torch;
transports and LCAs
off Azeu beach near
Oran. (A12820)

of the beach. In Grandage's case he had two Assistant Beach Masters (ABM) who were to land ahead of him, with, or very close behind, the leading waves, to set up lights to guide in subsequent waves. Grandage:

I left the ship in a Landing-Craft Mechanised (LCM), a type used for carrying vehicles, with half my party, while the remainder were with the Assistant Military Liaison Officer and his party in a similar craft. Besides us in the craft were the Colonel [he does not say of what unit] and his HQ, two American jeeps [these could be jeeps belonging to a British unit. Jeeps had only just arrived in Britain] and one 37mm gun. After running four miles, we expected to find a submarine which was stationed as a guide, and two miles further a motor launch. To my consternation we found neither. By then the land was plainly discernible, but as we approached nothing could be recognised as being anything like what was expected, neither could we see the lights which should have been placed by the ABMs to mark the beach. There was no firing in the vicinity so I presumed the Fort at Sidi Ferruch had fallen, which our latest intelligence reports had told us we might expect. I then saw a motor launch coming out from shore and ordered the coxswain to close her. We were told by the people in the launch that we were off white beach, so that meant our green beach was a mile away to the south-west.

I did not like the look of things at all because no part of the land looked anything like the model and photographs which I had studied so carefully. We went carefully down the coast hoping to recognise something, until we came to a small village showing quite a few lights. I then consulted with the Colonel who had relied on us so implicitly to put them down at the right place at the right time. I had to confess that we had failed, but to my surprise I found him quite happy, or not as unhappy as I had expected. He suggested I landed him there.

Eventually we beached about a mile north-east of the village and the Colonel went ashore with his party. I also went with my bodyguard in the hope that I might be able to recognise something from ashore. On shore I found we were amongst vineyards and eventually returned to our craft, no better off for our stroll ashore. The Colonel and his party went on inshore.

After motoring fruitlessly up and down off the coast for the rest of the night and meeting other craft who were similarly lost:

As it got light, we found ourselves off the same village we had approached earlier. With my glasses I could make out people standing about staring at us, and some in uniform running about giving orders. I decided to go ashore and ask a policeman where Sidi Ferruch was. I could see that the people ashore did not appear to be adopting a hostile attitude to us, instead just stared in amazement. Suddenly I saw a gun of about 37mm on the beach right ahead, trained on us with the crew ready to fire. I ordered full astern to get away. After all I only wanted to ask the way, and I hardly thought that warranted the risk of being blown to pieces.

As we steered away from the shore, I suddenly saw a large tomb on a hilltop, which I remembered well from cruising along that coast some years ago. I knew we were about 15 miles out. I realised what had happened. The motor launch had correctly said we were off white beach, but he meant Apple sector white, not Beer sector white. A strong current had set all the ships of the convoy to the west while lying stopped, so that unknown to us our point of departure when leaving the ships was about four miles to the west of where we were thought to be.

I eventually landed on Beer Green Beach feeling very small at 08.30, but was much relieved to find that nearly all the other craft had had much the same experience, except those who landed in the first half hour before the current had time to have much effect.

Lieutenant Dennis Brown RNVR was in charge of part of a Flotilla of Landing-Craft Assault (LCA), carrying American assaulting infantry. He was an experienced landing-craft officer, who had taken part in the Dieppe raid:

We were a little late, but deployed and landed our infantry safely. The landing was unopposed; that was another bit of luck. We now had the task of unloading men and *matériel* from the ships. Later some shelling started. We were not that far from Oran, and certainly within range of the French coastal defence batteries. The shelling went on all that day, it was bloody hairy, and I willed the Americans to get a move on and capture those batteries. We in *Glengyle* [mother ship for LCAs] and all our craft escaped damage, but some shells fell very close, too close for comfort. Our unloading did not stop of course. The guns were eventually silenced.

The French, after some initial dithering, threw in their lot with the Allies. Hitler invaded Vichy France in retaliation, and speedily reinforced Tunisia. The land campaign against tough German opposition did not end until the surrender at Tunis on 7 May 1943.

The Royal Navy was not always as compassionate as it might have been in its treatment of its people. George Blundell:

Sunday 10 January

The Captain called me down to his cabin and showed me a pink signal. On it was the message, 'Captain Jacomb is to be informed that their Lordships have no further employment for him and that he is to be placed on the retired list from 12 January.' What can one think of a service that gives 48 hours' notice to a man who has served it for nearly 40 years? All the officers and men loved him because he was so interested in them. But above all he was a magnificent ship handler. He handled clumsy old 'Nellie' like a pinnace, always incisive and quiet with his orders. I adored him.

Adjusting to a new Captain:

Wednesday 17 February

Our new Captain the Honourable Guy Russell came on board to join. He was received by Humphrey Jacomb. The turn-over between the two men of the flagship of the Western Mediterranean Theatre of war was brief. 'This is your commander,' said Humphrey. 'You'll find the ship works and works well.' That was all. The two had a light lunch together, and Humphrey came on deck to leave. When he went over the side and shook hands with me, it was too much for me and I wept.

Guy Russell must have witnessed my grief and somewhat imperiously ordered me down to his cabin. There he sat at his desk, rang for the Captain's secretary, and in my presence, opened every drawer and removed their contents, most of which he threw into the waste paper basket, handing any papers of importance to the secretary or me. When he had cleared every paper off the desk and drawers, he rose and said, 'Come, Commander, let us walk round the upper deck.' That was my introduction to this remarkable man.

Captain the Honourable Guy Russell RN (*top*) and Commander George Blundell RN, from a photograph taken on board HMS *Nelson* at Rosyth on 7 November 1943. (A20279)

Captain the Honourable Guy Russell was not overawed by Flag Officers:

Friday 7 May 1943

A constant stream of advice and queries streamed down to us from the Admiral's bridge above. At last the Captain could stand it no more. He tore the signal off the pad, saying, 'Commander, take this personally to the Chief of Staff.' I did so. On it was written, 'Captain Guy Russell is in command of this ship and not anyone in that rarefied atmosphere above.'

Operation Husky, the invasion of Sicily on 10 July 1943, was a tougher proposition than Torch. The island was held by nine Italian divisions of doubtful quality, stiffened by the Hermann Goering Division and 15th Panzer Grenadier Division. Although the Hermann Goering Division was not as good a formation as it was puffed up to be, it, together with 15th Panzer Grenadier, would certainly fight harder than the French in North Africa. Although the Allied Air Forces greatly outnumbered the Axis, the latter would be operating from bases in Sicily and Italy. There was also a question mark hanging over the

Italian surface fleet, and how it would react. Italian and German submarines were likely to be a greater threat, but the Italian warships could not be ignored. The aim was to land US Seventh Army under Patton in the Gela area of Sicily, and British Eighth Army in the south-east corner, south of Syracuse. By this time Cunningham was back in his old job as C.-in-C. Mediterranean, with overall responsibility for the Allied naval part in Husky, with Ramsay as Allied Naval Commander Expeditionary Force. Some 279 warships took part (199 British, 68 US, and 12 from other Allied nations), 2,074 landing craft of all types and 237 merchant ships. To protect the invasion force from interference by the Italian Fleet, the battleships *Nelson*, *Rodney*, *Warspite* and *Valiant*, together with the fleet carriers *Indomitable* and *Formidable*, six cruisers and eighteen destroyers were interposed between Taranto and Sicily.

George Blundell:

Friday 9 July
The Captain showed me a rather disquieting signal about air support for the landing craft and landing parties which [said] air support might be hampered by the weather. The message had the gaffe, 'Troops on the beaches must cheerfully accept enemy air attack.' The gaffe: the word 'cheerfully'. In the afternoon we turned north and went on to 18 knots. In diamond or open formation. The two carriers are in extended order to starboard, and the destroyers ahead in a great fan. It is blazing hot, the sea gently ruffled blue, sky cloudless. It seems strange that hundreds of men will be dying on the beaches tomorrow. [In fact casualties actually on the beaches were remarkably light.]

Later:

The wind has been steadily getting up and at midnight was blowing about Force 5, which is not good for those landing, altho' luckily it is from the NW.

It is at times like this that I'm glad I'm a sailor and not a soldier. Just think of the poor devils huddled in landing craft, wet with spray, feeling seasick, waiting to land in the grey of dawn on an unknown beach, having just spent 14 days in a cramped, blazing hot transport.

Lieutenant Dennis Brown RNVR, now in charge of an LCA Flotilla, about to embark from the Landing Ship Infantry (LSI) SS *Orontes*:

We had an hour or two's sleep. At 23.30 we had breakfast. Then at 00.15, and with the inside of our ship almost in darkness, we went to embarkation stations. Only a few blue lights were in evidence inside the ship, to accustom the eyes of everybody to the darkness outside.

This, the grim preamble and anticipation, was always the worst part of it all. The ritual loading of my revolver, putting on my lifebelt and steel helmet, and making my way to my boat. It was by no means the first time I had been through all this, only this time there was a difference. This time I had the burden of a greater degree of responsibility than I had previously, and, with the weather conditions outside to add to my worries, my mind

was in something of a turmoil. I was able to draw some consolation, as I had usually done, that I was not alone. Hundreds of thousands of minds would be experiencing their own problems and fears, and just had to overcome them. One overriding thought, as no doubt in everyone else's, never let anyone see that you might be concerned in any way.

Having embarked our assaulting infantry, all boats were lowered into the blackness and the heaving seas below.

Although I did not know it then, the ships were at least six miles further off the coast than they should have been. Also, instead of the two LSIs being in line abreast with their bows heading towards the land, the wind and sea had swung them into line ahead, and beam on to the land. The two flotillas of LCAs were in confusion, with the Motor Launch (ML), our navigational leader, in the middle of it all. For some reason, the ML moved away to get clear, but to seaward. Nothing like this had been envisaged in all the planning, or indeed in any of my anticipations. The inside of my mouth felt dry. I could hardly go back on board to try to sort it out. I was on my own; oh boy was I on my own. I had to make a snap decision. It was very dark; and I decided I must follow the ML, on no account must I lose it, and I must avoid getting mixed up with the 54th Flotilla. I believe I took the right decision, because having taken her wide sweep to seaward, our ML set a course towards the shore, but just belted off without waiting to ensure that she had her brood safely in station behind her.

After sorting his boats out behind the ML:

The sea was pretty foul, we were shipping it green over the bows. At 02.30, and twenty-five minutes late, having passed two marker submarines, the ML reached what was presumed to be the release position. This was the point where I altered course to head for

Hunt-class destroyer HMS *Tetcott* engaging shore batteries at Augusta, Sicily, while commandos land. Operation Husky. (A18089)

my beach, taking my six LCAs of the initial assault with me, to land the first wave of infantry. The rest of my flotilla were to be released half an hour later to land their men, the second wave.

Now I had to pick up a tiny light which would keep making the letter J to seaward of the course. This would come from a little folboat [two-man canoe] sitting about 500 yards from our beach. With, according to plan, less than two miles to go, it should not be too long before I picked up that signal. I held my course, not daring to increase speed to catch up time, because of the heavy sea. Already many of the soldiers were very sick. We went on and on, and I still could not pick up any semblance of the coast, let alone the folboat.

It was well over an hour before I was eventually able to pick out the coastline. From the silhouette, I was able to estimate that I was a little to the south of where I should have been. Suddenly, I picked up that flashing letter J just slightly to the north of me. Good old patient, faithful folboat. Although we were about ninety minutes late, the two chaps in the boat had still kept to their station and were still sending their signal. It seemed to me that that wonderful folboat was just about the only part of the plan that truly worked properly.

During the run-in, between my release and the folboat, I heard many desperate cries for help coming from the water. At the time I had no idea what it could be. My instinct was to go to their aid, but I had to ignore them. I could not stop, or I might have buggered up the entire operation in my sector. It was heart-rending.

Ninety minutes late, my troops were ashore, slightly out of position, but at least on the right beach in the right order. The second wave of my Flotilla also landed on the right beach. The initial landings did not encounter much opposition, although there was a little machine-gun fire. I suffered no losses. We had to be thankful that our enemy were the Italians, and not many Germans at this stage.

The landings were reportedly not too good in some other areas, and not all flotillas landed on their correct beaches. I had of course been shitting myself with worry. Everything that could possibly go wrong, had gone wrong.

The shouts for help heard by Dennis Brown on the run-in were from the British 1st Air Landing Brigade, carried in gliders, whose objective was the Ponte Grande, a road bridge south of Syracuse. Many gliders were released far too early by the tug aircraft; some because of trigger-happy sailors in the Allied Fleet who fired on them. Of 144 gliders carrying the Brigade, 78 landed in the sea, and 252 soldiers were drowned. Some swam ashore to take part in the battle.

George Blundell:

Saturday 10 July
There is no sign of a move by the Italian Fleet. I believe all these Continental countries are scared of the sea, and have an inferiority complex about the Royal Navy. There were no enemy reports and no RDF contacts. RDF is now called Radar to conform with the Yanks. The air is absolutely jammed with American chatter. They talk incessantly.

The Italians did play a part in the battle, but only their submarine service and coastal forces. Commander Vere Wight-Boycott RN, the captain of the destroyer *Ilex*:

At 05.30 we got a good contact [on a submerged submarine], and attacked, dropping five shallow set charges. We repeated the attack. *Echo* also got contact and attacked. After another attack *Echo* made a signal suggesting that the target was not a submarine.

Ilex was on the point of abandoning the hunt, to return to escorting a cruiser squadron, when:

Echo regained contact and was making another attack, and a U-boat popped up like a jack-in-the-box on *Echo's* wake. *Echo* was turning at the time, and opened fire with her B Gun. Her first round was plainly the result of the intense excitement of the gunlayer, and landed about three miles over [beyond]. The second pierced her hull below the conning tower, a very neat and satisfying shot.
Echo closed to pick up survivors.

As always, there were some instances of what today we call Blue-on-Blue, or 'friendly fire':

We sighted a strange aircraft. I gave the order to the Oerlikons to open fire, but as I did so, the plane turned at right angles so we could see the markings, which were British. I immediately pressed the cease-fire gongs, but to my horror, almost every gun in the ship opened up. Even the two 4.7-inch guns' crews who were not closed up came rushing up and got a round away. Having tasted blood, they took a lot of stopping. When we got back to Malta, I was sent for to be told that the C.-in-C. wanted my reasons in writing and that the AOC Malta was furious.

There were some new weapons encountered; George Blundell:

Leaving the swept channel, we passed the poor *Eskimo* being towed by *Tartar*. She has been hit by a 'glider' bomb from a JU88 attack and her back is broken with 16 dead and 22 wounded. This is a new form of attack; the bomb glides and is directed on to its target by the aircraft.

Wight-Boycott:

17 September
Warspite was hit yesterday by two glider bombs. The cruiser *Orion* has been disabled by one. It is a small wireless controlled aircraft with wing span of about seven feet, controlled by the parent aircraft up to a distance of about six miles. It is thought to be propelled by rocket apparatus and can be directed by W/T [radio] on to its target.
This casualty will lend weight to the (to my mind) very mistaken view, that Admiral Cunningham needlessly exposes his ships to unreasonable hazards. I heard it first after Crete, strangely enough from FAA officers from *Illustrious*. More recently we heard the

Glider bomb under test
(German photo).
(HU780)

same kind of thing in *Aurora*. Some may think their lives are being needlessly exposed. It is probably true that the C.-in-C., having a complete disregard of danger himself, cannot allow for it in others of his own kind (although he may assess the enemy's morale very astutely). I am personally not particularly keen to have my life exposed needlessly or otherwise, but I strongly feel that it is the C.-in-C.'s belligerent outlook that has maintained the Fleet in the Mediterranean in face of overwhelming air superiority, and has resulted in the present plight of the Italian Fleet, whose commanders probably had a more intellectually correct sense of values.

The glider bomb was the FX-1400 radio-controlled armour-piercing bomb filled with 1,400 lb of explosive, usually launched from a Dornier Do-17 and an exceedingly potent weapon.

The plight of the Italian Fleet, to which Wight-Boycott refers, was brought about by the Italians suing for peace on 8 September 1943. The Italian Fleet was ordered to rendezvous with the Mediterranean Fleet to be led into Grand Harbour. The Germans had reacted with their customary speed, and disarmed the Italian Army. The Luftwaffe now demonstrated their scorn for the Italian Fleet's inability to subdue the Royal Navy over the past two-and-a-half years. On 9 September, an FX-1400, one of several launched by Dornier Do-17s at the Italian battle-fleet on its way to the rendezvous, sank the battleship *Roma* with all her company, and another FX-1400 damaged the *Italia*. The next morning, the surviving battleship, six cruisers and eight destroyers made their rendezvous. Acting Captain Manley Power RN to his wife:

10.9.43
I have just returned from watching the Wop fleet. Went out with C.-in-C. and Eisenhower in a destroyer & we watched *Warspite* and *Valiant* leading the major portion of the Wop

A composite of the Italian Fleet as it approaches to surrender to Admiral of the Fleet
Sir Andrew Cunningham at Malta:

1. A general view of the Fleet; 2. The Italian flagship *Italia*;
3. The 35,000-ton Italian battleship *Vittorio Veneto*; 4. The Italian destroyer *Oriani*;
5. An Italian *Avieri* class destroyer; 6. A 7,800-ton Italian *Garibaldi* class cruiser;
7. *Eugenio Di Savola*, Italian cruiser. Prince Eugene of Savoy, the great ally and friend
of the first Duke of Marlborough, had the distinction of having two ships named
after him, both serving against the Royal Navy in the Second World War.
The other was the German heavy cruiser *Prinz Eugen*;
8. The *Emanuele Filiberto Duc D'Aosta*, 7,282-ton cruiser;
9. HMS *Hambleton*, with General Eisenhower and Admiral of the Fleet Sir Andrew
Cunningham aboard watching the Italian Fleet approach.

(AX14X)

fleet away to Malta. What a show! They are magnificent ships and looked well kept enough.

In Malta already were the battleships *Andrea Doria* and *Caio Duilio*, with two cruisers and a destroyer. Cunningham sent a signal to his Fleet:

Med Station (R) C.-in-C. Levant to C.-in-C. Med

I have this day informed the Board of Admiralty that the Italian Fleet now lies at anchor under the guns near the Fortress of Malta. So ends another chapter of the War. For just over three years the Royal and Merchant Navies in close concert with the sister services have fought the battle of the Mediterranean so that our object has now been achieved and the Mediterranean is once more fully in our control.

The way has been long. We have had our great moments and our bad times when the horizon looked black. During that time except for a short break it has been my privilege and pride to command the main forces at sea in the Mediterranean. At this moment when all for which we have worked so long has at length come to pass, I send every Officer and Man in the Royal and Merchant Navies who have contributed my thanks and admiration for the resources and resolution and courage which have made these things possible. In doing so I address my words to those whom it has been my honour to command, but let us not forget what we owe to our Sister Services, in particular to the devotion of those in the Royal Air Force, to whose loyal support we owe so much of what has been achieved.

(TOO 111556B/9/43)

In the letter to his wife on 10 September, Manley Power wrote:

But although the enemy fleet is disposed of, there is much planning and fighting to be done before we are masters of Italy.

Italy was not to be completely mastered, thanks to the fighting qualities of the German Army, until May 1945. As he wrote, the bloody battle of Salerno was in progress, yet another amphibious landing courtesy of Allied, mainly British, sea power. The following January there was to be another landing in Italy, at Anzio. But the main event was about to be staged in Normandy in June 1944. To lead the Allied Naval Team, Admiral Ramsay had already left for England, before the Salerno landings. Cunningham left the Mediterranean on 17 October, to take over the post of First Sea Lord from the dying Pound.

George Blundell:

The Americans have a large hospital at Bonsville beach. Part of the beach is reserved for hospital staff and the nurses. Some of our sailors swam in the reserved part, and an American major put on his cap and swam out to them and ordered them off. One of our sailors pointed to the shore, and said, 'That effing land may belong to General effing Eisenhower, but this 'ere sea belongs to Admiral effing Cunningham.'

SUBMARINE OPERATIONS

British Submarines in their traditional ship-hunting role served in all the theatres of war, but principally in the Mediterranean, the North Sea, the Norwegian and Barents Seas, and the East Indies and Indian Ocean. Here the enemy merchantmen and warships were to be found. In addition, submarines laid mines and carried out clandestine operations, including landing agents, small raiding-parties and beach reconnaissance teams. Submarines also towed midget submarines to the positions near the target, and brought surviving crews and boats back.

British submarines in all theatres almost invariably patrolled in areas which were unfavourable for submarine operations. Whether off the coast of Norway, the Adriatic, or in the Malacca Straits, they were always near the littoral, in areas that were well patrolled and often thick with mines. Even surfacing at night for a battery charge could be fraught with risk, and there was rarely a moment for relaxation. It was very different for the Axis, and particularly the Germans, in the vastness of the Atlantic.

Submarines in the Mediterranean, based in Malta, sunk millions of tons of Axis shipping destined for Rommel and the Italians in North Africa. Lieutenant Michael Crawford was the First Lieutenant of *Upholder*. Her commander, Lieutenant-Commander Wanklyn, was one of the most brilliant submarine COs of the War. Crawford:

Lieutenant C. Christie RNR, First Lieutenant, and Lieutenant A. A. Duff RN, the Commanding Officer of HMS/M *Stubborn* with the ship's company. She had a very lucky escape off the coast of Norway. After sinking two German coasters on 11 February 1943, she made an unsuccessful attack on a convoy in Folden Fjord. The escorts counter-attacked dropping 36 depth-charges in quarter of an hour. Eventually, heavily damaged she was stuck on the bottom at 500 feet (*Stubborn*'s test depth was 300 feet). After some nine hours, with air almost exhausted, the crew managed to get her to the surface. The enemy had gone. After a hair-raising six-day trip on the surface, part of it under tow, and escorted by destroyers and Beaufighters for some of the way, she arrived at Lerwick in the Shetlands. On her return to Scapa Flow, she was ordered to secure alongside HMS *Duke of York*, the flagship of Admiral Sir Bruce Fraser, C.-in-C. Home Fleet. When *Stubborn* sailed next morning, after the officers had dined on board the flagship, Admiral Fraser signalled; 'I am proud to have laid alongside you in my flagship.' (A21954)

207

The star attack was in May 1941, after which the Captain was awarded the VC. We were off the east coast of Sicily, with only two torpedoes remaining, and our Asdic out of action. I was on watch as it was beginning to get dark, and saw a dark shape. I called the Captain to the periscope. In a remarkable attack, with destroyers coming at him very close, he dodged through, and fired his last two torpedoes to sink the 18,000 ton liner *Conte Rosso*, carrying troops. This was followed by a heavy depth charge attack. Our crew bent their knees waiting for the crunch as we heard the escorts' screws passing overhead.

Upholder survived two hours of attacks in which some forty depth-charges were dropped. In mid September 1941, precise information on an Italian convoy of three troop-carrying liners was received. Four submarines sailed from Malta. Three were positioned across the convoy route, with *Upholder* in the middle, and *Ursula* about fifty miles to the east. Early in the morning, *Unbeaten* reported the convoy in sight but too far away from him to attack. Crawford:

We closed at speed on the surface. There was a heavy swell running. The boat was yawing about. Wanklyn fired at about 5,000 yards as the boat swung, first one torpedo, then another, then two more. We dived, and heard two explosions. Nothing came near us. We surfaced and saw one ship on fire, one lying stopped, and one retreating. Because of the heavy swell, we had to dive to reload the torpedo tubes, before re-surfacing. By now it was daylight, destroyers were circling the stopped ship. We were put down by destroyers coming at us. We were too close to the stopped liner to fire, so Wanklyn said, 'We'll go underneath, and fire from the other side'. We fired two torpedoes and sank the ship. Unbeknown to us, Teddy Woodward in *Unbeaten* found the convoy and was just about to

Lieutenant M. D. Wanklyn RN with some of *Upholder*'s ship's company, Malta, 13 January 1942. (A729)

fire, when he heard our torpedoes explode. He was extremely irritated at being done out of a sitting duck.

Lieutenant Michael Lumby, the First Lieutenant of *Ursula*, referring to Wanklyn:

His great art was to be in the right place at the right time – others were not so cunning.

Crawford:

The strain of operating against the North African convoys was considerable and not helped by any time in harbour in Malta being far from peaceful. Air raids increased in intensity, and after I left for my CO's course, submarines in Malta had to spend all day sitting on the bottom of the harbour.

On 18 April *Upholder* was posted missing, on Wanklyn's last patrol. He had written home:

Count the days, they are not many.

Sometimes crews escaped; Michael Lumby, CO of *Saracen* counter-attacked off Bastia, Corsica on 14 August 1943:

The stern was holed by depth charges, lucky it wasn't the bow. We were so deep we would never have come up. As soon as we surfaced, I put all the crew on the casing at the stern of

Lieutenant Michael Lumby, CO of *Saracen*, talks to Captain Submarine Squadron 8, Captain G. B. H. Fawkes RN before a patrol on 7 February 1943. (A16002)

HMS/M *Tempest* depth-charged near the Gulf of Taranto by the Italian destroyer *Circe* on 13 February 1942. The photograph shows *Tempest* being towed by *Circe* after the attack, and shortly before *Tempest* sank. (HU2278B)

the boat, while I and two others opened all the main vents to scuttle her. We only lost two men, both non-swimmers. Everyone else was picked up by the Italians.

Petty Officer Ian Nethercott describes being under depth charge attack:

We went to silent routine and started creeping away. We'd got about half a mile away, and one of the stokers dropped a bloody great wheel spanner, it could have been heard miles away from up top. The whole lot came charging down. You could hear the chuffle of the screws coming over. We were at about 300 feet and stopped. I actually heard the splash of the depth charges going in, and the click of the hydrostatic pistols just before they went off. We all looked like snowmen, covered with the white cork from the deckhead.

Lieutenant Commander Aston Piper RNVR, CO of *Unsparing* in the Aegean:

My worst experience was being depth-charged when we were pushed down 400 feet, 100 feet lower than the design depth. A lot of damage was done, including all the compasses. When we eventually surfaced, we had to use a hand-held magnetic compass to steer by. When you are depth-charged, you wonder if you are going to come out of it. I thought of my family. At 2 o'clock in the morning, my wife was woken by my photograph falling off the chest of drawers in her bedroom. She was very shocked and immediately said, 'Aston is in trouble.' Later I compared dates and times with my wife, and it was exactly the same time.

Operating off Norway was cold in winter, but summer brought its own hazards. Lieutenant Hugh Haggard RN, CO of *Truant*:

There is no darkness. We had to surface at some time to recharge our batteries. It was very dangerous.

Crawford, after his CO's course, the 'Perisher', spent a week as First Lieutenant in a captured U-boat acting as a training submarine:

They had superb periscopes, far better than ours. But they were terribly wet boats on the surface. In the slightest swell, water came down into the boat from the hatch on the bridge. They were very cramped inside too.

Conditions in British submarines were always cramped, but especially unpleasant in the tropics, when dived; Ian Nethercott:

Utmost at attack stations, the CO, Lieutenant-Commander R. D. Cayley RN, at the periscope. This is a posed photograph taken on her return to England after a year's service in the Mediterranean. (A7721)

On the big boats, the T-boats, you had to be at sea for two months, so you only carried enough water for drinking. You could wash in salt water with salt water soap. But it depended on your chief stoker, if he was prepared to flood up a tank with salt water. I was never on a boat where you could do that, so all you ever did was wipe yourself down with an oil cloth now and again. So of course if it was very hot – in the tropics where we had no air conditioning, and the humidity was terrific – you were just one mass of prickly heat

and sweat rash. Between your legs and under your arms it was just great running sores of blood and sweat. We used to buy loads of talcum powder.

A young South African Sub Lieutenant went to the Coxswain, and said he'd got a dose of crabs. The Coxswain said, 'Just sit over a bucket of salt water.'

'What does that do?'

'Well', replied the Coxswain, 'they keep looking down at the water and as it's moving about with the motion of the boat, they get dizzy and fall off.'

So he's sitting on this bucket, with his trousers down, and the Captain comes in, and says, 'What are you doing, subby?'

He told him.

'Yes', says the Captain, 'that takes a long time. The best thing is to go and get a drop of rum from the Coxswain, mix it with sand and rub it in.'

'What will that do?'

'They get drunk on the rum, throw rocks at each other, and brain each other.'

Lieutenant Geoffrey Tibbs RNVR, navigating officer in *Tantalus* in the East Indies:

We all wore sarongs. When the hatch was opened on surfacing at night, you could almost see the smell disappear in a green cloud. After the diesels were started, the sweet tropical scents were sucked down into the boat.

The bridge at night on patrol in *Tantalus* was manned by the officer of the watch and two lookouts. The Captain always slept in his sarong on the deck of the bridge on a small mat to be instantly ready if needed. We couldn't think how he stood it, he was terribly old; at least 32.

Every now and then someone would come up from below and ask to use the pig's ear on the bridge, the pee funnel. This was better than using the heads which were pumped out by compressed air when on the surface. When dived it was more complicated. You pulled a lever which let the contents into a chamber underneath, opened a sea-cock to let in water from outside the boat, closed it, opened another and blew the contents out into the sea with compressed air, relieved the pressure by pulling a lever, and finally shut the sea-cock. If you got it wrong you got the lot blown back at you. You had to ask the officer of the watch's permission to use the heads when dived, because it made a disturbance on the surface, visible even from the air, unless the sea was rough.

British submarines wreaked havoc on Japanese shipping in the East Indies and Indian Ocean. Lieutenant Mervyn Wingfield RN, CO of *Taurus*:

The Malacca Straits were shallow; on one occasion I was being harassed by a Japanese sub-chaser. I got fed up, ordered surface action, and sank him with my gun. Their anti-submarine techniques were not good.

On another occasion, thanks to good intelligence [the Allies were reading the Japanese Naval Codes], I sank the Japanese submarine I 34, on the surface in the Indian Ocean. She was carrying VIPs from Singapore to Germany, and a load of gold bars and tin.

Like all submarines we could lay mines very accurately, firing them from our torpedo

tubes. The mine was set to sink, and the timing mechanism set to arm when we were clear. We laid magnetic mines outside harbours, and in places where ships had to pass.

If submariners were often individualists, those in midget submarines, or X craft, were often more so. X craft were 51 feet long, could dive to 300 feet and had a crew of three officers and an engine room artificer. They were armed with two side charges, each containing two tons of explosive which could be dropped under a target and set to detonate by clockwork time fuses. Lieutenant H. P. 'Percy' Westmacott RN volunteered for X Craft after winning the DSC as the First Lieutenant of HMS *Unshaken* in the Mediterranean. Westmacott was a stickler for protocol, and was dubbed 'Pusser Percy'. He regarded most of the others on his training course with wry distaste. He described his introduction to X Craft:

Our training with Nobby Clark consisted of sloping off to the nearest area, which he always allocated to himself, opening main vents, dropping to the bottom, putting on the kettle for tea, and settling down to a game of dice. All very wrong and inexcusable, but fortunately it did not matter, I had a very good idea of the essential standards before one could be satisfied, and it only remained to familiarize ourselves with the nuts and bolts of X Craft, which from their resemblance to a large submarine was not difficult. But it always amused me to think of authority looking down the loch at the unbroken surface of water,

HMS/M *Statesman* after sinking a convoy of Japanese lighters off Sumatra. (AX152A)

to satisfy itself that we were all hard at work, when in fact we were sitting quietly on the bottom, drinking tea and playing dice.

Westmacott would brook no such behaviour in his own command. Eschewing social contact with others on his course, he put the time to good use to produce standing instructions for X Craft. On 11 September 1944 'Percy' Westmacott took his boat, X24, into Bergen harbour in an attempt to sink a large floating dock which was vital for the repair of U-boats based in Norway. The facilities in French Atlantic ports were by now denied the Germans thanks to the advance of Allied armies in France since 6 June 1944. After a very skilful passage down the West Byfjord, Westmacott dived to avoid detection in daylight, and ran into Puddefjord:

About 09.00 I sighted the floating dock, and the water became restricted and the traffic denser. The surface was glassy. I was crawling around poking the periscope up like a billiard cue; prohibited from showing more than two inches and only for about ten seconds at a time.

It was about 09.30 when we went astern under the north end of the dock, and I let her settle on the bottom, while we released one charge, then manoeuvred up two hundred feet under the other end to let go the other. All was done by 10.15. With the boat feeling in my hand like a whippet, I let her go for a thousand yards clear, took one fix [a sight to establish position], tucked her head down, and ran like a race horse to the entrance of the Byfjord.

The next morning, having negotiated the coastal minefield for the second time, he rendezvoused with his towing submarine, *Sceptre*, and eventually returned to base at Rothesay. The dock was completely destroyed. Westmacott was awarded the DSO, and his crew decorated.

Westmacott also commanded XE5, a larger version of the X Craft, in the Pacific. On 30 July 1945, he successfully put out of action a Japanese undersea telegraph cable connecting Hong Kong with Singapore and Saigon. This forced the Japanese to resort to radio transmission, allowing the Allies to decode the messages.

9
Operation Neptune to VE Day:
1944–1945

Previous page: MTBs returning from patrol off Cherbourg, 12 June 1944. (A24047)

Although the Battle of the Atlantic was won in May 1943, and Doenitz temporarily withdrew his U-boats, it was not long before they returned. They were never to be so near winning again, but it would be wrong to imagine that they did not pose a serious threat to Allied shipping right up to the end of the war. Indeed had the War in Europe not ended in May 1945, new boats such as the Type XXIII coastal submarines and the even more potent Type XXIs might have swung the pendulum back.

Only by holding shipping losses down could the invasion of north-west Europe be mounted and sustained. Admiral Sir Max Horton, the C.-in-C. Western Approaches since November 1942, had never let slip the initiative gained in the war against the U-boat in the North Atlantic in May 1943. Commander Evelyn Chavasse RN spent the last year of the war in Europe in Derby House in Liverpool, Admiral Horton's Headquarters:

A type XVII U-boat with a submerged speed of 25 knots. Hydrogen peroxide was used to heat water to produce steam to drive turbines. This was an air-independent engine. These boats were never used operationally. They were probably more dangerous to the crew than the enemy, because hydrogen peroxide is so toxic. The British encountered the hazards of hydrogen peroxide when they experimented with captured type XVIIs and this experience helped influence the decision to build nuclear-powered submarines, rather than pursue the development of hydrogen-peroxide propulsion. (HU2274)

There day after day, Max sat in his glass cage, with a round, wise, almost humorous face, brooding on the vast map before him. A few hundred miles away, the hard-faced bleak-eyed Doenitz was no doubt doing the same. This was not a battle of wits between two men; have no doubt, the battle was won at *sea*.

Dear Max, sitting benignly but concentrated in his glass cage above my frantic desk, where there was another exactly similar cage, immediately to the left of his. Without the

Admiral Sir Max Horton, C.-in-C. Western Approaches, addressing the ships' companies of the escort group commanded by Captain Frederic Walker RN after his death. The tactics devised by Captain Walker were one of the key factors in turning the tide in the Battle of the Atlantic. His group alone was responsible for sinking 20 U-boats. After his death on 9 July 1944, ships of his group went on to sink eight more. (A25139)

co-operation of the RAF we might have lost the Battle of the Atlantic, and the whole war with it. In the left-hand cage, alongside Max, was the Air Officer in Command 15 Group, Coastal Command, Air Vice-Marshal Slatter.

So this extraordinary year under the streets of Liverpool proceeded. I watched my old mates at sea doing their stuff, and wished I was with them. When I had been at sea, I had not the foggiest idea of the efficiency of our Intelligence service.

Chavasse was one of a small group of officers admitted to the secrets of what in Derby House was called Z intelligence:

The few of us who were in Z gathered daily in a special room where we had a loud-speaker telephone report from the U-boat tracking room underneath the Admiralty in London. By and large we knew almost exactly where the enemy were and what their orders were. Why then didn't we wade in and sink the lot? Supposing Doenitz ordered a 'milch cow' U-boat to go to a certain position at a certain time; and a few hours later half a dozen British destroyers came zooming up and sank it, the Germans would have known we had broken their cipher. The whole thing was a matter of trying to use our knowledge to the best advantage without letting on to them what we were up to.

Beginning in mid 1943 the Allied planners bent their minds to the task of landing the Armies of the United States and Britain in France. Until General Eisenhower was appointed Supreme Commander Allied Expeditionary Force in December 1943, overall responsibility for planning was borne by Lieutenant-General Frederick Morgan, the Chief of Staff to the Supreme Allied Commander

U-744 returning to Brest early in 1944. (HU2269)

U-744 a few weeks later, sinking after a 30-hour hunt by a mixed Royal Navy/Royal Canadian Navy group. The escort crews are rescuing survivors. (HU2270)

(COSSAC). Until Eisenhower arrived in England, Morgan, a British officer, was a Chief of Staff without a Commander. He was therefore in the difficult position of making plans to be carried out by somebody else. That person, who, under Eisenhower, was to command the Armies for the assault, was General Sir Bernard Montgomery. Fortunately Morgan had the benefit of Admiral Ramsay's presence at his Headquarters since October 1943 as Allied Naval Commander Expeditionary Force (ANCXF). Ramsay's considerable experience was invaluable, and he was able to progress the planning and a number of other measures. But in an amphibious or joint operation, the Naval plan waits upon the production of the Army plan. Ramsay's opposite number, the C.-in-C. 21st Army Group, Montgomery, did not return to England from Italy until 2 January 1944. He at once grasped the reins, and having judged 'the present plan is impracticable', had it changed in a few days [see *The Imperial War Museum Book of Victory in Europe: North-West Europe 1944–45*]. Time was short, almost too short, to find the extra landing-craft and crews to land two armies, each of two corps, five divisions up, on a fifty-mile front; to complete the planning that would take them to the right place; and put them ashore fit to fight the minute foot, track or wheel hit the beach. The array of special craft and equipment, including the Artificial Mulberry Harbour, is familiar to many. Suffice it to say that many of the plans for this equipment had been laid years before, and were the outcome of hard-won lessons in earlier operations, especially the disastrous Dieppe Raid in August 1942. Perhaps most critical of all, by the time both Ramsay and Montgomery appeared on the scene, the landing place had been decided upon: Normandy.

Firming up the details was bedevilled by the American wish to carry out a landing in the South of France (Operation Anvil) simultaneously with the landing in Normandy (Overlord). Not only would this divert assault shipping needed for Overlord, but other resources as well, such as naval gunfire support. The decision to postpone Anvil to July was not taken until 24 March, and D-Day for Overlord was early June. Thanks to Ramsay the plan for Neptune, the naval part in Overlord, despite being produced against the clock with many unwelcome interruptions and tussles with other staffs, was a masterpiece. The operation involved 1,213 warships and 4,126 landing ships and craft moving to the beaches of Normandy, having started from ports all round the United Kingdom from Oban to the Forth. Nearly 80 per cent of the maritime effort was British and Canadian.

The five beaches were from left to right (east to west): Sword (British), Juno (Canadian), Gold (British), Omaha and Utah (US). The time of landing was sequential starting with Utah on the right, because of the differing time of high water on each beach. The aim was to land at about half tide to enable beach obstacles to be cleared. One British and two US airborne divisions would be dropped very early on D-Day, starting soon after midnight to secure the flanks of the invasion.

Originally planned for 5 June, D-Day was postponed to the 6th because of bad weather in the Channel. The assault technique is shown diagrammatically

Admiral Sir Bertram Ramsay. In 1935 he resigned as Chief of Staff Home Fleet as a Rear-Admiral, because his C.-in -C., Admiral Sir Roger Backhouse, insisted on dealing with all the staff work himself. In 1939 Ramsay was brought back as an Acting Vice-Admiral as Flag Officer Dover, although still on the retired list. He masterminded the evacuation of Dunkirk and the other Channel Ports. He was Deputy Allied Naval Commander Expeditionary Force for the landings in North Africa in 1942, commanded the Eastern Naval Task Force for the Sicily landings, and while still on the retired list became the Allied Naval Commander Expeditionary Force for the Normandy landings. He was finally restored to the active list, promoted to full Admiral and knighted. He was killed in an air crash on 2 January 1945, and never saw the fruits of his great contribution to victory. (A23442)

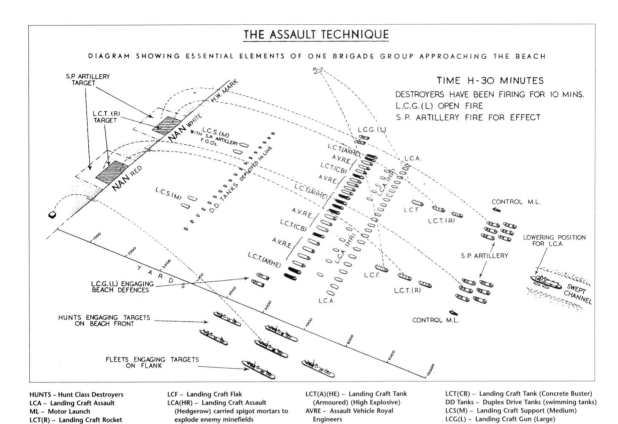

THE ASSAULT TECHNIQUE

DIAGRAM SHOWING ESSENTIAL ELEMENTS OF ONE BRIGADE GROUP APPROACHING THE BEACH

HUNTS – Hunt Class Destroyers	LCF – Landing Craft Flak	LCT(A)(HE) – Landing Craft Tank	LCT(CB) – Landing Craft Tank (Concrete Buster)
LCA – Landing Craft Assault	LCA(HR) – Landing Craft Assault	(Armoured) (High Explosive)	DD Tanks – Duplex Drive Tanks (swimming tanks)
ML – Motor Launch	(Hedgerow) carried spigot mortars to	AVRE – Assault Vehicle Royal	LCS(M) – Landing Craft Support (Medium)
LCT(R) – Landing Craft Rocket	explode enemy minefields	Engineers	LCG(L) – Landing Craft Gun (Large)

Diagram from *Normandy to the Baltic* by Field Marshal The Viscount Montgomery of Alamein. Printed April 1946 by Printing and Stationery Service British Army of the Rhine. Department of Printed Books Imperial War Museum. © Crown Copyright/Ministry of Defence.

above. Essential to the plan were ten lanes swept clear of mines. Ahead of the minesweepers there was only a force of MTBs. Coastal Forces had seen a good deal of very hard fighting, and by June 1944 Petty Officer Frank Coombes, now a coxswain in MTB 624 in the 55th Flotilla, had been at sea in various Coastal Forces boats since 1939:

Think that most of our nerves were getting a little ragged by the summer of 1943 when Fred [twin] came home. He had wife trouble and solaced himself by spending his leave aboard us and wanting action, it was just what I did not want. I went down with a body rash from head to toe. They put me in isolation for a fortnight. I nearly did my nut when they told me it was to give me a break, as I was suffering from nervous tension. I had been having nightmares, being woken up by alarm bells, and when I rushed up on deck, heading for the bridge in my vest and pants, found the boat snug alongside in harbour, but thought nothing of it.

Fred, after fighting in the Mediterranean, was soon in the thick of it as an MTB coxswain in the North Sea and Channel. Frank went to meet his boat:

Fred's boat was last in about 9 o'clock, and I saw five long canvas sacks being carried ashore to the meat wagon. Going on board to Fred still on the bridge, I was shocked to see his yellow goon suit, old PO's cap, head and face were smeared by black blobs of hair and brain, obviously from the head of the Port .5-inch gunner who had taken one through his tin hat. All I could do was talk sympathetically as I wiped the blobs off him. From then on it was a different Fred to the one who had come aboard a bit too all for it for my liking.

Commander Donald Bradford, commanding 55th Flotilla:

I had been tremendously pleased to discover that my boats of the 55th Flotilla had been given the place of honour in the Invasion Fleet. We were to scout ahead of the mine-sweepers who were to clear a path for the destroyers protecting the first wave of assault craft. We were actually to be the spear point of the Assault.

I with four of my boats was to escort and if necessary fight clear a route for the minesweepers of Force J (Juno Beach) until they reached the lowering position, where the small assault craft would be put in the water from their mother ships. Then we were to take station between them and Le Havre to protect them from any surface attacks from that quarter.

Bradford's four boats, including Frank Coombes's 624, sailed

out into Portsmouth harbour into the Solent to take our places ahead of the mass of shipping already jockeying for position in the fairway. The weather was definitely not ideal; a small sea was running even in the sheltered waters of Portsmouth approaches, and the strength of the wind told of a nasty chop in the Channel.

Minesweeping is a dangerous, unglamorous job, and demands great skill, especially at night. Successful sweeping was absolutely crucial if huge losses were not to be suffered from the extensive minefields in the Bay of the Seine, off the Normandy coast. The tide does not run in the same direction constantly so to avoid being swept off course, navigation must be spot on. Having swept a clear channel, it has to be marked with dan buoys, each with a light on top. Lieutenant J. W. Main RN, the navigating officer of the fleet minesweeper HMS *Fraserburgh*, the leader of 15th Minesweeping Flotilla, was leading down lane 0, the most easterly lane of all, off Ouistreham, on Sword beach:

Dan laying especially at night is a very tricky job, and ensuring that the lights on top of the dan stave are burning and the wires clear of the ship's screw is very difficult. The tide was half springs, and started off to the eastward, and midway through our run changed to the westward. Our swept channel was to be four cables [800 yards] wide.

From our point of view the operation proceeded excellently. We sighted what was afterwards confirmed as a German convoy proceeding into Le Havre, but it took no notice of us, and we naturally kept very quiet not wishing to advertise our presence. During the hours of darkness we heard our aircraft passing overhead. Many were towing gliders and formed the spearhead of the army. Some were our bombers which carried out a heavy bombardment of Havre just before we arrived at the lowering position. The explosions

X Craft, X25, under way.
Her Commanding Officer was
Lieutenant J. E. Smart RNVR.
(A22903)

and fires on shore were tremendous. After completing our channel, we anchored just to the west of it. The Captain let the anchor go underfoot, but it would not hold, so we steamed about in small circles.

The first Allied craft in the area were two midget submarines, X20 and X23, arriving 48 hours before, whose task was to provide navigation beacons for Sword and Juno beaches.

Bradford in 55th Flotilla:

I could easily distinguish the low lying coast of Normandy without using my binoculars. It seemed utterly fantastic that all the conglomeration of warships that by this time were prowling within a few miles of the enemy coast could have arrived and taken up position without the knowledge of the Germans. Not a shot had been fired from the shore batteries.

At the lowering position, troops climbed into their landing-craft, or embarked down scrambling nets into boats surging up and down alongside the parent ship. Lieutenant Dennis Brown RNVR was taking his LCA Flotilla into Gold beach:

I led the first wave, and we formed up into two columns in line ahead to the rendezvous area. The sea was very rough, but so far everything had gone to plan. Meanwhile the bombardment of enemy gun positions ashore by cruisers and destroyers had commenced after the LSIs had anchored and even before my LCAs had been lowered into the water.

The LCAs were to link up with a procession of craft forming up and heading for the shore. Ahead of us were several groups designated to give heavy cover during the approach and then actually on the beaches. These included a force carrying DD tanks. This was something quite new. These tanks had been fitted with inflatable skirts, and were to be launched from LCTs while still at sea. The skirts, filled with compressed air, would keep them afloat while they reached the shoreline firing beyond the beach while the LCAs carrying the assaulting infantry touched down among them. A great idea, but in the event the sea was much too rough to attempt to launch them, so this force pulled out of line [the LCTs went in and beached and the tanks drove ashore, having dropped their skirts].

We were on time, in good order, and kept excellent station on our ML. As promised its skipper played his signature tune for us, which blared out over his loud-hailer, the tune: 'We don't know where we're going until we're there', a popular tune at the time, and not bad for a navigational leader.

We were released by our ML about a mile or so offshore, and soon after I deployed my boats to port and starboard, in line abreast for our touch-down on the beach. Gunships were firing over our heads, and LCTs firing huge clusters of rockets, hissing over our heads. Our aircraft had not been idle; I saw buildings of the village of Le Hamel just to my right disappear in bomb bursts. All of this fire, with that from destroyers, was intended to stun the enemy by sheer weight of concentrated gunfire, and thus hopefully make them keep their heads down, while the first wave of assaulting infantry landed and, with any luck,

LCAs landing Canadians on Juno beach, 6 June 1944. (MH4505)

stormed and cleared the beach. It had been planned that mine should be the third or fourth group to touch down, but because of heavy seas and consequent loss of support I was actually the second. First ashore was a tank landed by LCT equipped with chains (flails) which pounded up and down the beach with its flails thrashing in front of it to blow up any mines and clear a path for the infantry. This tank beached at exactly the appointed time of 07.25. I timed it myself. My ten craft touched down on exactly the right beach at the appointed time of 07.32, in the right order and disembarked my troops. The disembarkation was not as swift as it might have been, it could not be helped. The sea was pretty awful, many men had been sea-sick and just could not be hurried. The beach was shallow, only gradually shelving, and with a most unpleasant surf, so that boats actually grounded about fifty yards offshore, and the troops had to wade this distance through breakers. All my boats got off safely, and we turned and headed out to sea. As my boat left the beach, a shell or mortar bomb burst on either bow, but no damage was done.

By the end of D-Day, over 130,000 men had been transported from England and landed on the Normandy beaches in one lift: 72,215 British and Canadians and 57,500 Americans. This stunning display of seapower was a tribute to the seamanship, fighting spirit and skill of the Royal Navy, Royal Canadian Navy, United States Navy and Merchant Navy, who with the ships of other Allied nations put into effect Ramsay's master plan. In addition some 23,000 Allied airborne troops had been landed by the air forces. It was now the task of the navies, principally the British and Canadian with the Merchant Navy, to maintain the flow of troops, equipment and supplies to enable the armies ashore to hold off German counter-attacks, while expanding the bridgehead, and eventually break out and advance into Germany to finish the war. The battle at sea off the beachheads was harder after D-Day than on the day itself. The Germans had allocated thirty-six U-boats for anti-invasion tasks. Some of these submarines were fitted with *schnorkels* and could stay underwater much longer running on diesels. They also had torpedoes adapted to shallow water. But so good were the Allied anti-submarine measures by now, especially using land-based aircraft of Coastal Command, that it was not until three weeks after D-Day that U-boats sank their first ship in the area. German Coastal Forces operating out of Le Havre and Brest were a far greater menace, and the Allies deployed 138 MTBs to cope with them. Donald Bradford:

Late in the afternoon of our first day off the Assault beaches, we made for the cruiser *Scylla* [Flag Rear-Admiral Sir Philip Vian, Commander Eastern Task Force] to attend conferences on the night's dispositions. We were assigned our patrol positions where we were to lie with engines cut, and to which we were to return immediately we lost contact with the enemy, should we be fortunate to have a brush and chase them. HMS *Scylla* would provide us with radar cover from her berth on the edge of the anchorage and inform us of any unidentified craft moving outside the Eastern Flank, giving us a range and bearing.

We arrived at our patrol position as dark set in. It was roughish and by no means comfortable to be stopped beam on to the swell. After a few minutes of it I had to howl

On the bridge of an MGB.
(A12903)

for my own special bucket, always kept handy at the back of the bridge, and invariably in use during some part of each trip to sea I made.

Scylla warned Bradford of the approach of six enemy craft:

They were obviously out on a minelaying sortie. I ordered illuminant rockets fired and crash started. My unit slipped into quarter-line for battle, without orders – they knew what it was going to be and how it would be fought without being told.

The Germans opened fire at the same time as us. The range was 500 yards and closing rapidly as we got into our stride. From their shooting and the fact they had immediately altered course I guessed their hearts weren't in their work and I don't blame them. They were caught in a gun battle, each boat with six or eight mines on board, some five tons of highly temperamental explosive ironmongery on deck where it wouldn't do the least good if hit in the right spot. They scattered as we charged into them.

The German boats fled, jettisoning their mines as fast as they could. Bradford's boats pursued, firing:

In the excitement of the clash I had completely forgotten about the minefields [German and known to the British], but not my Navigator who howled up the voicepipe from the charthouse, 'Sir, we are a mile inside.' However so were the enemy, so there couldn't be more danger to us than them. I felt certain we had them in the bag and was really elated; our first meeting with our German opposite numbers in the Assault Area, we had them on the run as if we were a pack of foxhounds out for a day's cubbing.

Suddenly there was a tremendous explosion followed by a gigantic column of water between us and the enemy, then another close astern of us. Mines! Life was starting to be difficult. I was left with a choice of risking a known and self-advertised danger to my boats and men, by continuing at full speed, or breaking off the action without a definite kill to teach the Germans a lesson. I decided to go ahead and risk it.

More mines went up, some near, some far away. Then, in a vast inferno the last R-boat in line disappeared, leaving nothing but a flurry of water and a pall of smoke. Either it had hit a mine, or our shooting had detonated one of the mines on its deck before the crew could throw it overboard.

I decided it was time for us to think of self and devote our attention to getting out of the dangerous waters into which we had so gaily headed. I ordered the helm put over and reduced speed to a mere crawl, and we commenced to pick our way out of the minefield content with our victory and thinking, 'We'll live to play another day.' We nosed our way out daintily. Everyone on my boat was talking in unaccustomed whispers and walking around on tiptoe.

German destroyers also took a hand in the early days. Bradford a few days later:

Scylla ordered my unit to investigate vessels moving out from Le Havre, informing us that the vessels were probably a destroyer force. We were all on our mettle for a scrap with the

The 6-inch guns of the Colony class cruiser HMS *Mauritius* during a night action between Brest and Lorient on 15 August 1944. HMCS *Iroquois* and HMS *Ursa* under Captain W. W. Davis RN (*Mauritius*) sank eight German minesweepers, an escort and a supply ship.
(A25321)

German destroyer men. Our last brush with these chaps left bitter memories and we were aching to repay them. I ordered preparations for a torpedo attack, and reduced speed to give us a chance of slipping up on them unobserved.

There were three all right and they were too big for E- or R-boats. Suddenly I saw another dim shape on the opposite bow to the destroyers. We were steaming between two units. I could see the destroyers to the south of us, an *Elbing* and two *Möwe* class, the latter the equivalent in size of our *Hunt* class destroyers. They were moving slowly up towards the north-west apparently closing the ship to the north of us.

The three German destroyers were stalking a lone British corvette, which was well outside the convoy route. The corvette fired star shell, attempting to take on all three destroyers at once:

It was obvious neither side knew we were there, they were both too occupied with their feud. It was our chance. I led in immediately, my boats opening out into a torpedo firing formation, a broad quarterline.

As soon as we opened out the Germans spotted our bow waves, we were 700 yards away. They immediately swung away to the southward to put their sterns towards us, increasing speed, following round one after the other. It was now or never. Away went six torpedoes, a zone shot, each boat firing her fish with slightly different deflection. It was tricky, the destroyers were altering away rapidly, and had switched all their guns onto us. We could see them firing torpedoes at the corvette as they swung. For a moment I thought we had been beaten and our fish had all missed. I gave the order to swing back into fine quarterline and follow me in for a gunnery attack and open fire. Suddenly a plume of smoke and spray shot up from the bridge of the first *Möwe*; we had done it. Immediately the *Elbing* started to alter towards us with the obvious intention of tackling us while the other *Möwe* went to her sister's help. She got hit on the bridge and forward gun position by a nicely placed burst of pom-pom shells from one of my boats; but we had shot our bolts, one boat had just reported an engine out of action. It was time to disengage. I altered to the north, giving the *Elbing* a parting burst of Oerlikon, which spattered the bridge, and away we went towards the corvette. The *Elbing* turned back to help the *Möwes*.

When I got within hailing range of the corvette, I was greeted with a storm of abuse for firing torpedoes at her. The captain calmed down a little when I pointed out that ours had gone the other way.

Perhaps the most serious problem was mines. After D-Day, the Germans dropped parachute mines into the anchorages and shipping lanes. These included magnetic [activated by the ship's magnetic field] and acoustic [activated by the noise of propellers], which by now were familiar enough. But among them was a new type, which sat on the bottom and was activated by the pressure wave of a ship passing overhead. The Allies, who called them Oyster mines, had no counter to them, other than steaming at very slow speed when in shallow water.

Finally, despite the Allies having almost complete air supremacy in the skies over Normandy, the Luftwaffe still got through, mainly after dark, when the

**HMS *Rodney*, off the coast
of Normandy, bombarding
German battery positions.**
(A23958)

Allied fighters had gone home for the night. The Allies were also wary of the
glider bombs they had first encountered off Italy. Warships also provided gunfire support for the armies ashore until the advance took them out of range. In
the 6-inch gun cruiser HMS *Arethusa*, Bandsman Arthur Webster, Royal Marines
was Port Watch in the gunnery control post. With his opposite number in the
Starboard Watch, Bert Baker, he kept a combined diary of events:

June 9th

07.00 Action breakfast

11.45 Given target by FBO [Forward Bombardment Officer ashore]. Enemy mortar positions. Our troops are very near, so careful firing is necessary. Third broadside well hit target
and out of action. We used up 42 x 6-inch HE.

12.00 New target. Enemy observation post. Range 180, almost as far inland as Caen.
Target well hit, 63 rounds of HE used.

13.30 Rocket ship blast at shore and start fires. Shore battery fires on destroyer who moves
out of way

14.55 New target enemy mortars.

15.05 Opened fire on observation post in chimney

15.40 Stand by for next target. Enemy transport, poor visibility. Shore batteries fire at us
but are 1,000 yards short.

15.50 Ready to fire again at more mortars. Target well hit.

17.00 Air Raid [warning] Yellow

17.05 Air Raid [warning] Red

17.30 Twelve bombs dropped near to merchant ship. Bofors and Oerlikons let rip, hit
nothing.

17.30 Twenty fighter-bombers over beachhead. Thought to be FW.

18.40 6-inch target enemy area

18.44 Air Raid [warning] Red

18.52 *Sumatra* an old Dutch ship sunk in fairly shallow water to form breakwater [part of Mulberry].

18.57 Air Raid [warning] Red

20.00 bombarding again

21.00 Air Raid [warning] Yellow

21.10 Air Raid [warning] Red. Bomb dropped astern of liberty ship. Heaps of flak going up.

21.25 Under way going to anchorage. When cable party was on fo'c's'le, A and B turrets fired a broadside. I'll bet that shook them up [the unfortunate cable party].

21.35 Heard on bridge from enemy bombers [intercept?] 'enemy fighters attacking, where are ours?'

21.50 Last shooting of the day against enemy OPs. Very good shooting today.

22.30 Closed up in CP

22.50 Air Raid [warning] Red

22.52 Make smoke [to cover anchorage against air attack]

23.00 Glider bomb warning

23.05 Glider bomb [warning] cancelled

23.10 All ships firing at planes, but also at shore battery searchlight

23.10 Enemy plane coming down

23.25 Another one coming down. Fleet putting up terrific AA.

There were some lighter moments:

June 16th at Pompey [Naval slang for Portsmouth]

07.30 Knobs came aboard. Sir Charles Portal, Admirals Ramsay and Cunningham, Generals Ismay and Laycock, Lord Lascelles [*sic*] [the King's private secretary], Old Uncle Tom Cobley and all.

08.00 The King came aboard

08.05 Left Pompey. We went over at 28 knots. Rolled like blazes. Some of the knobs were said to be looking sick when they left the ship. They went ashore to dine with Monty.

21.00 Arrived in Pompey, stayed outside in Spithead where King and Knobs disembarked.

June 17th

Ship's company 'chocker' [fed up] because no leave. No boats and under steaming orders.

June 18th

08.00 Colours. Played for leaving harbour [the Royal Marines Band in its other role].

The *Arethusa* left the assault area on 25 June, after suffering mine damage.

The Navies' task in support of the Armies did not end with the break-out from Normandy in mid August 1944. Most supplies were still coming over the beaches and through the surviving (British) Mulberry Harbour. The American Mulberry had been wrecked in the great gale of 19 to 21 June. Although ports such as Cherbourg were captured and opened – usually weeks later, thanks to extensive German sabotage – convoys still had to be escorted, U-boats and

Minesweepers clearing the River Scheldt. (A26548)

coastal forces sunk or driven off. As the Brittany and Biscay ports fell to the Allies, so the U-boats were driven to using German and Norwegian ports, and the pressure eased slightly. E-boats operated from the Dutch ports of Den Helder, Ijmuiden and Rotterdam until almost the end of the War. On 16 October 1944 Field Marshal Montgomery, as he had become, gave the clearing of the Scheldt estuary top priority. Ramsay had been prodding him to do so for weeks, in fact ever since Antwerp, with all its port facilities intact, fell to the Allies in early September. The first Allied ship steamed into Antwerp on 28 November. (For an account of the opening of the Scheldt Estuary see the *Imperial War Museum Book of Victory in Europe*.)

While the Allied Armies were fighting in north-west Europe, succoured by the Royal Navy, the Royal Canadian Navy and the Merchant Navy, the Battle of the Atlantic had still to be fought, Russian convoys maintained, and the war in the Far East (described in the next chapter) involved an increasing commitment by the Royal Navy. But the end of the tunnel was in sight, although some way off when Ordinary Seaman Vincent Brennan a Southern Irishman wrote to his mother on 5 July, from the minesweeper *Fraserburgh*:

And so we have come back to France again. The first step on the road down-hill. Greater strides will be made as time passes on until the whole thing will turn into a catastrophe for the Germans. In the meantime we still have to work harder than ever, while you at home must show greater patience. Just keep your hearts up, especially now that we have reached the final highway. All will be well, please God, and soon peace will once again be our reward for those long years of patient waiting, working and yearning. Your prayers have indeed been great and given me courage to face whatever might come.

Tons of love to you both

Your loving son

Vincent XXXXXX

The Royal Navy still had to keep capital ships in northern waters to guard against the possibility of the mighty *Tirpitz* sallying forth from her Norwegian fjord and attacking convoys. These capital ships were urgently needed in other theatres of war, increasingly in the Far East. *Tirpitz* had only once been attacked at sea, in March 1942, in the abortive operation described by Lieutenant Friend in Chapter Seven. It was this attack which had led Hitler to restrict her sorties to times when the British carriers were well away from the area, so it was not as fruitless as at first thought. A further series of attacks were made on *Tirpitz*, in attempts to get rid of this menace for ever.

On 22 September 1943 an attack was made on *Tirpitz* in Kaa Fjord by X craft. Six of these 35-ton midget submarines, each with a crew of four, were towed across the North Sea by S- and T-class submarines. X9 sank on passage and X8 had to be scuttled because of damage. Four boats entered Kaa Fjord, and two, X6 commanded by Lieutenant Donald Cameron RNR, and X7 commanded by Lieutenant Godfrey Place RN, both succeeded in placing charges under *Tirpitz*. Both charges exploded. X5 was never seen again. X10, sent to attack *Scharnhorst*, thought to be nearby but actually at sea, returned to the parent submarine, but sank under tow on the homeward journey. Thanks to Ultra, the Admiralty learned that *Tirpitz* was out of action for six months. Both Cameron and Place were taken prisoner, survived the war and were awarded the VC.

The next attack on *Tirpitz*, Operation Tungsten was planned for April 1944, as a strike by the Fleet Air Arm. Taking part were the carriers *Victorious* and *Furious*, and escort carriers *Emperor*, *Fencer*, *Pursuer* and *Searcher*, with a total of fifteen Fleet Air Arm Squadrons of Hellcats, Wildcats, Barracudas, Corsairs, Seafires and Swordfish aircraft. The Fleet Air Arm had come a long way since the dismal days of the Norwegian campaign four years before. Hellcats, Wildcats and Corsairs were modern American aircraft, designed to operate off carriers. The Barracuda was the Fleet Air Arm's first monoplane torpedo bomber. The Seafire was a Spitfire adapted for deck operations, by the addition of a hook to catch the arrester wires on landing and bring the aircraft to a stop, and folding wings so that it would fit on the hangar lift. Although the Seafire put in sterling service, it was not really suited to carrier operations. Its long nose blocked the pilot's view of the flight-deck during the last critical seconds of the approach on landing. Its undercarriage was not strong enough for the 'controlled crash' that so many carrier recoveries [landings] involved.

The plan involved two strikes, each of twenty-one Barracudas carrying bombs, rather than torpedoes, covered by forty fighters, and more aircraft on flak suppression and other tasks. Out to sea, Seafires from *Furious* flew Combat Air Patrol (CAP) over the fleet, while Swordfish from *Fencer* were allocated to anti-submarine patrols. Captain T. J. N. Hilken RN commanding the escort carrier *Emperor* launched her Hellcats:

3 April, Operation Tungsten
Perfect weather, light breeze, calm sea. Numerous hits seen on *Tirpitz*. All our [*Emperor*] air-craft returned safely, but one (Hoare) had to ditch as his hook had been damaged by flak.

Operation Tungsten: Hellcats on board HMS *Emperor*. The other ships are the carriers *Furious* (nearest camera), *Searcher*, *Pursuer*, and, in the distance, the cruiser *Jamaica*. (A22649)

Picked up safely by destroyer. Expected enemy air attack all day, but none came. Similar strikes ordered for tomorrow, but later cancelled.

A total of fourteen hits were obtained with a combination of 1,600- and 500-lb bombs, and *Tirpitz* was seen with her stern on the bottom, blown from her moorings. Only four Fleet Air Arm aircraft were lost. Many bombs did not penetrate *Tirpitz*'s armoured deck because they were released too low; perhaps pilots flying low to avoid the flak, we shall probably never know. *Tirpitz* was out of action for three months. It says much for her construction that she was not sunk. But it was a great achievement by the Fleet Air Arm.

The Fleet Air Arm made eight more attempts to sink *Tirpitz*. On only one were any hits achieved. The ship was very difficult to approach because of high cliffs, flak and smoke that obscured the target. It was realized that a big bomb with great penetrating power was needed to finish her off. Three strikes were mounted by Bomber Command Lancasters of 617 and 9 Squadrons carrying the giant Tallboy 12,000 lb (5 ton) bombs. The first, flown from a Russian airfield, as UK airfields were not within range of Kaa Fjord, damaged her. She was moved to Tromsö, and two strikes were launched from Lossiemouth. The second, on 12 November 1944, caused her to turn turtle. Of her company of 1,700, some 1,000 were trapped, only 86 being rescued through holes cut in her bottom. At last the menace had been removed.

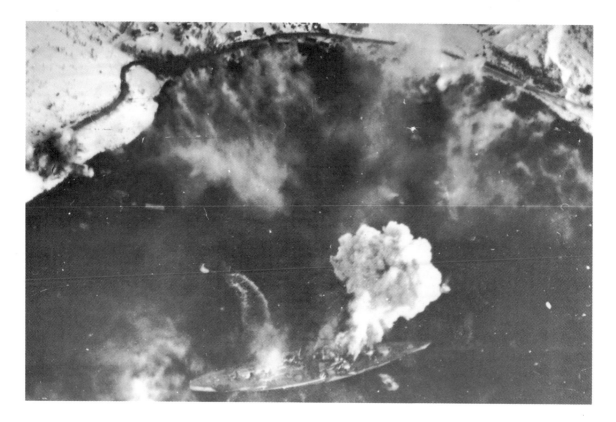

Tirpitz **hit by Barracudas.** (A22633)

Attacks on shipping in the fjords and inshore waters of Norway from 1942 onwards were not confined to attempts to sink major units of the German fleet. Numerous attacks had been made by both the Fleet Air Arm and submarines on all manner of shipping. Aircraft from HMS *Emperor* alone carried out four anti-shipping strikes between 26 April and 15 May 1944.

On 15 August 1944, the postponed Operation Anvil renamed Dragoon, the invasion of the South of France, took place. It was a huge operation, second only to Neptune in its size, and warships of the Royal Navy were overwhelmingly in the majority. Over a hundred warships took part, and seven Fleet Air Arm squadrons in seven escort carriers. Hilken was there in *Emperor*, and aircraft from his ship alone flew 252 sorties in eight days, not only covering the landings, but supporting operations up the Rhône valley.

The Russian convoys continued. Leading Signalman Butler in *Matchless*:

I received an urgent message that our sister ship *Mahratta* had been torpedoed. Big seas were running and a blinding snowstorm was raging in utter darkness. None of us hardly slept that night. We were still edgy the following night, and as we tried to rest in our mess decks the ship was shaken by a loud bang. All lights, except for the emergency lights, went out, and I thought like everybody else that the ship had been torpedoed. The disciplined abandon ship drill was forgotten as we fought to be first up the ladder and through the hatchway. When we reached the open deck we were told that the ship had been shaken

HMS *Furious* taking it 'green' over her flight deck. (A23043)

by one of our own depth-charges which had been quickly dropped on a contact. Unfortunately we weren't doing the required speed, and had almost blown off our own stern. We returned to our mess deck shamefaced at our undisciplined reaction.

Our big convoy of empty ships battled through and eventually reached Loch Ewe on 6th May [1944] with 44 merchantmen. On our way back, I was passing through the seamen's mess deck on the way to my own. I noticed a large 'fanny' of pot mess, a stew of odds and ends, standing ready to be served. It was heavy weather, the ship was rolling badly, and a young seaman in obvious distress staggered over to the 'fanny', thinking it was the gash bucket, and added his lot to it. Only me and an old three-badge killick [leading seaman with three good conduct badges] saw it. Old stripey winked and said, 'You didn't see that did you, bunts?' I stood puzzled for a moment and hurried on when I saw him nonchalantly stir in the lot with a big wooden spoon.

The war in the Atlantic and Arctic continued despite the catastrophic defeats suffered by the German Army in Europe at the hands of the Western Allies and Russians. But the techniques, on both sides, had improved out of all recognition since the early days. Lieutenant-Commander John Mosse RN in HMS *Mermaid*:

For some months U-boats had been using an acoustic torpedo called Gnat, which homes on the noise of a ship's propellers. One countermeasure was to tow a noise making decoy called Foxer.

At 23.00 on August 23rd [1944], a Swordfish from *Vindex* [escort carrier] reported two U-boats 56 miles distant. *Keppel*, *Peacock* and *Mermaid* went off in search, later joined by

Loch Dunvegen from the close screen. At 02.07/24 [02.07 hours 24th August], *Keppel* gained Asdic contact, and shortly after a Gnat exploded close by. This U-boat was hunted by *Keppel* and *Peacock*, while *Mermaid* and *Loch Dunvegen* went to search for the second one.

I was swallowing a mug of cocoa at 03.21, when suddenly, 'PING', the sound I had been waiting to hear for five years! We took immediate anti-Gnat precautions; just in time. Ninety seconds later a Gnat exploded close astern, followed a minute later by another. The hunt was on.

Our first attack at 03.51 was not a good one. Asdic conditions were difficult, and for a while both ships lost contact as the U-boat went deep. Suddenly at 04.50, there was a yell from X gun's crew that a conning tower had broken surface very briefly, and then dived again. I was unsighted by the mast and didn't see it.

Contact was lost and regained:

At 05.13 range was opened for a careful deliberate attack and a Foxer was streamed. The U-boat fired two bubble targets [to fool the Asdic], which were easily recognised. No depth was recorded and [a] ten charge pattern was fired because it was thought the U-boat was on its way down. This attack produced a patch of oil. Immediately after the attack the Foxer was cut adrift with an axe, because it would have been dangerous to keep it out with the U-boat astern.

Loch Dunvegen attacked with Squid, but her Asdic broke down, leaving the field to *Mermaid*: from Report of Group Commander:

Mermaid's third attack was considered the best of the day. The depth of the U-boat was again recorded as 600 feet, and pattern JIG was used. This started a leak in the U-boat's tanks which exuded diesel oil steadily for the next twelve hours, eventually covering an area five miles long and one mile wide.

At this point Rear-Admiral Dalrymple-Hamilton, commanding 10th Cruiser Squadron (CS10), ordered the attacking ships to rejoin the convoy at 08.00. Mosse:

But we still had no evidence of destruction. The depth of water was hardly sufficient to burst the hull if he was lying on the bottom. Then began a tug-of-war between a Senior Officer who was concerned for our safety in the event of attack by enemy surface forces or aircraft, and an anti-submarine officer who was not going to let go of his first U-boat. The following signals tell the story:

07.30 To CS10. STILL IN CONTACT OIL WELLING UP. HAVE CARRIED OUT FIVE ATTACKS AND WILL DO MORE AS SOON AS I CAN PREPARE DEPTH CHARGES. WILL STAY HERE TILL I KILL HIM.

Our time limit was extended till 09.00.

08.52 To CS10. U-BOAT STILL VERY MUCH ALIVE AND BUBBLING OIL. IT MAY TAKE TWELVE HOURS TO EXHAUST HIM.

Time limit extended till noon. Three hours to go but still he would not surface. Shortly before noon *Keppel* and *Peacock* arrived on the scene, but neither could get contact, and *Mermaid* conned them into a close order attack on the bubbles. With hindsight the U-boat was already dead on the bottom at 900 feet. I wanted to wait, but *Keppel*, the senior officer present, said, 'would like to but we have to get back'. I was dragged away, but with *Keppel*'s permission I signalled to CS10:

HAVE LEFT U-BOAT STILL GUSHING OIL AND PROBABLY SEVERELY DAMAGED. REQUEST RUSSIAN AIRCRAFT BE ASKED TO SEARCH. HE HAS BEEN SUBMERGED SINCE 04.50.

Keppel and *Peacock* were sent back for one hour and confirmed oil still rising from same position.

Throughout this long hunt which lasted for some twelve hours *Mermaid* carried out ten attacks. We were able to maintain Asdic contact most of the time, although sometimes very faint.

Postwar Assessment: U-344 Kapitan Leutnant Ulrich Pietsch. Definitely Sunk.

On the return convoy from Kola Inlet, they again encountered U-boats that went deep; Mosse:

Depth-charges were slow to sink, and it was possible for a deep U-boat to take evasive action if he knew the moment they were dropped. This he could estimate from the frequency of the Asdic pulses and the propeller noise of the ship passing overhead. To counter this Johnnie Walker and his Anti-Submarine Officer Michael Impey had devised a Creeping Attack which could be carried out by two or more ships.

All four ships manoeuvred for such an attack. All ships reduced to a silent speed of 7 knots, *Peacock*, directing from astern, guided us like a ploughman with three horses. *Keppel* and *Whitehall* each fired 22 depth-charges from their outboard throwers and rails, and *Mermaid* dropped 18 down the centre. Charges were set to make a sandwich explosion between 500 and 850 feet.

At first it appeared that the U-boat had survived, and *Mermaid* still in contact was about to direct another creeping attack, when at 18.13 there were three loud explosions. *Mermaid* made one more attack, after which bubbles and wreckage came to the surface. *Peacock* recovered some positive evidence of destruction, which her doctor classified as blood group four.

Postwar Assessment: U-394 Kapitan Leutnant Wolfgang Borger. Definitely Sunk.

In the U-boat, as its pressure hull was riven or crushed by the explosions, or by sinking below the depth it could sustain, men choked or were mashed to death in the dark and cold. The end might take hours, as they sat listening to the sound of their remorseless hunters overhead; perhaps knowing that their boat was damaged beyond hope of surfacing and the only future was a lingering death. The casualty rate among U-boat crews in the Second World War was 85 per cent, the highest of any service in any nation on either side in that War.

Operations in the North Sea also continued. On 12 December 1944, at the age of twenty-six, Lieutenant Dennis, recently engaged to be married, took command of his own ship, the First World War vintage destroyer *Valorous*:

Interior of U-boat,
searching for damage after
a depth-charge attack.
(HU2235)

Modernised and in good shape, her pennant numbers were L00, and she was always known as the 'Lucky Loo'. Perhaps then a lucky third ship for me. She was usually employed escorting coastal convoys between the Firth of Forth and Sheerness. These convoys were unlike those in the Atlantic or Russia. Because of the heavily mined areas all down the coast, the ships, usually thirty to forty small coasters or colliers, proceeded in two lines, keeping inside the narrow swept channels, marked by buoys. Lately the Germans had been perking up a bit, and had been sending E-boats over to the southern end of the run with mines and torpedoes, and U-boats to the deeper waters off Scotland. But it was comforting to be so near to friendly ports, especially after that cut-off feeling in the Kola Inlet, where even the friendly port was hostile in a sinister way.

Valorous having recently been in dock, I had not expected a refit for months, by which time it looked as if the war in Europe might end. It looked as though I would not get any leave to get married. On 18 January, as I passed under Forth Bridge, I received a signal ordering us in for a boiler clean. I came to the conclusion I had better get married right away. If I were to miss this chance, I might not get another before being whisked off to fight the Japanese. So I telephoned Wales. Faith and her parents were out. Polly the cook took the message that I wanted to get married in two days. I arrived chez my own parents at midnight. They were very good about it. I hadn't even got a ring, and had ten shillings and sixpence in the bank [55p].

To their lasting credit, my in-laws got everything organised and we were wed on January 20th 1945, at 48 hours' notice. I had arranged for the necessary banns to be read some time before. Indeed I had read my own on board, with no man daring to object.

Just as I was girding myself to return to the ship, I received a message that because of troubles with the dynamo, *Valorous* could not leave the dockyard for another ten days. Loo was indeed lucky and old.

Eventually it was not until February 3rd that I was off to sea again, leaving my forlorn bride to the mercies of Uncle Cyril Colthart, who liked comforting young grass widows. He chased Faith round a haystack later, but didn't catch her, I was told. He remained a good friend.

It wasn't until February 21st that I ran into a spot of bother with the enemy who had been laying mines down our route, between Immingham and Sheerness. The senior officer in *Verdun* was ahead, I was in the rear trying to keep the stragglers in the swept channel. It was dark, blowy and cold. A little after 01.00, there were several heavy explosions somewhere up ahead. It became clear to me that at least two ships were sinking. I closed one of them, and they reported that they had been hit by a torpedo from one of a number of E-boats, which were still around.

By now we were a long way behind the convoy. A nasty decision had to be made. If I stopped to pick up survivors from the coaster, I would leave the rest of the convoy naked to the enemy. So very reluctantly I dropped off our Carley Floats right by the wreck, called for a rescue boat from Immingham, and told the survivors that help would be on the way. With that, we raced off to rejoin the convoy.

We arrived just in time. There were several E-boats milling about. The situation became *mouvementé*. A lot of tracer fire from both sides and then a shattering explosion in our boiler room, which at first I could only imagine was a torpedo. On these occasions there always seems to be an earsplitting escape of steam, which certainly happened now and didn't help one to think clearly. We were stopped in the water, a target for our erstwhile targets. But, after a few minutes of all kinds of gunnery, they shoved off. We couldn't pursue them.

We suffered one man killed, and two seriously wounded. Unfortunately the Surgeon Lieutenant was sick ashore, but the sick berth attendant did very well indeed. On investigation we found we had been struck by a 5-inch shell from one of the merchantmen in the convoy, who must have mistaken us for the enemy in the mêlée. I expect they still think they got in a good shot.

By now the War in Europe was drawing to a close. The U-boats remained potent to the end; Alec Dennis:

When we got back on the convoy cycle we found things warming up a bit. The E-boats were having their final fling at the south end of the run, and north of the Humber the new Type XXXIII U-boats were appearing with their high underwater speeds and sophisticated torpedoes.

Our sister the *Viceroy* was sure she had sunk one in the Firth of Forth, the recorder readings were so good. Another pattern of depth-charges was dropped and, lo and behold, up came a rubber raft with some unbroken bottles of brandy with it, undoubtedly of U-boat origin. She was later identified as U-1274. On the other hand the Germans had scored by sinking the Free French destroyer *La Combattante*, along the route, probably by mine.

As April progressed it was evident that the war in Europe was nearing its end, though the U-boats kept at it until the last moment. Indeed the last merchant sinking of the war occurred the day before VE day, just in the entrance to the Firth of Forth. So I'd been with it to the end.

Commander Evelyn Chavasse RN, in Derby House:

Came the ultimate vindication of all that we had been trying to do, at sea, in the air, on shore. Germany surrendered. As far as we were concerned, our long and horrible battle of the Atlantic was won. The nightmare was over. Every U-boat was ordered by Germany to surface, report its position en clair, hoist a large black flag, and steam on the surface to Scottish waters, mostly Loch Erriboll. They nearly all obeyed, and were often thankful to do so. A few scuttled themselves; a few sought sanctuary, but didn't find it in neutral ports. With my companions, I stood one day in Derby House, and gazed at the huge dark

'Lucky Loo', HMS *Valorous*, pennant number L00.
(Papers of Commander J. A. J. Dennis RN 95/5/1 negative number DOC521)

The end of the Battle of the Atlantic. A German sailor throws a heaving line to fellow U-boat crewmen while coming alongside to surrender at Loch Eriboll. Royal Navy officers and ratings are grouped forward of the conning tower of the right-hand boat. Both fly the White Ensign.
(A28528)

green map of the North Atlantic Ocean. It was now studded with U-boats steering to the north-east. The final convoys had reached their destinations unmolested. The war was won.

Lieutenant Commander Mosse RN in *Mermaid*:

At dawn we met the frigate *Loch Tarbert* and set course for the Western Approaches, where we found the U-825 lying stopped on the surface flying a large black flag as they had been told to do. It was an eerie feeling approaching this black monster, which had so recently been our mortal enemy, and he was probably as apprehensive as we were. We kept our guns trained on him, but he gave no trouble, and we set him on course for Loch Alsh. Until this moment it had been hard to believe that the war against Germany was over.

But we were very quickly reminded that a fierce war was still raging in the Pacific where the Japanese, fighting to the last man with fanatical ferocity, were defending every inch of every island they held. An important requirement was to have suitable AA armament to deal with Kamikaze suicide bombers. We went into Portsmouth for a brief refit, and to be equipped with extra Oerlikons.

I took the opportunity of inviting friends and relations on board for lunch parties. But overhanging this lighthearted revelry was the black cloud of Japan, and it was with some foreboding that we sailed for Malta en route for the Far East.

10
The Defeat of Japan – The Far East and Pacific: 1942–1945

The Japanese strategically went over from offence to defence once they had reached the outer rim of their conquests, in May 1942. There were of course local offensives, primarily in Burma, but in the main they had hoped to win the war by making any Allied offensives so costly in lives that in the course of time they would be left to enjoy their territorial gains undisturbed. As we saw in Chapter Six, all hope of this was lost when they attacked the United States. It is not within the scope of this book to cover the vast sweep of the campaign in the Pacific fought by the United States. Suffice it to say that without the participation of the United States, Japan, and Germany, would have remained undefeated. Japanese strategy had in fact placed the country at a disadvantage when confronted with such a major seapower, soon to be the greatest in the world. Germany, a continental country, could not be defeated by seapower, however powerful. Indeed two of her three principal enemies, the United States and United Kingdom, were totally reliant on seapower to bring their armies to battle on the continent and sustain them; and the United Kingdom depended on command of the seas for her very survival, as did Japan. Every ounce of the materials for which she had risked the wrath of the United States by going to war, had to be shipped back to Japan, which the Americans recognized at once. When, with remarkable speed, they recovered from the first shocks, they set about cutting Japan's sea lines of communications, and retaking, or bypassing, her newly won island bases, as a precursor to invading the home islands. So extensive were these bases and defended with such fanaticism, that the process took over three years, from 7 August 1942, the first American offensive at Guadalcanal, to mid August 1945 when the Japanese surrendered, their homeland as yet uninvaded. The American submarine service, given clearance to wage unrestricted warfare within hours of the attack on Pearl Harbor, sank millions of tons of Japanese shipping, including escorts. Japanese anti-submarine tactics were rudimentary, and they did not introduce a convoy system until 1944.

From December 1941 to mid 1944 the Royal Navy in the Far East, driven back to Ceylon after the fall of Singapore, was on the defensive, and played a very minor role in the war against Japan. Admiral Sir James Somerville, of Force H, was sent to take command of the Eastern Fleet after the loss of Admiral Sir Tom Phillips in *Prince of Wales*. His second-in-command was Vice-Admiral Algernon Willis, once Cunningham's Chief of Staff in the Mediterranean Fleet, and C.-in-C. South Atlantic for a while. On his way to the Indian Ocean, Willis prepared a strategic appreciation for discussion with Somerville. The key point was:

The preservation of the Eastern Fleet was more important than Ceylon. If we lost Ceylon, it would be certainly difficult, though not impossible, to safeguard the shipping routes off the coast of Africa and to India. But if the Eastern Fleet, or a large part of it, was destroyed, both Ceylon and the shipping routes would be wide open to attack.

Admiral Willis was proposing a policy of 'The Fleet in Being', which as he said,

has often been practised by our opponents against us, but not often by ourselves, for in the past the Royal Navy has usually been strong enough to take the offensive. But now in March 1942, the hastily constructed Eastern Fleet was about all we had left in battleships and carriers allowing for the essential missions in home waters and the Mediterranean.

Yet again the 'chickens' of British Government policy between the wars had come home to roost, when a British admiral had, perfectly correctly, to adopt the strategy of a lesser seapower. Somerville agreed with Willis's strategy, although he must have found it hard to bear, and indeed took a number of risks with his fleet soon after.

The Eastern Fleet certainly is a mixed lot,

was Willis's comment on seeing it:

it comprised:

Battleships:	*Warspite* and the four R Class; *Valiant* to join later after repairs.
Aircraft Carriers:	*Formidable*, *Indomitable* and *Hermes*, the latter very small and slow and cannot be described as a fleet carrier
Cruisers:	8-inch *Dorsetshire* and *Cornwall*
	6-inch *Emerald*, *Enterprise* and two others
Destroyers:	About a dozen in various stages of disrepair
AA Cruisers	The Dutch *Heenskirk*

Somerville divided the Fleet into two parts:

Force A	*Warspite* (C.-in-C.), the two fleet carriers, the 8-inch cruisers, two 6-inch cruisers *Emerald* and *Enterprise* and six destroyers.
Force B	3rd Battle Squadron, with my flag in *Resolution*, *Revenge*, *Royal Sovereign* and *Ramilles*, *Hermes* with about 12 Swordfish, two 6-inch cruisers, *Heenskirk* and five destroyers.

I considered making a revised will as I reckoned if the old R Class Battleships met a Japanese Fleet we would be for it.

The Fleet was in Addu Atoll, in the Maldive Islands, south-west of Colombo. His battleships were not in good order:

Conditions in these 26-year-old ships [built for service in the Grand Fleet in the North Sea] in the tropics were very bad, the heat in engine rooms and boiler rooms and between decks generally being intense.

We joined Somerville on 2 April. He greeted me with a signal, 'So this is the Eastern Fleet. Never mind. There's many a good tune played on an old fiddle.' Which my ships' companies felt was rubbing in our antiquity!

On 4 April a Catalina reported a large Japanese force heading for Ceylon. Willis:

We were caught completely on the wrong foot.

The Japanese force which proceeded to launch an air strike on Colombo consisted of four fast battleships, five fleet carriers, three cruisers and eight destroyers, although this was not known at the time because the Catalina was shot down before it could complete its report. Both Willis and Somerville left Addu Atoll as soon as possible. At one time it seemed to Willis that Somerville was heading for a battle with the Japanese, but:

apparently Somerville's idea was, having located the enemy, to try and keep clear by day and close after dark to deliver aircraft torpedo attacks from our carriers.

Fortunately contact was never made, because the Japanese aircraft both outnumbered and outranged any of the obsolete types in the Eastern Fleet, or anywhere in the Fleet Air Arm at the time. Neither, mercifully, did the Japanese find the ancient battleships of 3rd Battle Squadron, who had put back into Addu Atoll because of a water shortage. They did however find the cruisers *Dorsetshire* and *Cornwall*.

Herbert Gollop was an AA gunner second class in *Dorsetshire*, manning A Defence Position under command of a midshipman:

Over 50 Japanese dive bombers attacked us and *Cornwall*. The first wave of three bombers came out of the sun, released their bombs at a low height, and all three hit the ship. Communications were disrupted. I shouted down to P1 gun, 'Why have you stopped firing? Get it firing.' One of the crew shouted back, 'How can we fire? All the rest of the crew's dead.' We were hit by about thirty bombs. Everything was a shambles. The ship's siren stuck and was wailing away. Captain Agar gave the order to abandon ship. She sank in a few minutes.

Cornwall was also rapidly despatched to the bottom.

Willis believed that Somerville's aggressiveness, which was contrary to what they had agreed earlier, might have been in part due to his being criticized by the Admiralty two years before, in the incident described in Chapter Five. Eventually it was agreed that the battle squadron should be based at Kilindini near Mombasa in Kenya to protect the Middle East convoys which at that stage in the war were routed round the Cape. Here they would be safer than forward in Ceylon. By this time the Japanese had sunk the *Hermes*, two fleet tankers and the destroyer *Vampire*. Willis:

So all in all we had lost control of the Indian Ocean, except perhaps the area west of Ceylon. However the bulk of the Eastern Fleet had been preserved.

In early May 1942, the port of Diego Suarez on the island of Madagascar, a French colony, was seized by an amphibious assault to deny it to the Japanese as a base. Operations to occupy the whole island were complete by 6 November 1942.

The threat to Ceylon and the Indian Ocean shipping lanes was reduced to negligible proportions, not, it must be said, by the Eastern Fleet, but by events thousands of miles away. On 7 June 1942, the United States Navy inflicted a crushing defeat on the Japanese in the battle of Midway. The Japanese lost four carriers, the Americans one. In October 1944, at Leyte Gulf, in the greatest naval battle in history, the United States Navy sank three Japanese battleships, four carriers, six cruisers and numerous other ships including transports.

Not until May 1943 at the *TRIDENT* Allied conference in Washington were the joint Anglo-American staffs ordered to prepare a joint strategy for the defeat of Japan. The plan that eventually emerged envisaged the advance of the Americans in two prongs; one across the Pacific islands, and one from New Guinea, through the Philippines, both aimed at Japan. The British would advance through Burma and Malaya. At the *SEXTANT* conference in Cairo in November and December 1943, it was decided that in prosecuting the war against Japan, the campaign in the Pacific would take the higher priority for joint assets, and therefore the main effort of the Royal Navy, once ships could be spared from other tasks, would be to form the British Pacific Fleet (BPF). The BPF would be based in Australia, with a forward base, whose location would be decided later. The Eastern Fleet would be maintained at a strength sufficient only to support operations in the Burma, Malaya and East Indies theatre.

The Eastern Fleet's first offensive foray in two years took place in April 1944, when Somerville led it to attack oil storage facilities at Sabang, an island off Sumatra. After a highly successful attack in which the Fleet Air Arm played a leading part, Somerville went on to attack Sourabaya. This was followed by eight more such strikes in the Dutch East Indies.

On 28 October a remarkable attack was carried out on two ships in Phuket harbour in Siam [Thailand] by two Chariots.

The Chariots were taken to the target area by the submarine *Trenchant*. Lieutenant Tony Eldridge RNVR commanded the attack:

From four and a half miles off all Chariot crews made a visual recce of our targets through *Trenchant*'s periscope. I was to attack the recently salvaged *Sumatra*. *Trenchant* surfaced at 19.00 on a perfect night with a brilliant moon: super for finding the target but we were concerned with being spotted. We were dripping with sweat inside our diving suits. Our

escape kit included a cyanide capsule in case we got captured and things got rough. At 22.10 hours, 'open fore hatch, up divers'. We mounted the machines which were ready on the chocks on the casing. The submarine opened her vents with a loud hissing of air, and slowly sank, leaving us on top. As we motored towards the harbour, I surfaced from time to time, to check our position. About 500 yards from our target, I dived for the final time. At 00.30, we were below our ship. My number two clamped the explosive head to the bilge keel, set the clock for six hours, and we shook hands. The time was 00.45. It had taken fifteen minutes.

On the return trip, we shone a red light out to sea at the agreed distance from shore. As we approached the submarine they flashed us in Morse. They thought they were being approached by an MTB, but it was only our engine the Hydrophone operator had heard. We ditched the machines and climbed inboard.

The next morning *Trenchant* went in closer; we heard two explosions and through the periscope saw wreckage fly into the air. It was the only completely successful British Chariot operation in the whole war.

When the war ended in Europe, it was expected that the war against Japan would last well into 1946, or even 1947. The outline for operations in the East Indies was the invasion of northern Malaya, Operation Zipper, in August 1945, culminating in the capture of Singapore by January 1946. In the Pacific, the amphibious assault on the southern island of Japan, Kyushu, was planned for November 1945, and on Honshu, near Tokyo, in spring 1946. The British

Above: Chariot Mark I without its 700-lb charge on the front. The charge could be attached to the bottom of a ship and detonated with a timer. Crewed by two men, the Chariot was battery powered and could motor at three-and-a-half knots for 20 miles. The Phuket raid was carried out in Mark IIs, in which the crew sat back-to-back in an enclosed cockpit. (A221221)

Left: Charioteer in Sladen suit and fitted with oxygen breathing apparatus. (A22117)

Fireflies on *Indefatigable* after a strike on Pangkalan Brandan, Sumatra, 4 January 1945 by ten Fleet Air Arm squadrons. The other two carriers were *Indomitable* and *Victorious*. The wings are being folded manually. and the forward lift is down. The Firefly carried a crew of two, pilot and observer. (A27167)

Government intended that the BPF as well as substantial British ground forces would take part in the American-led operations against the Japanese mainland.

In March 1945 the BPF arrived and came under command of Admiral Nimitz, C.-in-C. United States Pacific Fleet. En route to the Pacific the BPF carriers, commanded by Rear-Admiral Sir Philip Vian, launched a devastating attack on oil refineries at Palembang in the Dutch East Indies. Although Admiral Sir Bruce Fraser was C.-in-C. BPF, the complicated political tasks he was expected to undertake, involving the British, Australian and American Governments, led him to appoint his deputy Vice-Admiral Sir Bernard Rawlings as fleet commander at sea, while he flew his flag at the Fleet Base in Sydney, Australia. The BPF forward base was Seeadler harbour, Manus Island, in the Admiralty Islands. This was 1,800 miles away from Sydney, and a further 2,000 miles from the area of the BPF's first operation under US command as part of Admiral Spruance's US 5th Fleet at the invasion of Okinawa. Support for the BPF was supplied by the Fleet Train, a collection of oilers and supply ships that would rendezvous with the warships whenever they needed replenishing with fuel, ammunition, spares and food. These techniques had been practised by the USN for the last three years. They were new to the Royal Navy, who throughout the war so far, except for some rudimentary refuelling operations at sea, had operated from fixed bases. We have seen what problems this caused; for example during the *Bismarck* chase when ships had to be detached to refuel; and on many other occasions when the imperatives of refuelling and re-ammunitioning overruled all else. It was not until July 1945, one month before the end of the war with Japan, that a British warship carried out a beam RAS from a tanker, using the techniques practised to this day, instead of refuelling from astern.

At Okinawa the BPF first encountered Kamikaze attacks which had become such a feature of maritime war in the Pacific. On that operation alone, 28 USN ships were sunk by Kamikazes and 171 damaged, including the US carriers *Wasp*, *Yorktown* and *Franklin* with their wooden flight decks. The British carriers *Indefatigable*, *Formidable*, *Indomitable* and *Victorious* were hit, but saved from serious damage by their armoured flight decks.

Vernon Day, now a Petty Officer in *Formidable*:

The first Kamikaze landed in the middle of the flight deck, made a small hole in the deck, and killed about twenty people. We pushed it over the side and carried on. Some weeks later another Kamikaze landed among parked aircraft on the rear of the flight deck and set them on fire. It didn't damage the ship. We pushed the damaged aircraft over the side and carried on.

Lieutenant-Commander Ian Easton RN, Fighter Direction Officer of *Indefatigable*:

We had fifteen dead, but were back in action within an hour.

A Seafire, hook down, approaches *Indomitable*. The deck landing officer or 'bats' signalled with two ping-pong type bats to correct the attitude of the aircraft, such as trying to land with one wing too high. Finally he would signal 'land', or if in his opinion the aircraft was too high or too fast to have a chance of catching one of the wires, give a 'wave off' indicating 'go round again'. The long nose of the Seafire obscured the pilot's vision, making carrier landings difficult. The batsman was replaced in 1954 by the mirror deck landing system (invented by the British). (EA7568A)

A Seafire crashes into the barrier on *Indefatigable*. This was designed to prevent an aircraft whose hook had missed all the wires from doing what is happening in the next photograph: crashing into parked aircraft forward of the 'island'. The angle deck on modern carriers (a British invention), allows aircraft to be parked clear of the approach line of those recovering (landing on). (A27171)

On completion of these operations, the bulk of the BPF returned to Australia to refit for the invasion of Japan.

The East Indies Fleet, the new name for the Eastern Fleet, also dealt the Japanese Navy several severe blows. Captain Manley Power RN commanding 26th Destroyer Flotilla wrote to his wife on 18 May 1945:

Now on our way back again loaded with congratulations. I can't tell you about it yet, except that we have been fighting Japs again. It was an exclusive flotilla show, and a howling success, at the cost of only two killed and wounded, all in this ship. My PO Steward, who is sick, was in his mess until he couldn't bear to listen to the racket any longer without looking [seeing what was going on]. He got up and was just out of the door, as an 8-inch shell came in through where he had been lying. As he was wounded three years ago when the *Pakenham* was sunk, he is evidently born to be hanged.

The action had involved *Saumarez* (Captain Power), *Venus*, *Verulam*, *Vigilant*, *Virago* and the escort carrier *Emperor*. The Japanese 8-inch-gun cruiser *Haguro* was trying to supply the Andaman Islands, and having failed, she and a destroyer were sighted by a Fleet Air Arm aircraft steaming down the Malacca Straits. Power's Flotilla was sent to intercept. Power, in a later letter to his wife:

We got the aircraft sightings in the forenoon and they presented a nice problem of inter-ception. After a desperately anxious day, which nearly drove me round the bend for fear

The deck party scatters as a Seafire crashes into the forward deck park on *Indefatigable* after operations against Kamikaze aircraft. Either the barrier was not up, or the aircraft bounced or 'floated' over it. (A29715)

we should miss him, we made contact at about 23.30, after covering over 300 miles at maximum speed.

The *Venus* had picked her up on radar at 34 miles.

It was a pitch dark night, with dense black clouds and occasional tropical rain, lit fitfully by vivid lightning. A proper stage setting for a rather desperate venture. We were south of Penang, further into enemy waters than any surface ship had been before. After shadowing for a bit, and jockeying for position, I got him surrounded, and sent the Flotilla in to attack at 01.00. He'd got wind of us by then and was dodging like a snipe, so we didn't all get our shots off together. Nobody on either side opened gunfire for fear of disclosing our position until I got so close to his destroyer (which was in the way) that there was a danger of collision. I opened fire on him and dodged under his stern at 30 knots. That put the fat on the fire. The cruiser opened up on me at 5,000 yards with the whole of her armament, and the destroyer joined in on the other side. We went bald-headed for the cruiser which came into sight looking enormous and with a huge bow wave and wash as she cracked on speed to break through the ring. The rest was about the maddest ten minutes of my life. The sea was spouting with shell splashes all round us. We were drenched to the skin with near misses and water streaming everywhere as we closed the range. Our guns still firing rapid broadsides into the destroyer and hell's delight going on with enemy salvos screaming over the ship. Before I got to my chosen range, we got hit in the boiler room. There was a roar of escaping steam and clouds of smoke and steam.

Right: Ship's company of *Trenchant* which sank 21 enemy vessels including the 11,500-ton cruiser *Ashigara* of the *Nachi* class. (ABS429)

Below: The Japanese cruiser *Ashigara* at the 1937 Spithead Review. (DS595/34)

Leading Seaman Rhodes at diving stations in midget submarine XE4 in the Far East. (A30568)

A lot of instruments went out of action and the way started to come off the ship. I smacked the helm over to get the fish away before we stopped or sank (which appeared to be on the cards). Off they went, while the enemy continued to throw everything he'd got. The engine room, by magnificent work, got the engines going almost without a pause. With the helm hard over and full speed on the telegraphs we turned away under smoke, enemy salvos still cracking down at rapid intervals. Then, astern, through our smoke screen, three enormous pillars of flame and spray went up (like a Prince of Wales's Feathers) as the torpedoes struck home. The enemy never fired again. *Verulam* a short distance to the south of me had attacked simultaneously, unseen and unfired at. She is believed to have been responsible for one of the hits, and us for two. A few minutes later *Venus* and *Virago* crashed in on the other side and hit again.

By this time I was drawing away clear to sort myself out, what time Bill Argles in *Vigilant* had also rolled up into the fray, and I left the four of them snarling like wolves over the carcass. They polished her off and away we went.

We are not quite sure what happened to the enemy destroyer.

The destroyer was damaged, but got away. Total casualties in Power's Flotilla were two killed and three wounded.

On 8 June the British submarine *Trenchant*, in what is universally regarded as the most technically perfect attack of the War, sank the heavy cruiser *Ashigara*. On 19 July X craft sank the cruiser *Takao* anchored off Singapore. All the Japanese heavy ships in the East Indies were now at the bottom of the sea.

On 15 June, a task group of the BPF consisting of the newly arrived fleet carrier *Implacable*, five cruisers and five destroyers carried out air strikes and bombardment on the Japanese base at Truk in the Carolines. Commanding a squadron of Avengers on *Implacable* was Lieutenant-Commander Alan Swanton RN:

After the Barracuda, with which we had previously been equipped, the Grumman Avenger Torpedo/Bomber/Reconnaissance (TBR) was a great step forward. At first sight it looked huge, but I very soon learned to appreciate it. No longer those delays on deck after landing while the hookman struggled to disengage the hook from the arrester wires and others manually folded the wings in winds over the deck that almost blew them off their feet. I could retract the hook by the flick of a switch and fold the mainplanes while taxiing into the deck park, knowing the next aircraft to land would be relying on me to clear the landing area as soon as possible.

A little over a month after VE Day, we learned that our first strike was to be against the Japanese occupied island of Truk. We heard rumours that the beleaguered inhabitants were so short of food, they had resorted to cannibalism. I'm not quite sure what I had in mind as I strapped on my revolver, but presumably I aimed to avoid appearing on some Jap menu. In the event it did little to buoy up my spirits.

A fleet carrier can accommodate four squadrons, and practically every serviceable aircraft was taking part. Even though they were packed as tightly as possible, there wasn't room for those at the head of the range to make a free [running] take-off. The Seafires and Fireflies would be launched by catapult. The carrier altered course into wind and increased speed. I could see Charles Lamb, the Flight Deck Officer, standing near the catapult on the port bow, while preparing to flag off the first of the fighters. No sooner was the first off, than the next was brought into position on the catapult. Everything seemed to be going like clockwork, as I glimpsed the green flag being waved aloft as another fighter opened to full throttle, down would come the flag, and a split second later the aircraft would hurtle forward and sail into the air.

The sensation of being catapulted is quite unlike anything I have ever experienced. From start to finish the launch lasts no more than a second or two, and in that time the aircraft is accelerated from standstill to flying speed. The acceleration is quite smooth but so rapid one feels powerless in the grip of such a giant force. For those few seconds one is scarcely capable of blinking. During my earliest launches, I used to think, 'If this lasts much longer, I can't stand it.' Then, suddenly, it's over; you're briefly imbued with a feeling of complete euphoria.

Just occasionally something goes wrong, and that happened during the launch of our strike on Truk. Charles Lamb was on the point of despatching an aircraft, when it fell off the catapult cradle. As it hit the deck, the propeller shattered and part of one of the blades almost severed one of Charles's legs. It took a little time to lift the damaged aircraft by crane and clear the flight deck. The rest of the fighters were launched successfully, and it was my turn as CO of 828 Squadron to carry out the first free take-off.

The Avengers were powered by Pratt and Whitney air-cooled engines, and they had all been running for some time, not too fast or they would overheat, and not too slowly or the plugs would oil up. I was waved forward to the centre line of the deck. Being first meant that I would have the shortest run, so I held the aircraft on brakes while I ran the engine up to full throttle. Even so the engine seemed a bit sluggish, and the revolutions weren't building up as fast as they should. By the time we were abreast the island, I was

certain we weren't going to make it with our full bomb load. For the first time in my life I decided to abort a deck take-off. Snapping the throttle shut, I braked hard, but an oil spillage from a previous accident may have left the deck greasy. Instead of coming to a halt somewhere near the bows, I found to my dismay they were getting alarmingly close. I just couldn't stop in time and the aircraft trickled gently over and dropped into the sea directly ahead of the ship which was cleaving its way through the water at something like 30 knots. As it hit the sea, the aircraft righted itself momentarily, and automatically I carried out the drill: releasing my harness, I abandoned the cockpit and was groping my way towards the dinghy release panel, when the ship's bows sliced their way through the aircraft. The next few moments were a battle for survival, but fear didn't seem to enter into it. The water down the ship's side was very turbulent, and I swallowed a lot of it, as a succession of eddies sucked me downwards. At one point as I was on my way down, I encountered what must have been the port wing of the aircraft going the other way. I made a grab at it, and was dragged back up again. Unfortunately as the wing surfaced, it straightened out and trapped my fingers. I was lucky they weren't severed.

On the bridge there wasn't much the Captain could do to avoid slicing us up in the ship's propellers. He didn't even know if we had all been swept down the same side. My observer Nigel Matthews and CPO air gunner Ward both found themselves on the starboard side, and we all met bobbing in the wake. I was grateful for the help they gave

An Avenger crash lands in the sea after engine failure on launch; June 1945. (A29167)

255

Beam resupply at sea (RAS), taken from *Formidable* which is doing a stern RAS, while *Euryalus* is 'Rassing' abeam. (ABS626)

me in inflating my lifejacket, and they discovered I was being weighed down by my personal dinghy, attached to me by a lanyard. They soon had this inflated too, and having shoved me into it, hung on the sides. We didn't have to wait long before the destroyer *Terpsichore* came along and picked us up.

For some reason the experience seemed to have shaken me up more than the other two. When they were transferred to the carrier, I was kept on board until the following day. I certainly felt pretty grim, and a bout of seasickness didn't improve matters.

By the time I was transferred back to *Implacable*, I discovered that Nigel had taken in a second air strike against Truk. I wondered what sort of Squadron Commander I appeared in the eyes of my young aviators. It was a bad start to our Far Eastern operations, and the last thing I wanted was to be thought chicken-hearted or lacking in moral fibre. Nigel on the other hand showed the right spirit in getting back to his ship and on with the job. If he had any misgivings in his commanding officer, he certainly never voiced them. He had already received a painful wound when we ran into AA fire during our earlier operations off Norway, when we successfully torpedoed a merchant ship.

On 6 July, the BPF, designated Task Force 37, sailed to join Admiral William Halsey's US 3rd Fleet, to take part in strikes against targets in Japan as a prelude to the invasion on 1 November. While refuelling from the fleet train on 13 July,

Captain Brian Schofield RN commanding *King George V*, exasperated by the constant bursting and parting of hoses in the astern RAS method, positioned his ship abeam of the tanker. Both ships steamed parallel, the battleship maintaining station on the tanker. Until that moment it had taken the twenty-four warships of the BPF three days to refuel.

On 16 July, the 3rd Fleet, consisting of over 100 ships, including 7 battleships, 9 fleet carriers, 21 cruisers and 60 destroyers, was sighted. Admiral Rawlings was transferred in a bosun's chair by light jackstay to Admiral Halsey's flagship, the battleship *Missouri*.

Halsey offered Rawlings three options: operate as part of the 3rd Fleet; or semi-independently; or entirely separately. Rawlings chose the first without hesitation. Alan Swanton:

By this time the Japs had their backs to the wall, and there was a very real threat from Kamikaze attacks. Every precaution was taken to keep these suicide attacks at bay. Returning strikes could only approach the task force from seaward, and even then only after being checked by the fighter defence to make sure no uninvited guests were tagging along with us. Strikes continued throughout July against shipping and harbour installations. We also flew inland and attacked airfields and industrial targets. There seemed no shortage of

Fleet Air Arm Avengers on their way to bomb Japanese shipping. By the end of the war against Japan, of the 59 carriers in the Royal Navy, 34 were operational in the Far East and Pacific, with more on the way.
(ABS633)

aircraft on the ground, and I was only too happy that most seemed to remain there. One could only conclude that an acute shortage of fuel kept them grounded. There was no shortage of ammunition and anti-aircraft fire took its toll all too frequently.

During our briefings we were warned on no account to jettison bombs on Hiroshima or Nagasaki. Since none of our targets had been as far south as either of these towns, I felt that was hardly likely, though I thought it possible there might be POW camps in that area which we should avoid. I didn't have to wait long to find out that these two towns had been selected for the most devastating attack of all time. The first atomic bomb was dropped on Hiroshima on 6 August, and three days later Nagasaki was given the same treatment.

On 9 August we carried out two strikes, and were in the air for a total of eight hours. On the following day, we made our last strike on the Japanese mainland against an airfield at Koriyama. It seemed particularly tragic that we lost an Avenger, two Fireflies and a Corsair, on what was for us the very last day of World War 2.

The cease-fire came into effect on 15 August and the surrender was signed on board Halsey's flagship, the *Missouri*, on 2 September 1945. The Second World War was over.

Ian Easton:

Our reactions to the atom bomb were absolute delight. We regarded the Japanese as expendable. They had fought a filthy war, murdered our captured pilots, and we had no feeling for them.

Lieutenant-Commander Alec Dennis brought HMS *Tetcott* back to Portsmouth from Malta, the nearest he got to the Far East:

The war was over for me. There wasn't much of a hero's welcome; half a dozen wives and a handful of scruffy dockyard mateys. But who cared?

Opposite: Seafires over Japan, Corsairs below. 17 July 1945, BPF's first strike on Japan in the Tokyo area. (A29964)

GLOSSARY

AA

Anti-aircraft (gun) (fire)

Asdic

From the initials for the Allied Submarine Detection Committee, set up in the First World War to find the most effective method of detecting a submerged U-boat. It was, and is, a device incorporating a transmitter and receiver, suspended in a dome on the ship's bottom. It transmitted a sound pulse, which was reflected on hitting a solid target with an audible ping (through head-phones). By measuring the time the sound took to return to the receiver, the range of the submarine could be worked out, exactly as dolphins do. Finding the target's depth using the same principle was more difficult, but it could be done. Asdic operators had to be well practised and skilled to be of any use. Asdic is now called sonar, in line with American practice.

Bubbly

Rum, because when mixed with water it has a frothy appearance. Every sailor over twenty years old, of Leading rate and below, was issued with a daily ration of three fingers of rum mixed with three parts of water. Chiefs and Petty Officers were allowed it neat (known as 'neaters'). Men under punishment had their rum ration stopped. The rum ration was abolished in 1970. Naval Rum was far stronger than its civilian equivalent, being 54.5 per cent by volume compared with 40 per cent. The proper stuff can still be found at Threshers wine shops; ask for Pussers Rum, Blue Label.

Commander

A rank and an appointment. In the latter sense, the executive officer or second-in-command of a major warship, cruisers and above.

Coxswain

The senior Chief Petty Officer or Petty Officer in a small war vessel, such as an MTB or submarine. Usually took the helm in action.

Dinner

The midday meal.

Divisions

The ship's company was split into divisions for administration e.g. Stokers, Air. When the ship's company paraded on formal occasions, known as 'divisions', they formed up by divisions. In peacetime, 'divisions' were held every Sunday for inspection by the Captain.

DSM
Distinguished Service Medal. An award for gallantry for ratings.

First Lieutenant
The second-in-command of a small ship, vessel or submarine, which does not carry a Commander. Sometimes known as the executive officer. In a large warship, there was, and is, a First Lieutenant and a Commander. In these circumstances, the First Lieutenant could be a Lieutenant-Commander.

Fix
To 'fix' one's position on the chart by taking bearings from objects on land, or by astral navigation.

Flak
German slang (picked up by the Allies and copied) for anti-aircraft fire, from the German *fliegerabwehrkanone*.

Flat
An open space below decks in a ship. Not an apartment.

High Angle
The term High Angle gunnery was used to denote what later became generally known as AA gunnery.

Hydrophones
Underwater listening device, to detect a ship's or submarine's propeller noise.

LCA
Landing-Craft Assault, with a maximum load of an infantry platoon. Designed to be carried at a ship's davits and to land infantry in a beach assault. Armoured to give its passengers some protection against small-arms fire and shrapnel, but not air burst.

Mess deck
Space in which ratings slept, ate and spent their time off. The size depended on type of ship, the number of people in the mess deck and the space available.

MGB
Motor gun boat, a small, fast vessel mainly armed with guns.

MTB
Motor torpedo boat, a small, fast vessel mainly armed with torpedoes.

Glossary

Naval Rank

Naval Rank was as follows:

Admiral of the Fleet *equivalent to*	Field Marshal
Admiral	General
Vice-Admiral	Lieutenant-General
Rear-Admiral	Major-General
Commodore	Brigadier
Captain	Colonel
Commander	Lieutenant-Colonel
Lieutenant-Commander	Major
Lieutenant	Captain
Sub-Lieutenant	Lieutenant
Midshipman	No equivalent[1]
Warrant Officer	No equivalent[2]
Chief Petty Officer	Colour Sergeant
Petty Officer	Sergeant
Leading Seaman	Corporal
Able Seaman	No equivalent
Ordinary Seaman	Private

1. Midshipman was not, and is not, a commissioned rank.

2. A Warrant Officer Class 1 (WO1) in the Army was not quite the same as a Warrant Officer in the RN in the Second World War. Now the RN has WO1 and WO2 ranks like the Army.

Oerlikon

A 20mm quick-firing gun of Swedish design.

Pipe

An announcement; in the Second World War usually over the ship's broadcast system, known as the 'Tannoy', because of the maker's name on the equipment. Before the days of ships' broadcast, announcements would be passed by bosun's mates shouting, preceded by the appropriate 'pipe' on his bosun's whistle or call.

Pusser

From Purser, the officer responsible for stores at sea in the old Navy and in the Merchant Navy still. The word is still used in the Royal Navy to describe anything official or issued by the Service ('Pusser's Planks' – issue skis). By extension used to describe a person with a reputation for always doing things the official or proper way.

RAS

Resupply at sea. RAS(L) for Resupply at Sea (Liquids) when refuelling, and RAS(S) for Resupply at Sea (Solids), for taking on other supplies such as food, ammunition and spares.

Rating(s)

All non-commissioned personnel, i.e. Chief Petty Officers and below, were ratings.

Sippers

Allowing one's messmate to have a sip of one's rum ration. A sailor would normally be given sippers of all his messmates' tots on his birthday; all too often with disastrous consequences.

Stripey

Usually an old sailor with three good conduct badges, or stripes. A good conduct badge was awarded for every four years of unblemished behaviour, or as sailors would say, four years of 'undetected crime'.

Tot

Rum ration.

VC

Victoria Cross, the highest award for gallantry for all ranks.

Mediterranean

Alexandria
Red Sea

Leningrad
Baltic Sea

Kola Inlet
Murmansk
White Sea

Barents Sea
North
Cape
Altenfjord
Tromsö
Gällivare
FINLAND

Wilhelmshaven
Antwerp
Dunkirk
Le Havre

Bordeaux
*Bay of
Biscay*

Casablanca

Freetown

NORWAY
SWEDEN
Bardufoss
Narvik
Kristiansand
Oslo
Namsos
Trondheim
Andalsnes
Bergen
Stavanger
Jossingfjord

Dover
Brest

Gibraltar

Dakar

Bear Island

Liverpool

Jan Mayen

Faroe
Islands
Scapa Flow

Madeira
Canary Islands

Denmark Strait
GREENLAND
Reykjavik
ICELAND

Azores

Cape Verde Islands

NORTH
ATLANTIC
OCEAN

Halifax

Bermuda

Trinidad

New York

San Juan

Miami

PANAMA

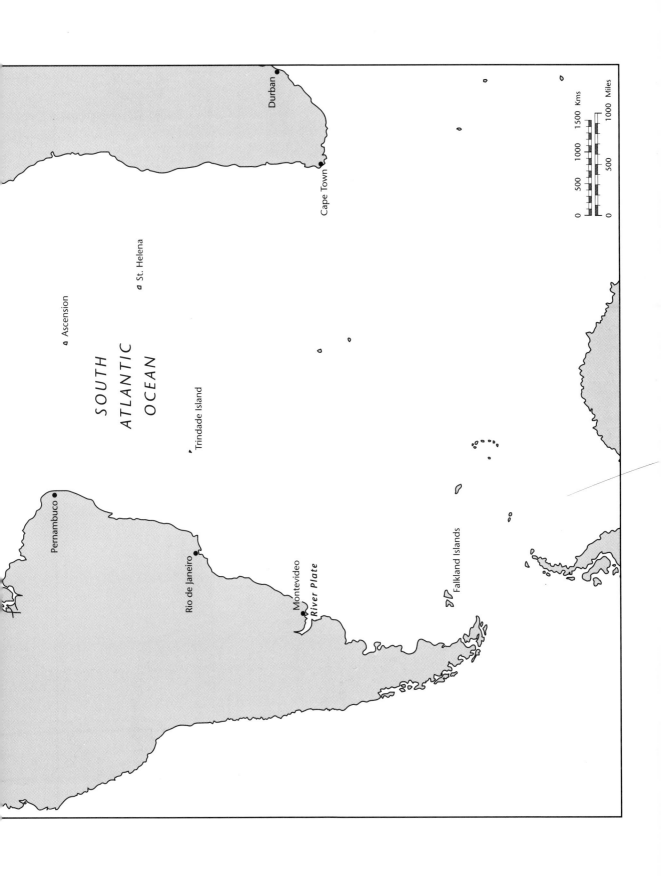

SOUTH
ATLANTIC
OCEAN

Pernambuco

Rio de Janeiro

Montevideo
River Plate

Trindade Island

Ascension

St. Helena

Durban

Cape Town

Falkland Islands

0   500   1000   1500   Kms

0   500   1000   Miles

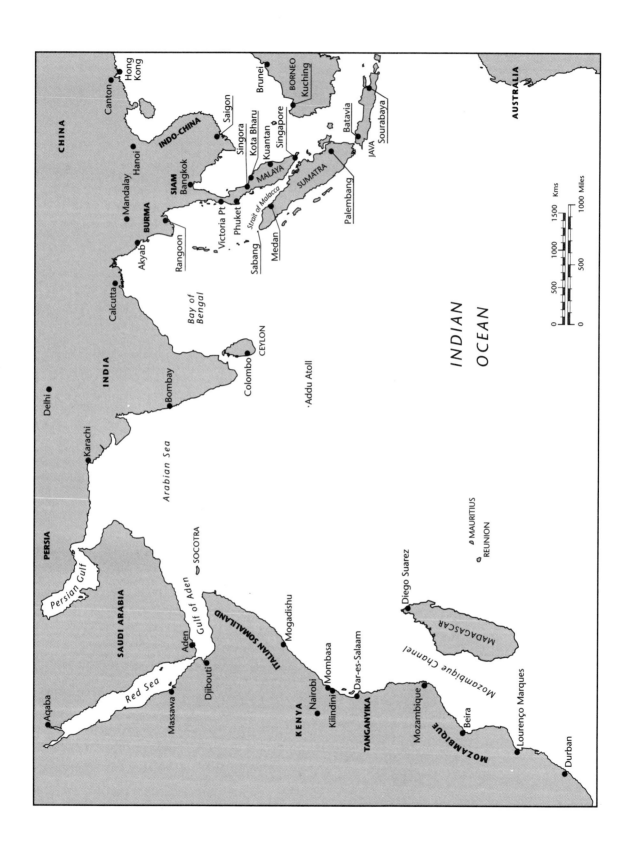

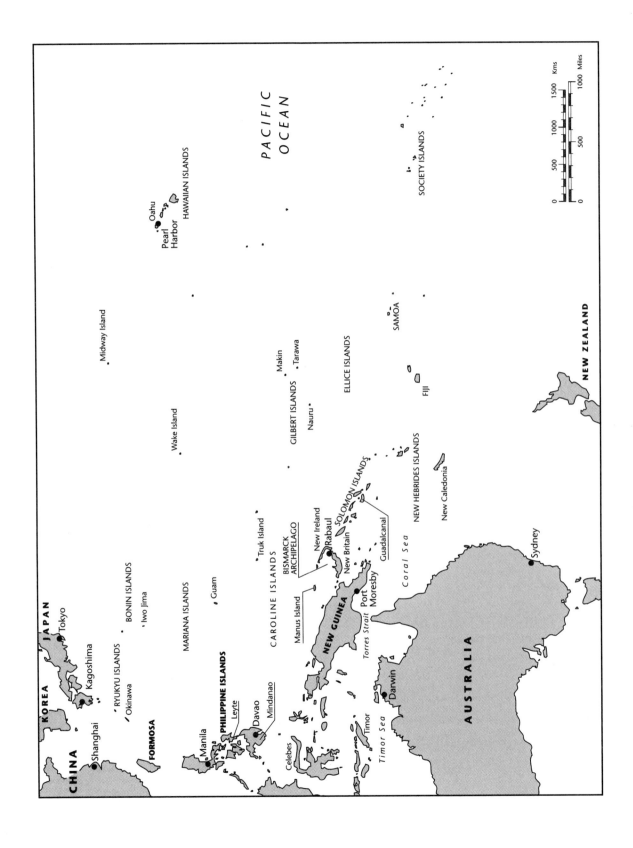

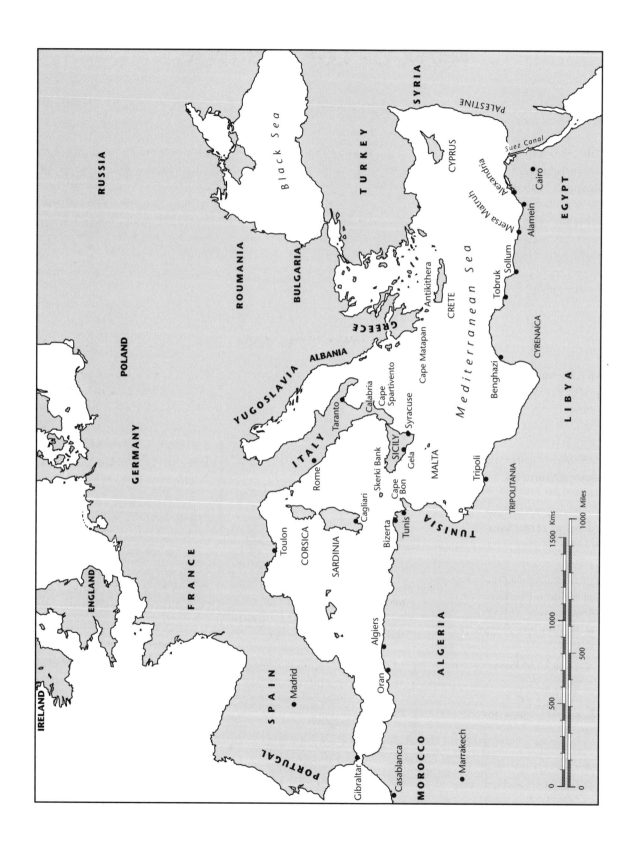

INDEX OF CONTRIBUTORS

This index serves two purposes: it lists those whose writings or recordings are here quoted and gives due acknowledgement to the copyright holders who have kindly allowed the publication of material held in the Museum's collections. If the copyright owner is not the contributor, their name appears in round brackets after the contributor with whom they are associated. Where the papers quoted are not contained in a collection under the contributor's name, but form part of another collection, this is indicated in round brackets. Every effort has been made to trace copyright owners; the Museum would be grateful for any information which might help trace those whose identities or addresses are not known. The number in square brackets is the accession number in the collection. Ranks are as they were at the time of the experiences described. Decorations are not shown.

DEPARTMENT OF DOCUMENTS

Index of Contributors

SOUND ARCHIVES

INDEX

Individuals have been allotted their most senior rank mentioned in the text, even though they may have subsequently reached a higher rank. Page numbers for illustrations are shown in bold print.

Index

Index

Three fleet carriers take part in Operation Pedestal 11–13 August 1942, the biggest Malta convoy of the Second World War. HMS *Indomitable* and HMS *Eagle* taken from HMS *Victorious*. A total of 72 fighters were carried. Sea Hurricanes can be seen ranged on the end of *Victorious*'s flight deck. The Second World War saw the end of the battleship's supremacy at sea, which had begun in Tudor times. Aircraft carriers became the major maritime striking force. At the start of the Second World War, the Royal Navy had one modern and six old carriers in commission. Five of these carriers were sunk in the war. All the Royal Navy's 232 aircraft were obsolete by 1939 standards. By the end of the war the Royal Navy had 59 carriers and 3,700 aircraft in service, the majority modern types, and many of American manufacture. Today the Royal Navy possesses three small carriers.

(A15963)